A fine dining chef who flipped his chops into a railroad-car diner at the edge of the Pacific, Clark shares 130 recipes for seasonal, down-home cuisine. This is a visual storybook of free-spirited Californian living, set against the surf, peaks, curving roads, and sunsets of the westernmost United States.

Through the transporting photographs by fourth-generation Californian Cheyenne Ellis, we're scrabbling for pink peppercorns and huckleberries in a thicket off Highway 1, plucking wild seaweed along the beach, casting line for lingcod in Half Moon Bay, and toeing aside pine needles to reveal a clutch of morel mushrooms near Big Sur. We take our haul home—whether from the woods, the farmers' market, or the grocery—and apply Clark's "aha!" techniques and flavors. We make glorious Bacon-Gouda Dutch Babies and Furikake Popcorn, big-flavored sandwiches and steaks, hippie salads spilling over with candied kumquats and creamy avocados. We end the day with an Earl Grey Icebox Pie that tastes like a symphony but contains only ten ingredients.

Clark's recipes deliver the adventure of the California coast in smart, creative, unfussy, and delicious ways. Home cooks and roadtrippers alike will find their soulmate in *Coastal*.

STAL

130 recipes from a road trip

Scott Clark
with Betsy Andrews

CHRONICLE BOOKS
SAN FRANCISCO

Photography by
Cheyenne Ellis

Library of Congress Cataloging-in-Publication Data available.

ISBN 978-1-7972-2664-4

Manufactured in China.

MIX
Paper | Supporting responsible forestry
FSC™ C169962

Food styling by Scott Clark and Beth Protass.
Prop styling by Beth Protass.
Design by Lizzie Vaughan.
Typesetting by Wynne Au-Yeung.

10 9 8 7 6 5 4 3 2 1

Chronicle books and gifts are available at special quantity discounts to corporations, professional associations, literacy programs, and other organizations. For details and discount information, please contact our premiums department at corporatesales@chroniclebooks.com or at 1-800-759-0190.

Chronicle Books LLC
680 Second Street
San Francisco, California 94107
www.chroniclebooks.com

contents

Introduction 17
Rules, Gear, and Ingredients 27

the go-tos

Ghee 42
Homemade Yogurt 43
Crème Fraîche 44
The Best Mayonnaise 45
Umami Oil 46
Confit Garlic 47
Pickled Onions 48
Pickled Mustard Seeds 50
Pear Butter 51
Seasoned Vinegar 52
Hippie Vinaigrette 53
Shio Koji 54
Sweet Soy Glaze 55
Coastal Kraut 56
Whole Napa Cabbage Kimchi 58
Chile Jam 60
Fermented Hot Sauce 62
The Best Chicken Stock 63
The Best Bacon 65
Oven-Dried Tomatoes 67
Tajin-Style Spice 68
Furikake 70
Everything Seasoning 71
Homemade Tortillas 72

afternoon at dad's

Dad's Potato Chips 79
Curried Carrot Soup 80
Mac 'n' Cheese with Puffed Rice Topping . . . 82
Shrimp and Chicken Liver Grits 84
Smoked Chicken with Smoked Chimichurri . . 87
Hen of the Woods or Hamburger Sandwich . . 91
Smoked Tongue Reuben 94
MEET UP • The Crew at Dad's 97
Earl Grey Icebox Pie 100
Yeasty Drop Donuts 103
Rhubarb Brownies 105

road trip snacks

Perfect Meyer Lemonade 111
Furikake Popcorn 112
Shio Koji–Cured Jerky 115
Herby Buttermilk Ranch Dip 116
Shredded Potato Salad 118
California Kimbap 122
Confit Tuna Salad with Sea Salt Lavash . . . 126
White Chocolate, Pistachio, and
   Rose Cookies 128
CA Muddy Buddies 131

post-break breakfast

Pre-Surf Fire Cider 136
Goji and Hemp Overnight Oats 137
Brussels Sprout Latkes 140
MEET UP • Dee Harley, Harley Goat Farm . . 143
Asparagus Grain Bowl Benedict 146
Lox 'n' Tacs 148
Smoked Mussel Custard 151
Duck Egg Brie Bake 154
Bacon-Gouda Dutch Baby 156
After-Surf Sundae 157

visit to the seaside farmers

Fried Artichokes with Artichoke Dip 164
Summer Squash and Plum Salad 167
Jimmy Nardello Panzanella 168
Fig, Feta, and Radicchio Hand Salad 169
Roasted Corn and Smoked Blue Cheese
    Salad 170
MEET UP • Cristóbal Cruz Hernández and
    Verónica and Cole Mazariegos-Anastassiou,
    Brisa Ranch 173
Miso-Braised Gigante Beans 179
Falafel Party 181
California PBLT 183

fishing and foraging on the coast

Smoked Huckleberry Old Fashioned 190
Seaweed-Shiitake Miso Soup 191
MEET UP • Spencer Marley,
    Marley Family Seaweeds 195
Albacore Pea Shoot Bowl 198
Porcini with Guanciale Ravigote 200
Chicken-Fried Morels with Red-Eye Gravy . . 202
MEET UP • Anthony Gerbino,
    Mushroom Hunter 206
Lingcod Ceviche 210
Fries with Eyes 213
Oyster Po'boys with Smoked Padrón Mayo . 216
Dungeness Crab Rice 218
Red Miso Caramel Apples 222

after the hunting trip with pals

Blooming Shallots with Wasabi Dip 228
Kumquat and Kale 229
Charred Broccolini with Melted Anchovy
    and Garlic 231
Bacon Fat–Roasted Turnips 234
Salt-Roasted Purple Potato Salad 238
Seared and Sauced Kuri Squash 241
Sage-Grilled Yardbird with
    Miso-Maple Grits 243
Peppery Sausage Bánh Mì 245
MEET UP • Brooke and Clay Avila,
    Frontera Hunting 249
Roasted Beef Tenderloin
    with Chanterelle Cornbread 253

lunch in the vineyard

Chamomile–Pink Peppercorn Spritz 261
Country Toast Bar 262
Smoked Mackerel with Lemon-Dill Relish 263
Cured Salmon with Roe and Crème Fraîche . . 267
Deviled Quail Eggs 268
Chicken Liver Mousse with
    Persimmon Pudding 270
Head Cheese with Charred Onion Mustard . . . 271
MEET UP • Tyler and Rachel Eck,
    Dunites Wine Company 276
Seasonal Herb Salad 278
Barley and Wine Grape Salad 281
Shio Koji–Roasted Goat Leg 282
Meyer Lemon Curd with Blueberry Sauce . . . 283

grilling on pismo beach

Tamarind Mezcal Americanos 288
Grilled Eggplant Yakitori 289
Roasted Snap Pea Salad with
    Yakult-Style Dressing 291
Ember-Roasted Sweet Potatoes 292
Grilled Spot Prawn Cocktail 295
MEET UP • Neal Maloney, Morro Bay
    Oyster Company 296
Ghee-Roasted Oysters with
    Fire Cider Mignonette 301
Korean BBQ Pear Butter Ribs 304
Hard Cider Clam Bake 306
Santa Maria Rib Eye and Mustard Greens . . . 307
Grilled and Chilled Melon 309
Horchata Paletas 311

sailing to the channel islands

Kimchi Mary 316
Raw Scallops with Citronette 318
Homemade "Tinned" Fish 321
Sea-Blanched Broccoli 322
Sea Urchin Cacio e Pepe 325
Rockfish Curry 328
MEET UP • Wally Kluhgers, Queen of Hearts
    Sportfishing 333
Kimchioppino 337
Pretzel Crispies 340
Onboard Oreos 341

back home with the kid

Watermelon Agua Fresca 349
Pumpkin Bread with Salty Butter 350
Dry-Fried Green Beans 352
MEET UP • Downtown Santa Cruz Community
    Farmers' Market 355
Fish Stick Hand Roll Bar 358
Date, Sopressata, Arugula, and
    Smoked Gouda Pizza 361
Taquito Party 364
Matcha Mochi Waffles 366
Miso, Walnut, and Chocolate Chip Cookies . . 369
Dad's Sleepy Time Nightcap 371

Acknowledgments 374

Index 376

introduction

Here's the first thing you should know about me: I cook in a rented caboose on the side of the highway. If you come to Dad's Luncheonette, you can get a killer burger, a soulful bowl of soup, and a slice of homemade pie. But Dad's Luncheonette isn't your average mom-and-pop shop, and the highway it sits on isn't any old highway. It's California's Route 1, a ribbon of asphalt that stretches and twists and climbs cliffs with the waves crashing below for 656 miles alongside the Pacific Ocean. That's the water I'm in every day of my life, fishing and kayaking, foraging and surfing. ● The house salad at Dad's is a seasonal herb salad, with stalks and leaves and flowers hacked up wabi-sabi style and hit with a funky Meyer lemon vinaigrette. Our mac 'n' cheese has a crunchy, earthy, chivey blanket of puffed wild rice that you dig down through into creaminess. The veggie analogue to our burger is a maitake sandwich, made with mushrooms grown and harvested right here in Half Moon Bay. We griddle them, dripping with ghee, and top them with melty cheese, a soft egg, pickled red onions, and our mustardy Dad's sauce. It's a visceral experience—if you're not wearing it, we didn't do it right. The press loves that sandwich and regularly throws it on best-of lists. Californians come from all over the state to line up and order it. And me? I'm busy making sandwiches and being happy. It took a while to get here. I ran a Michelin-starred kitchen. I almost died along the way. ● An East Coast dropout, I started cooking professionally in Washington, DC, and northern Virginia, not far from my childhood home. But the Californian food I make today—using ingredients just pulled from the ground or yanked from the sea and coaxed into something comforting, elemental, and fun—goes back to what I ate as a kid and the wild way I grew up. ● I was a little rascal in cutoff jeans raising hell in the Virginia woods. Every weekend, rain or shine, my old man, a hulking guy with a Magnum P.I. mustache, would load my older brother and me into his truck and take us to the Potomac River. We'd climb rocks, jump off waterfalls, swim in creeks, and piss off my dad while he fished. I have so many photos of him from those days, standing in the front yard, bronzed and shirtless in too-short shorts, holding a stringer full of bass with a big-ass smile behind that impressive facial hair. Fresh fish was always on our table. ● My pop's parents lived on a sprawling farm in Maryland, near the Chesapeake. My grandma grew fava beans and tomatoes and tended a gargantuan blackberry patch. My grandfather raised alfalfa and corn for feed. There were bulls and chickens everywhere. I spent summers chewing on honeysuckle, stepping on cow patties, shooting stuff with my BB gun, and collecting rotten tomatoes to throw at my brother. My grandmother's gingersnap cookies were rock-sugar crunchy on the outside, chewy on the inside, and so spicy, I'd sneeze from eating them. After running around with busted knees and riding donkeys all day, we'd come home to her house knowing those cookies were waiting for us. ● When my parents split up, around the time I was in middle school, my mom got a gig as an event coordinator at a Maggiano's Little Italy in DC. I would visit her at work, walking through the kitchen with steam tables hissing, fryers sizzling, and cooks turning out countless bowls of softball-size meatballs. Then we'd sit down on tall-backed chairs to eat under massive chandeliers. On those days, I got a glimpse of a world that other diners didn't see. ● I fell in love with the chaos of restaurants then. I started getting serious about cooking when I learned to make crêpes to impress a cute girl in my home ec class. Still, when I brought up cooking as a career to my friends, they called me a loser. I wasn't brave enough to push back. Instead, I went to college for creative writing, where I learned early on that I couldn't sit down and write anything for more than twenty minutes without being distracted. Turns out I have pretty severe ADHD. I bailed on classes and started partying hard. ● I was acting like Hemingway but not writing like Hemingway. College was no use for me, so I dropped out. The night I packed to leave campus for good, I reached into a coat pocket, found a big bag of blow, and threw myself my own private send-off. The last thing I remember was my feet feeling as if they were on fire. I came to with my best friend, Jake, doing mouth-to-mouth resuscitation on me. I OD'd on cocaine and suffered an aneurysm. I'm lucky to be alive. ● When I moved back home, my mom said, "What are you gonna do now?" I didn't know. "I suggest you figure it out," she said. I googled "best restaurant in DC," stole my mom's car and knives, and drove downtown. For some reason, the chef let me in. "You can come and do your stage tomorrow," he said. I didn't know what a stage was. "Great," I thought. "I'm hired!" ● That's how I started at Vidalia. Chef had me picking thyme and scrubbing tiles with a toothbrush for no pay. He had a paddle for stirring lobster stock. One day when I had been giving him lip, he beat my ass black and blue with that thing. Then the dishwashers held me down, and Chef buzzed my head with an electric razor. ● It was game on. Restaurant cooking engulfed me in a thumping, pounding, crushing drum of energy. I needed that pain and chaos. It was what I was used to from partying and being a wild little kid. I devoured every morsel of the culture of restaurant cooking. I ate it whole and licked my fingers. As long as I could enter a kitchen and leave most of myself at the door, and as long as I could take simple commands and stand on my feet for sixteen hours, I could be weird and loud and

reap the glory of hammering beers with the most wholesome group of debauched animals I could hope to hang out with. For the next twelve years, the intensity never stopped. ● A year to the date of my first day on the job, I quit Vidalia and moved to Restaurant Eve in Alexandria, Virginia. The chef, Jeremy Hoffman, had worked with Thomas Keller at Per Se in New York. As with Keller, under Hoffman you were only as good a cook as you were a human being. At Restaurant Eve, I discovered where chaos met professionalism. We got our vegetables from a cooperative of Amish farmers in Pennsylvania. They'd drive down in a box truck full of the most incredible produce imaginable. The guy who sold us goat meat and chèvre would come to the kitchen with a bleating kid under his arm. Chef taught us to show respect to the people producing these ingredients. That's when I started switching from the life of a line cook to the life of a chef. ● I spent three years at Restaurant Eve, working my way up to sous, expediting on the line, ordering ingredients, developing the menu, and, finally, taking charge of the kitchen when Chef had his first child. Things were good, but there came a point when I realized that I had never left home. If I wanted to see what I was really made of, I needed to get off the East Coast. ● Around the same time, I read an article about Corey Lee, the chef at San Francisco's Benu. When he was a kid, his Korean grandma walked around his neighborhood collecting acorns to make jelly. He was embarrassed by her, but when he learned how to cook, he realized she embodied technique and history. Corey's story—and his rad grandma—really spoke to me. I started sending notes to any email address I could find at Benu, begging for a job. When that failed, I sent handwritten letters. I hounded them until they let me stage for a couple of days, and when they didn't have a position for me after my stage, I hounded them again until, one random day, they replied, "Someone is leaving, and you can start on pastry." ● I quit Restaurant Eve, packed my truck, drove across country, and went down a rabbit hole. I stopped answering my mom's calls. I forgot about my friends. I grew incredibly close to my coworkers. We'd go out and gorge ourselves on everything that was California. It was a dream, and it was horrifying all at once, because that kitchen kicked my ass every single day. ● I have a visceral memory of working Benu's fish station. There was an abalone dish on the menu. It was cooked sous vide, braised, fried, and served with diced Meyer lemon and a purée we made by pressure cooking cauliflower until it was mega-tender and then blending it with a milk jelly and exactly 1 percent of its weight in salt. The whole process was foreign to me. I'm more of a "let's put it in the pot and figure it out" kind of guy. I came from a place where, if you wanted to make purée, you just rocked cauliflower down in cream until the cream almost broke, and then you blitzed it in a Vitamix. So, I misfired the abalone. Corey made me eat it in one bite in front of the whole kitchen. That was the first time I tasted abalone. ● The chef de cuisine took pity on me and told me about Saison.

"It might be a better fit for you," he said. He was right. At Saison, I stood searing pork belly over a roaring fire, sweating and coaxing flavor out in the most primal way. I felt at home again, going to the farmers' market, meeting producers, and understanding more deeply where the ingredients came from. Josh Skenes, Saison's chef-owner, taught me how to be precise, not by weighing ingredients out on a scale but by using my senses. ● I remember watching Chef braise potatoes in kelp water, along with sardines he'd dried in front of the fire, and then rice them so they were silky and fishy all at once. As I was furiously writing notes, trying to get the gram weights down, he said, "No. You have to taste the kelp broth, smell the sardines, look at the potatoes, move into this space with all your senses. Slow down and make yourself aware. Be in tune with all the things you're making." ● I started at the bottom, as morning prep cook, and worked my way up to chef de partie, then sous chef, then research and development chef, then chef de cuisine. But after four years at Saison, I felt cooked myself. I had moved to California in 2013 to work in Michelin-starred restaurants. I was laser focused. I worked eighty hours a week. I learned a lot. I did so much. But I was missing myself, and, man, was I burnt out and beat up. I'd had my ribs kicked in, my ankle bone stomped, I'd been elbowed and sucker punched by restaurant chefs. There were a few times when I gave it right back to them, and more times when I passed the abuse onward, beating on cooks who worked under me to vent the frustrations of a sixteen-hour workday fueled by cold brews and unfiltered cigarettes. It was my life, and I was committed to it. But if cocaine didn't kill me, cooking was going to. ● Late one night, I called Alexis, my then-girlfriend and the mother of my child, a baby girl named Frost, whom I barely had time for. Did I want to cook? Hell, yeah. Did I want to feed people and make them happy? Yes again. "But I don't know if this is what I need for my life," I said. ● I took the next day off, and we drove to Half Moon Bay to check out this spot Alexis had seen on Craigslist. Six weeks later, we signed a lease, and I quit Saison. We rehabbed, repainted, and rebranded the place, and a month after signing, we opened Dad's Luncheonette, which is situated in the most inspiring of locations: at the top of California's Central Coast. For a lot of people, California seems like a dream. And we've come to see "California cuisine" like it's a dream too. It's so fresh and so elevated. But you don't have to live in California to cook this way. California is an ignition point. The destination is a damned fine meal you've made yourself. ● I'm a guy from the East Coast. I chose California. But it hasn't turned out the way I thought it would. I thought I wanted Michelin glory. It turned out I wanted a life. Even after I moved to the Central Coast, it took me a while to figure that out. When you come from the world of excess and suffering that too often characterizes high-end restaurant kitchens, the pain holds onto you. It took some soul searching and some tough times for me to leave that pain behind and find

I'm a guy from the East Coast. I chose California. But it hasn't turned out the way I thought it would. I thought I wanted Michelin glory. It turned out I wanted a life. Even after I moved to the Central Coast, it took me awhile to figure that out.

better ways to communicate with myself. ● Along with leaving Michelin-starred kitchens, I had to put down the bottle. Don't get me wrong: There are cocktail recipes in this book, and if you drink, I want you to enjoy them. Let it rip. But it wasn't working for me, so I'm sober now, running ultramarathons on California's mountain trails and learning to fully embrace myself. The Central Coast gave me that. Its abundance, its beauty, its precariousness, its chill. Surfing, sailing, ocean kayaking, gathering your salad ingredients from the tide pools and the woods: This is the way of life offered by the Central Coast. I am goddamned grateful. ● I have the land and sea to thank, but also the people. The Central Coast is full of folks who steward the land and steward the sea: organic farmers, regenerative ranchers, hook-and-line fishermen, and sustainable foragers and hunters. You'll meet a lot of them in this book because we're going to take a road trip down the Central Coast, winding along the Pacific Coast Highway from Half Moon Bay to Santa Barbara County. Most people miss the Central Coast entirely when they're speeding down Interstate 5, hustling between San Francisco and Los Angeles. But it's a horn of plenty. You leave Devil's Slide at the bottom of the Bay Area, and for the next four hundred miles on the Pacific Coast Highway, what you're looking at is truth. You're in hardworking, food-producing country. This cookbook honors the coast's local places because, for all the high-falutin' ways of its Michelin-starred restaurants, California cooking comes from the ground up. ● Humans have dug into this place's abundance for at least fourteen thousand years, beginning with Indigenous people: the Ohlone in the Bay Area, down through the Carmel Valley; Monterey's Salanin; the Esselen at Big Sur; and the Chumash along the coast south from Morro Bay and out onto the Channel Islands. These First Nations folks feasted off the sea creatures and land creatures and plants here, making flour from acorns, which isn't easy, and thoughtfully using fire to clear space for more of what they wanted to eat. They were super successful, with towns of thousands and trading networks stretching from the islands to the mountain peaks. When the Spanish arrived in 1769 and established their missions, they destroyed these Native communities. But Indigenous people are still here, stewarding parts of the coast such as the Santa Ynez Reservation and Big Sur's Esselen Tribal Lands Conservation Project and protecting the ocean with their work to establish the Chumash Heritage National Marine Sanctuary. ● The rancheros eclipsed the Spanish missionaries when California became part of an independent Mexico in the 1820s. Cattle are still raised on the Central Coast, and that's where we get our Santa Maria BBQ (page 307). The Gold Rush brought more than three hundred thousand new people to California from all over the world. Many ended up on the Central Coast, lured by new gigs in farming, fishing, and back then, whaling. The Salad Bowl of the World, the Artichoke Capital of the World, the Clam Capitol of the World, Cannery Row—all of it's here on the Central Coast, along with sleepy surf towns,

The Salad Bowl of the World, the Artichoke Capital of the World, the Clam Capital of the World, Cannery Row—all of it's here on the Central Coast, along with sleepy surf towns, redwood and pine and lichen-draped oak forests, sage scrub and grasslands, tide pools, and a Pacific crazy with life.

redwood and pine and lichen-draped oak forests, sage scrub and grasslands, tide pools, and a Pacific crazy with life. It's been burned by wildfires, desiccated by drought, and swallowed by flooding and landslides. But somehow, this place perseveres, providing a cornucopia that chefs like me, and the people who eat our food, are fortunate enough to enjoy. It needs our gratitude and care in return. So, for me, this isn't only a cookbook. It's a love letter to my chosen home, California's Central Coast. ● The recipes in the book are organized around the adventures we'll have on our travels, the places we'll get to know, the ingredients we'll find there, and the people we'll meet. Starting with a tool kit of go-to recipes, a full belly from an afternoon at Dad's, and a cooler packed with road snacks, we'll hit the Pacific Coast Highway and head south along the Central Coast. We'll experience seaweed and mushroom foraging, oyster farming, kayak fishing, and diving for urchins. We'll hang out with the young vegetable producers growing beautiful crops a stone's throw from the ocean, and the goat farmer making feta that's so amazing, I eat it like it's a candy bar, just munching on a block of it. When I cook, I like celebrating those friends and treating the products they provide exactly the way they treated them to get them to me—like gold. ● Beyond the recipes, I also share my techniques. They're the kinds used in Michelin-starred restaurants. But they're not tricks. They can be learned. This is not fanciful food that you will never actually make. You'll come back to these recipes, because they're designed to make you and your people happy. ● You want a perfectly grilled, homemade sausage sandwich? How about having it Vietnamese style, spiked with cilantro, ginger, and chile? Whether you got your hands on some wild boar like I did hunting in Paso Robles or you grabbed some pork this afternoon at your local butcher, I'll teach you how to make it. Then you can enjoy it, smeared with ginger-spiked mustard and piled on a baguette with a pickled carrot salad. How about that? And you can follow it up with homemade vanilla ice cream bathed in caramel that I make with beer from Firestone Walker on the Central Coast, but that you can make with any hoppy brew from where you live. ● Because I'm Dad, these recipes are also for parents who want to put super fun goodness on the table for their kids—parents who like to show their kids some culinary adventure and let them throw whatever weird pizza toppings they choose all over the family pie with their grubby little hands; parents who might hop in the car and take the kids to a local farm to pet goats and pick strawberries, faces smeared with sticky juice. ● This book is for cooks and dreamers. It's full of scratch cooking of a high order, but there are no fancy gadgets or inaccessible science, just teachable techniques I learned working the line in restaurant kitchens. I'm constantly striving for the best and simplest way to make flavors sing, full throttle. If you can relate to that, then this book is for you.

● What I mean is, this book is like Dad's Luncheonette. I'm just gonna come kicking out the door with some food in my hands: "Here you go. Have fun. Let's talk." Take it from a guy who almost didn't make it, a guy who scratched his way up to running the kitchen at a restaurant named the twenty-seventh best on the planet, and who left that for sandwiches and happiness on the Central Coast: It's all just cooking. And it's all good.

"HERE YOU GO. HAVE FUN. LET'S TALK."

THIS IS THE PACK-YOUR-BAGS SECTION.

It's about getting organized, so it's stuffed with the things you need to journey through this book. You don't have to buy every piece of gear, but the tools I describe are super useful. And you'll use the pantry items time and again for cooking the recipes in this book and then some. To get us started, before we buckle ourselves in, I have a few overarching lessons to share with you from the kitchens I have worked in. Let's call them our Rules of the Road.

RULES OF THE ROAD

1 **Prep for your landing.** If you're going to take a leap and do something you haven't done before, jump with mindfulness. Where am I going to put this hot pot? Do I have a bowl for my kitchen scraps? Answer those questions before you start. Prepping for your landing ensures that when you're doing something outside your comfort zone, you have everything in place to know that you're safe.

In restaurant kitchens, the term for this is "mise en place." But it's not just measuring out ingredients beforehand. You mise en place yourself, your station, your kitchen. Come with an apron on and a kitchen towel folded over your apron strings. Set up a clean water bath, or what chefs call a bain-marie, full of spoons and a whisk. Get your kitchen timer in place. Put all those things in order, so you can get out of your comfort zone but still feel secure that you know where everything's going to go. Then you can crush it. You have to be organized to cook well. Not only will you do it better, but you'll also make less of a mess, wash fewer dishes, be all-around more comfortable, and have more fun.

2 **Read the recipe before you start cooking.** This is mise en placing your mind. Put another way, your recipe (yes, including the headnote) is your guidebook and road map to where you're going; it details everything you need to cook the dish successfully. I like to hit the road fully aware, especially when the journey takes a few hours, like a lot of the recipes in this book do. You don't want to discover you can't make it to your destination on time, no matter how recklessly you speed, just like you don't want to try to make Chicken Liver Mousse (page 270) last minute, only to find out you were supposed to brine the livers overnight. You don't want to find yourself stranded on the side of the road without a spare tire, just like you don't want to attempt to replicate Dad's Hamburger Sandwich (page 91) without Pickled Onions (page 48) in your fridge. We're after a chill ride, and hopefully, reading the recipes will be a pleasure in and of itself.

3 **If you're cooking, you're tasting.** The reason things taste so good at Michelin-starred restaurants is that someone put a spoon in the food and put that spoon in their mouth and kept doing that with more spoons about fifteen times before the dish got to the table. If you're cooking in one of these restaurants, you probably shouldn't need family meal because you taste food so many times during the day. At 4 p.m. every day at Saison, we'd call for tasting trays. Ice cream, caviar, diced grapefruit, lobster gelée, micro herbs—the sous chefs and I would taste every component of every dish we prepped. The thing that always got me is when people didn't clean their cutting boards between jobs. I would put that grapefruit in my mouth and taste shallots. You have to be able to catch those things. And with long-cooked dishes like soups and stews, you want to see how your flavors are developing and whether you need more seasoning. Taste as you go, always.

4 **Lavish attention on everything.** Cooking is like being in a long-term relationship. You have to keep dating your ingredients. You can't just expect them to be there every day if you don't keep the spark alive. Be a lover; open the door for your ripe tomatoes. Show them your passion. Wash them, appreciate their seasonality, and put them to bed lovingly.

5 **Store everything properly.** If you don't pack and stow foods correctly, then all of your good work turns sour. Throughout these recipes, I mention how long you can keep foods and how you should store them. Take my advice. Then give yourself the time to wrap and stack things right. Use airtight containers in your fridge and freezer. Label the containers so you know what's in them and how long it's been there. You're making all this fun stuff, and you want to keep it at the right temperature and in the correct condition to ensure its deliciousness.

6 **Your hands are tools.** It's a frowned-upon scenario for some people, but I'm telling you: Cooking is high touch. Wash your hands first, then touch everything. I'm a tactile human, anyway, because of my ADHD. I want to touch. But it's sensible too. It's as simple as knowing how soft a lemon is, or if a radish is woody. It's kneading dough, it's tossing salad, it's pulling the meat from the pig's skull for head cheese (page 271). If you just get in there and get after it, you learn a lot in the process. You can use the insight you gain to become a more capable cook. I also promote eating anything you can with your hands. Feel it, love it, grab it, get involved.

7 **Focus.** Hands on the wheel, eyes on the road. Slow down, think intentionally, and you'll learn a ton. Things that feel foreign at first will become your signposts, and small, even seemingly annoying techniques will reveal themselves to be wildly useful because you strove to understand what it is you're doing. Why do we peel fat asparagus and then cook it in a broth made with its peels? Do it carefully, taste it, and you'll know why. The first time you prepare a recipe, you're clunky, but if you pay close attention, by the third or fourth time, you're moving gracefully. So be present while creating a meal for yourself and your loved ones. You'll enjoy the process more.

In Front of You

Apron ● Once you start wearing one, you won't stop. It keeps you from ruining your clothes and from scorching your belly when you're balancing a pot in an awkward way. Get a collection of sturdy ones with pockets for stashing tools.

Cutting Board ● You need a bigger one than you'd imagine. A cutting board that comfortably fits a giant squash or a load of sweet potatoes is instrumental. Get a thick slab of wood and some mineral oil to keep it alive. Skip the germy plastic.

Kitchen Towel ● Always have at least two towels on hand. One is for cleaning up and one is for grabbing hot things.

Salt Cellar and Pepper Mill ● Salt shakers give you no control. A salt cellar lets you grab unrestricted fingerfuls for seasoning. A well-made pepper mill, with gears you can dial into the grind you want, is also essential. I prefer those made by Peugeot. They're consistent and come in rad colors.

Tasting Spoons and Bain-Marie ● In every station in every reputable kitchen, there's a hot water bath—bain-marie in French—for holding your tasting spoons. It might seem fussy, but try it out. Fill a big cup or a quart container with warm water, and you can throw every spoon, whisk, or fork you've used in there to rinse it off as you go. This is key for your tasting spoons because you should be tasting throughout the process of making each dish (see Rule of the Road #3). Dump the water and refresh it regularly. If the bain-marie doesn't work for you, at least keep a stack of spoons beside you for tasting, chucking them in your sink as you use them.

Cutting

Chef's Knife ● An 8-inch one will knock out most tasks. Preferably it's Japanese, because Japanese knives are well made, not clunky, and last forever.

Paring Knife ● It's essential for small prep and getting into tight, little spaces. I love a smaller blade for prying and pulling things apart.

Bread Knife ● A long, durable, serrated blade is the right thing for slicing country bread, but it also saws through melons and other hard-skinned produce. MAC makes one that can basically halve a tin can.

Cleaver ● I can break down thirty chickens in twelve minutes with one of these, no problem. It's thick, it's heavy, it can crack through anything.

Kitchen Shears ● Trim herbs and green onions right into your dishes, snip through small bones and skin, and use them to open packages so you don't dull your knife blades. Japanese shears pull apart so you can clean them easily, but Wüsthof makes a nice pair too.

Mandoline ● You're never going to do with a knife what you can do with a mandoline. A stainless steel surface embedded with a wicked-sharp blade, a mandoline allows you to be precise, fast, and efficient at cutting ingredients into paper-thin slices. Benriner mandolines are durable and come with different blade attachments for flat or matchstick slicing, as well as a guard to protect your fingers. But even with the guard, I push with the base of my palm instead of with my fingers. And I don't use downward pressure. Because the blade is so sharp, you don't need to press down. You're pushing through to the end of the mandoline rather than into the blade. Let it do its job, and you'll get consistent thickness and stay safe.

Honing Rod and Whetstone ● Your knives should be scary sharp. A honing rod takes the burrs off, smoothing and aligning the blade, but if you learn how to use a whetstone, you can keep your knives razor-edged every day. If you can't do it yourself, take your knives somewhere that specializes in sharpening kitchen knives.

Measuring

Kitchen Scale ● Although American home cooks measure by volume, chefs typically don't screw around with cups. Especially for baking and fermentation, weight is more accurate.

Kitchen Timer Get a digital timer you can set on your cutting board, so while you're prepping, you can easily check the cook times for what's in your oven. Some are magnetic, so you can throw them on your fridge or oven door. The best allow you to set multiple start times, so you can clock a few jobs at once.

Thermometers and Temperature Testers With its clip for hanging inside a pot, a candy thermometer is the easiest tool for testing temps when you're heating oil or making caramel. It's inefficient to use a probe thermometer for liquids, but you can jab it into big hunks of meat like the Shio Koji–Roasted Goat Leg (page 282) to check doneness. Personally, I prefer a turkey truss or a cake tester for checking most meat temps. You insert the metal stick into the meat, rest it on your bottom lip, and if it's cool to the touch, it's rare. Sun-kissed warm, not cool or burning, that's medium rare. Warmer still is medium, hot on your lip is medium well, and so hot it will singe you is well done.

Other Tools

Basting Spoon Get a good one. Hold onto it. In a restaurant kitchen, spoons are like gold. Everyone has their own set, and they get real upset when they go missing. For basting, scooping butter, and pushing things around in a pan, I like a deep-cupped, long-handled spoon with rounded edges.

Grabbers It could be kitchen tongs, long tweezers, or a nice pair of chopsticks, but you need something for grabbing foods that might be hot. Invest in a good pair of oven mitts, too, so you can handle pots and pans. For grilling, I suggest leather fireplace gloves.

Graters For fine grating, I use a Microplane all day. Don't want to chop garlic? Microplane it. Want sexy, long strings of cheese? Microplane them. Your dessert looks weird just sitting there on the plate? Microplane some chocolate onto it. But a box grater is essential, too, because sometimes you want a thick grate, and the slots on the side are good for shaving big curls of Parmesan.

Kitchen Twine You need it to tie up the meat for the Roasted Beef Tenderloin with Chanterelle Cornbread (page 253) to ensure even cooking and to make an herb brush to baste the bird for the Sage-Grilled Yardbird with Miso-Maple Grits (page 243), but kitchen twine is otherwise useful. You can use it to truss poultry, wrap herbs to dry them, and hang curd in cheesecloth to make fresh cheese.

Spatulas I'm all for a wooden spoon that has seen tons of love, with the burn marks to prove it. But a heat-resistant rubber or silicone spatula can get you into the crannies of blenders and mason jar bottoms. Invest in a bendy, metal fish spatula too. They are so wildly flexible, you can work them underneath anything sticking to a pan.

Strainers In addition to at least one colander for draining veg and pasta, get a chinois—a big, conical, fine-mesh strainer with a handle—for stocks and bigger jobs that require pressing on the solids. Essentially a strainer on a stick, a spider is useful for scooping foods from the pot when you're frying or blanching them. Use a smaller fine-mesh strainer to filter particles from oils, vinegars, and other infusions. Keep plenty of cheesecloth around to filter liquids even further and to let air into fermentations while protecting jar mouths from stuff that might fall in.

Tortilla Press This hinged gadget is cheap and easy to use, and you really can't make great tortillas without it. You line the top and bottom plates with plastic wrap, place a masa ball between them, then push down on the handle to flatten the ball into a tortilla that you then fry. Grab a wooden press at a Mexican store or go for an all-aluminum one, but avoid the plastic models, which can snap if you apply too much pressure.

Vegetable Peeler For peeling the living heck out of vegetables and making garnishes for cocktails. Kuhn Rikon Y-shaped peelers are my favorite.

Whisks They can make or break your sauces. Spend a little cash on them, and make sure they feel good in your hand. You need a tight, sturdy whisk for smaller projects and a medium-size whisk with a bit of give for incorporating air into a béarnaise (page 147) and other emulsifications.

Appliances

Blenders ● Your blender should have a few different settings, not just "on" and "pulse." I love Vitamix and Ninja blenders because they're monsters, but you can also dial in their power, going low for emulsifications and high for purées. Look for the same in a food processor, which is an all-purpose workhorse for making mayo, ribboning carrots, chopping, even mixing a decent dough. A stand mixer is a statement piece, but being able to walk away knowing stuff's still getting creamed is nevertheless a nice touch.

Coffee Grinder ● Fill your pantry with whole spices, so they're fresh when you crack them. Keep your old coffee grinder for coffee only, and buy another, good-quality coffee grinder to smash peppercorns, cardamom pods, star anise, whatever. If you're having a real party, you can grind up a bunch of weed in it too.

Dehydrator ● It's your snack machine. Buy an inexpensive one, plug it in, and make Shio Koji–Cured Jerky (page 115) and dried satsumas (see page 137), while keeping your oven free for other jobs.

Rice Cooker ● Of all the skills you have to perfect, I don't think boiling rice in water needs to be one of them. When you're cooking rice on the stovetop, it's painful trying to get that one temperature all the way through that cooks your rice just right. Buy an electric rice cooker. They're cheap and consistent, and you can throw the rice in and move on with your life.

Smoker ● I smoke a whole bird, bacon, even berries in a big barrel smoker. You can also use your backyard grill to smoke stuff, but don't just drop the food on there and pray for it to work. Watch some YouTube videos, read my instructions, and learn how first. If you're into gadgets, a stovetop smoker like Camerons is easy and cheap for small, quick jobs, such as the Smoked Mussel Custard (page 151) and Smoked Mackerel with Lemon-Dill Relish (page 263).

Cooking Vessels

Cast-Iron Pan ● Pick one up at a flea market, re-season it, put some love into it, and you'll have it for a lifetime. Cast iron can take a beating. Its heat retention is great. It can go in the oven. It's a multipurpose pan that can do almost anything.

Dutch Oven ● The sticker shock might get you at first, but a heavy-walled Dutch oven made of enameled cast iron from Le Creuset will last forever. They heat beautifully, and things don't stick to them like they do to other pots. I use them for braising, frying, and roasting. A medium one with a 6- to 8-quart capacity is a good, versatile size.

Hotel Pan ● In professional kitchens, we use these deep-pocketed, rectangular pans for cooking, carrying, storing—literally every task. You might have to go to a restaurant supply store, but particularly if you like cooking for a crowd, it's worth giving one of these a whirl.

Stainless Steel Saucepan ● Stay away from aluminum pans. If you boil milk in aluminum, you're going to get a scorched mess, and anything high-acid—vinegar, tomato juice, wine—corrodes it. Stainless steel gives you heat retention and easy cleanup.

Stockpot ● Get a big one. You're not going to fit a pig's head to make Head Cheese with Charred Onion Mustard (page 271) or all the stuff you need for the fumet for Kimchioppino (page 337) in anything else.

Landing Pads

Sheet Pans and Wire Racks ● Full sheet pans don't fit in home ovens. You should have a half sheet for bigger jobs and a quarter sheet for baking just a couple of cookies. But they aren't just for baking. They're for carrying all those carrots from the fridge to your station and peeling them onto the tray so you can compost the peels easily and not make a mess. They're for covering with a wire rack to rest steaks, season fish, or land whatever you've just pulled from the fryer. If you're peeling and dicing a ton of tomatoes, put the unfinished ones on a sheet pan so you can work on an unencumbered cutting board. A quarter sheet is perfect for trussing a chicken and not getting your cutting board full of chicken juice.

Silicone Baking Mats ● Save on parchment paper, which can burn in an oven grease fire anyway. Get silicone mats to fit your sheet pans instead. They last forever, and they protect pans from scorching and staining. My go-to brand is Silpat.

Stainless Steel Bowls ● These are a given. You need them to mix ingredients for just about every recipe ever. But as a landing pad, a metal bowl lined with paper towels is the place for chips and other small, fried stuff. Prop one on a saucepan with a couple of inches of simmering water in it and you've got yourself a double boiler for gently cooking the butter and sugar for the Rhubarb Brownies (page 105) and the béarnaise sauce for the Asparagus Grain Bowl Benedict (page 146).

Trivets ● Have a few on deck for hot pots. Put one in the center of the table, land your Dungeness Crab Rice (page 218) on it, lift the top off your Le Creuset, and say, "Bada bing, people!"

Storage

Cambros ● Square, high-walled, hard-plastic containers with measurements on their sides, Cambros are ubiquitous in restaurant kitchens because they store and stack so nicely that they keep you organized. Get two 2 quart [1.9 L], two 4 quart [3.8 L], and an 8 quart [7.5 L], and you can store anything you want. For smaller amounts, upcycle plastic deli containers.

Fermentation Vessel and Weights ● You can ferment the Whole Napa Cabbage Kimchi (page 58) or Coastal Kraut (page 56) in a mason jar or ceramic vinegar crock, but you will need fermentation weights (they look like glass hockey pucks) to keep whatever you're fermenting submerged in the brine. I prefer to ferment in a big, rectangular container made by the Korean company E-Jen. A plastic box with a vacuum lid and handle, it's like a fermentation briefcase. Because kimchi means business.

Freezer Trays ● I'll make a stock or broth, pour it into a silicone freezer tray with a lid, and freeze it in blocks. Then, when it's hard as a rock, I pop it out of the freezer tray and into a ziplock or resealable silicone bag, freeing up my freezer tray for more goodness. That's how you should roll, too. Deli containers crack in the freezer. Ice cube trays are too small, and they make a mess. Depending on their size, freezer trays let you store liquids in all different amounts. They stack snugly, and they don't easily spill. Souper Cubes are the ones I use.

Kitchen Tape and Sharpie ● Safety first, sanity second. Both depend on labeling. Label everything. Label, label, label. That's what kitchen tape, or masking tape, is for. Never second-guess what something is, where it came from, or how long it's been there. Don't just say, "I'll remember," because you won't. If you label your food with its name and date, you never have to wonder, "When and what is this freezer-burned thing I'm about to serve to guests?"

Mason Jars ● Upcycle these from whatever jarred foods you buy. They're for krauts (page 56), broths, cocktails, desserts, overnight oats (page 137), and layered dips (page 270)—anything liquid or creamy. Get yourself a few giant ones for bigger projects.

BUILDING-BLOCK INGREDIENTS

Aged Smoked Gouda • There's too much moisture in a young cheese to easily shave or grate it. With an aged cheese, the moisture has left the building, so you get a much better melt, a much better shave, and you can grate a metric ton of it easily. My go-to cheese is a well-aged smoked Gouda. It's so nutty and forward, it tastes like it came off a tree.

Arugula • I use arugula to cut the fat in the Bacon-Gouda Dutch Baby (page 156) and other rich dishes. It balances the sweetness of the Miso-Maple Butter (page 243) and the acidity of the Porcini with Guanciale Ravigote (page 200), helping the perfect bite come together. Salad arugula (*Eruca sativa*) is good, but it doesn't compare to the explosive flavor of wild arugula (*Diplotaxis tenuifolia*), which is a different species. Wild arugula is tender and unctuous, but you can eat a mouthful of it and sneeze from its intensity. If you can find it at a farmers' market, grab it.

Bay Leaf • With a flavor that tastes like oregano and thyme had a baby, bay leaf brings balance and piques interest. If you eat one out of hand, either fresh or dried, it's bitter and sharp. Cooked, it mellows to a strong whisper. In stocks and braises, it's like a bass note reverberating just loudly enough. There's a ton of it in the brine for the Pickled Onions (page 48), because with such pungent allium flavor, it's nice to have that earthy, herbal hum.

Bonito Flakes • To make bonito flakes, skipjack tuna goes through it. The fish is simmered, smoked, sun-dried, fermented, and finally, shaved razor thin. A lot of love has gone into it, and as a result, it brings umami big-time. It's the backbone to so many savory dishes in Japan. I use it to infuse oils (page 46), glazes (page 55), dashi (page 122), and dressings (page 167). You can find it at Asian markets, fish stores, and online, but also more widely, at food co-ops and Whole Foods.

Chervil • This tender herb is so lacy, it's just cute. It brings a green tone to things. It's not easy to find outside of California farmers' markets, though. You can sub in a mix of parsley and tarragon, but if you have a garden or a windowsill for some pots, why not just grow it yourself?

Garlic • Skip those plastic bags of pre-peeled cloves. Not only have there been accusations of labor abuse in that industry, but garlic doesn't need a plastic bag. It comes in its own wrapper. Its layers of papery skin protect it from dirt and germs. Buy whole heads, separate and peel the cloves yourself, and make sure to trim the woody root ends off them.

Green Onions (a.k.a. Scallions) • I have a soft spot for green onions. All alliums taste good, but the green onion is the above-ground "Hello, I'm right here, just grab me and put me in stuff" allium. There's nothing as fresh and flavorful as a green onion to throw on top of an ugly dish to make it pretty. I cannot stress enough, however, the importance of a sharp knife when cutting them. A lot of chefs have a dedicated green onion and chive knife, and it only does this one job. When you slice through it in one clean motion, each bit retains all that love and juice instead of it being pushed down and lost in the cutting board.

Honey • I buy honey like other people buy souvenir shot glasses or postcards from places they visit. There's a uniqueness to how the bees produce their miraculous concoction in each place, so it's a pure expression of terroir. Sugar is helpful in many things, but honey tells a different story. It's complex and ethereal with mouthfeel and viscosity. I use it to balance tons of savory dishes: the sauce on my Hen of the Woods or Hamburger Sandwich (page 91), the marinade for the Shio Koji–Roasted Goat Leg (page 282), and the dressing for Santa Maria Rib Eye and Mustard Greens (page 307).

Kombu • Kelp, or kombu, as the Japanese call it, is the king of seaweeds. A gargantuan alga, it forms jungles under the sea. In the Pacific, divers need compasses and knives to avoid getting lost or entangled in it. Dried and then plunged into oils (page 46), stocks (page 63), and dressings (page 167), it's a natural thickener, bringing silky texture and ocean notes. Plus, it's rich in vitamins A and C, iodine, iron, and calcium, so it's also super nutritious.

Meyer Lemons ● You become a lemon snob when you live in California, and the most available lemon to pick off a limb hanging over a fence is a Meyer. A lemon-mandarin cross, Meyers are sweeter, more floral, and simultaneously more complex and mellower than regular lemons, with a pith that isn't overly astringent. I juice and Microplane the hell out of them for recipes in this book, but because they can be hard to find outside of California, I list them as a preference, not as a must— except for in the Meyer Lemon Curd (page 283) and Perfect Meyer Lemonade (page 111), which rely on their particular flavor. When you can get your hands on Meyer lemons at a good grocery store, juice a bunch of them and freeze the juice in silicone freezer trays to have on deck.

Miso ● Highly salted soybeans or other legumes that are mixed with rice mold and left to ferment forever, miso pushes savory notes to 1,000. I fell in love with it when I became the R & D chef at Saison and started developing many types of miso with different kinds of beans and fermentation levels. Traditionally used for miso soup (page 191), white miso is made in springtime, when it ferments faster. It stays beautifully sweet. Red miso is made in winter, when it takes a lot longer for the soybeans to break down, and the paste has time to grow darker and saltier with more depth of flavor. The difference

between them is like the difference between the White Chocolate, Pistachio, and Rose Cookies (page 128), which include white miso and are lighter and more delicate in flavor, and the deep, nearly savory Red Miso Caramel Apples (page 222). But you'll find both types all over the recipes in this book.

Old Bay Seasoning ● Mostly celery salt and smoked paprika, with a sprinkle of mustard, mace, and other spices, this seasoning is ingrained in me. It defines an entire demographic. I grew up on fishing boats in the Chesapeake, eating crabs and shrimp covered in Old Bay and crushing bags of Utz "The Crab Chip" potato chips that tasted like it. I season the Oyster Po'boys with Smoked Padrón Mayo (page 216), Chicken-Fried Morels with Red-Eye Gravy (page 202), and the Shrimp and Chicken Liver Grits (page 84) with it because it takes me back. It's fun to bring that East Coast flavor to the Central Coast.

Red Pepper Flakes ● Adding heat without introducing new flavors, these are like hot sauce minus the vinegar. They give a poppy, skippy "hello" to the Smoked Chicken with Smoked Chimichurri (page 87), Hard Cider Clam Bake (page 306), and Duck Egg Brie Bake (page 154), without taking away or adding much else. Keep in mind, though, that I am the guy who guzzles Pre-Surf Fire Cider (page 136). If there's too much heat for you in a recipe, dial it back. Make yourself happy.

Sesame Seeds ● These are the Mighty Mouse of the kitchen. Fatty,

fragrant, and full of umami-flavored oil, they're tiny but pack a punch. You can get white sesame seeds raw or toasted, but the toasted have a deeper, nuttier flavor. They lend nice crunch to the California Kimbap (page 122), Sea-Blanched Broccoli (page 322), and about a gazillion other recipes in this book. Black sesame seeds are unhulled, so they taste slightly bitter and a bit like soil. They look really cool on dishes, including the lavash for the Confit Tuna Salad (page 126) and the Grilled Eggplant Yakitori (page 289).

Shallots ● What a beautiful little friend. I love shallots' crunch. I love their played-down sweetness. As opposed to raucous, abrasive onions, shallots give you what you want without overpowering everything. Raw, pickled, fried, braised, and everything in between, they're dainty and they deliver.

Vinegar ● Acid, in general, is important to my cooking, and we get that from citrus and salt, but also from vinegar. It's alive. It's good for your gut. And it brings a lot to the table. In this book, we use white balsamic, with its sweet-savory balance, to make vinaigrette for the Summer Squash and Plum Salad (page 167); hippie cure-all apple cider vinegar to marinate the rye for the Asparagus Grain Bowl Benedict (page 146); floral, flighty champagne vinegar for béarnaise (page 147); subtle, sake-like rice vinegar for California Kimbap (page 122) and Grilled Eggplant Yakitori (page 289); and sweeter, seasoned rice vinegar for mayo (page 45) and for the marinated

cucumbers on the Fish Stick Hand Roll Bar (page 358). We use vinegar anywhere we want its high-toned voice to sing.

White Chocolate ● I snack on white chocolate all day long, and for the Earl Grey Icebox Pie (page 100), the White Chocolate, Pistachio, and Rose Cookies (page 128), and the CA Muddy Buddies (page 131), it adds that unctuous chocolate mouthfeel without the cocoa powder flavor. Ghirardelli is our local SF brand.

White Onions ● Crunchier, sharper, and zingier but without the lingering gassy note that yellow onions have, white onions are used in Mexican marinades and Hawaiian poke. They're my preferred onion.

White Soy Sauce ● This is not low-sodium soy sauce I'm talking about. It is white soy sauce, or shiro shoyu, made by fermenting a higher percentage of wheat to soybeans. It's an umami tsunami. But it's sweeter and more subtle than other soy sauces, so I use it to bring pungency and salinity, without that obnoxiously salty kick in the mouth.

Whole Spices ● Everything freshly ground—that's our motto. A spice's flavor comes from volatile compounds that break down and diminish soon after you access them by breaking the spice into bits. If you buy a ground spice, you are buying something that's already oxidized. As it sits in your pantry, its potency fades, and you'll eventually have to throw it away. Waste less. You can store whole spices almost indefinitely, grind them as you go, and enjoy full, fresh flavor. Also, when you're dry-roasting whole spices, they won't burn like ground ones do.

the go-tos

The recipes in this chapter are building blocks for many of the other recipes in subsequent chapters. If you make some of them and have them on deck, you won't be scrambling when you need to incorporate them. Umami Oil (page 46), Seasoned Vinegar (page 52), Oven-Dried Tomatoes (page 67)—these will also bring flavor to so many other dishes you might cook outside of this book. That's why I give you tons of other suggested ways to use these staples.

The food I make is comforting. It's approachable from an eater's perspective. But let's face it: I'm a restaurant chef. I came up through the ranks in professional kitchens. A lot of what I do will be project cooking for you. You'll need to soak and rest and dehydrate some things overnight, ferment other things for days, smoke or roast some of them for hours. Multiple components make up one dish. You'll execute techniques you haven't tried before.

We're going on a trip and having adventures. And the payoff isn't just a glorious picture book of the Central Coast and a bunch of delicious stuff to throw at your friends. It's also skill and knowledge. Once you nail the techniques and get to know the ingredients, you can incorporate them into your cooking on the regular.

1 lb [455 g] salted or
unsalted butter

ghee

When you clarify butter, freeing it of its milk solids, it's pure, golden magic. Clarified butter, a.k.a. ghee, has a burn point much higher than regular butter, and it delivers mouthfeel and flavor in ways that avocado oil or canola oil cannot. The only problem is that it's damned expensive. So why buy it when you can make it yourself? You'll use ghee for recipes such as the California PBLT (page 183), Roasted Beef Tenderloin with Chanterelle Cornbread (page 253), the Albacore Pea Shoot Bowl (page 198), and of course, the Ghee-Roasted Oysters with Fire Cider Mignonette (page 301). Once you get the hang of it, you can play with your ghee: Push it past golden to where the milk solids start to brown for a caramelized ghee to toss with pasta and clams. Whip it in a food processor with smoked salt for basting ribs, veg, or whatever your ghee-making heart desires.

Put the butter in the smallest saucepan that will fit it, so skimming the solids is easy. Put a small bowl and a kitchen towel next to the stove. Melt the butter completely over low heat, 10 to 15 minutes. Then let it cook for 5 minutes more before you start skimming.

To skim, make 360-degree sweeps with a spoon or small ladle, gently removing foam and solids that bubble to the surface. Put them in the bowl, wipe the spoon with the kitchen towel, and repeat. Once the ghee is clear, with some solids stuck to the bottom of the pot like stalagmites, which should take 10 to 15 minutes more, turn off the heat. Rest the ghee for 10 minutes. Any solids still floating will sink to Davy Jones' locker.

Fold a piece of cheesecloth lengthwise, then crosswise, making sure it's big enough to overlap the sides of your fine-mesh strainer. Arrange the cheesecloth in the strainer, and gently pour the ghee through the strainer into a wide-mouthed jar or deli container. Let it cool before covering it with a lid. You do not need to refrigerate ghee. It will hang out for up to 2 months at room temperature if you keep it out of the sunlight in a cool, dark place. Then again, if you still have ghee after 2 months, you're not cooking enough of these recipes.

TIME
45 minutes

YIELD
About 1½ cups [300 g]

I make my own yogurt, because it's easy to do, it's cool to witness, and it's cost-effective. For the price of a half-gallon of milk, you get as much yogurt as would cost you double that at your local hippie store. To make yogurt, you start with yogurt—an organic Greek one full of live cultures. When it's ready, run wild. Spoon it onto the Curried Carrot Soup (page 80) and the Earl Grey Icebox Pie (page 100). Season it with Meyer lemon zest and as much black pepper as you can handle, and dip veg into it. Swirl in some Fermented Hot Sauce (page 62) for marinating chicken thighs. Spread it on a half sheet pan and freeze it for a crackly snack. Or just eat it straight out of the jar in the middle of the night. There's a lot of love to go around with homemade yogurt. And when your jar's nearly empty, you can use the last bits to start the process again.

homemade yogurt

8 cups [1.9 L] whole milk

½ cup [120 g] organic Greek yogurt

In a large saucepan with a candy thermometer attached, bring the milk up to 185°F [85°C] over medium heat. Kill the heat, and let the milk drop down to 110°F [43°C], about 30 minutes. Whisk in the yogurt. Once the yogurt is fully incorporated, pour the mixture into a large mason jar. Cover the mouth of the jar with cheesecloth and screw on the lid rim only or wrap a rubber band around the neck to keep the cheesecloth in place. Leave it on your countertop for as long as it takes to thicken to the consistency you like, from 8 to 15 hours, depending on the temperature of your kitchen. Remove the cheesecloth and screw on the full lid. The yogurt will last, in the fridge, for up to 2 weeks, gradually getting more sour because, technically, the cold doesn't stop fermentation; it just slows it down.

TIME
45 minutes active; up to 16 hours total

YIELD
About 8 cups [1.9 L]

2 cups [475 ml] heavy cream

½ cup [120 ml] cultured buttermilk

You need crème fraîche for the Lox 'n' Tacs (page 148), the Blooming Shallots with Wasabi Dip (page 228), and the Country Toast Bar (page 262). Beyond this book, you need it in your life for topping baked spuds, blending into sauces and soups, folding into pies, and anywhere you want creamy goodness. Spend the extra coin and start with high-quality, organic buttermilk and cream. If you're afraid to leave dairy out at room temperature, a pH meter can come in handy. This little gadget measures the acidity of a substance, and with crème fraîche, which doesn't thicken like yogurt, the pH reading can help you know as soon as it's ready.

crème fraîche

In a wide-mouth mason jar, whisk the heavy cream and buttermilk together. Cover the mouth of the jar with cheesecloth and screw on the lid rim only or wrap a rubber band around the neck to keep the cheesecloth in place. Leave the jar in a cool, dark place until its pH hits 6.3, which should take about 3 days. Remove the cheesecloth and screw on the full lid. Crème fraîche keeps, in the fridge in an airtight container, for up to 10 days.

TIME
10 minutes active; 3 days total

YIELD
About 2½ cups [600 ml]

SPECIAL GEAR
pH meter

the best mayonnaise

There's no reason to fight about it: Kewpie is the best mayonnaise. That's just how it is. It has an impeccable, high-fat mouthfeel. The salinity is perfect. The sweetness is perfect. We love some Kewpie around here. This is the homemade version. You'll fold it into the Confit Tuna Salad with Sea Salt Lavash (page 126), zhush it for the Fish Stick Hand Roll Bar (page 358), mix it into the sauces for the Smoked Tongue Reuben (page 94) and the Fries with Eyes (page 213), and use it in plenty more recipes. Stir Calabrian chiles into it for dunking your pizza crusts. Drizzle it over roasted broccoli and shake on sesame seeds. It goes anywhere. You need the Umami Oil (page 46) for this recipe, though, so make that first.

In a food processor or blender, in a medium bowl with a whisk, or with an immersion blender in a container just a bit wider than the blender, blend together all the ingredients except the umami oil. While blending constantly, slowly stream in the oil until the mayo comes together and is smooth and thick. It keeps, in the fridge, for up to 4 weeks.

2 large whole eggs

2 egg yolks

4 tsp seasoned rice vinegar

4 tsp sugar

2 tsp Dijon mustard

2 tsp fresh lemon juice, preferably Meyer

2 tsp kosher salt

2½ cups [600 ml] Umami Oil (page 46)

TIME
10 minutes

YIELD
About 3 cups [650 g]

2 cups [475 ml] avocado oil

2 cups [475 ml] grapeseed oil

1 oz [30 g] dried shiitake mushrooms

10 garlic cloves, peeled

4 by 2 in [10 by 5 cm] piece kombu

2 tsp peppercorns

1 bay leaf

1 cup [5 g] bonito flakes

1 cup [50 g] fresh parsley sprigs

PACKAGED DRIED SHIITAKES ARE MORE SUBTLE THAN THE SUPER-AROMATIC ONES IN CHINATOWN BULK BINS. IF YOU SCORE THE LATTER, USE HALF AS MUCH IN THIS RECIPE.

umami oil

California olive oil is a beautiful thing. But it isn't always the answer. When you beat it into an emulsion, its polyphenols can make your dressing taste bitter. Avocado and grapeseed oils don't have that problem. I blend them fifty-fifty to balance their thick and thin textures. Then I infuse the blend with a boatload of umami boosters. This oil is used in The Best Mayonnaise (page 45), the Shredded Potato Salad (page 118), the Miso-Braised Gigante Beans (page 179), and a whole lot of other recipes in this book. Confit meat and veg in it, blend it into vinaigrettes, and use it anywhere else you want that earthy, funky vibe. After you've infused your oil, the shiitakes are awesome chopped into eggs, stir-fries, or salads.

In a medium pot with a candy thermometer attached, heat the avocado and grapeseed oils, mushrooms, garlic, kombu, peppercorns, and bay leaf over medium-low heat until the temperature hits 300°F [150°C], about 20 minutes. Kill the heat and let the oil drop down to 250°F [120°C], about 10 minutes. Put the pot in your sink to catch any splattering, then carefully add the bonito flakes and parsley and give it a stir. Let the oil sit, uncovered, for 1 hour. Fold a piece of cheesecloth lengthwise, then crosswise, making sure it's big enough to overlap the sides of your fine-mesh strainer. Arrange the cheesecloth in the strainer, and strain the oil into a clean container. It keeps, at room temperature, for up to 1 month.

TIME
40 minutes active;
1 hour 40 minutes total

YIELD
About 4 cups [960 ml]

Spreadable and delicious, confit garlic is the Swiss Army knife of flavor. You can use it in salad dressings, slap it on veg, or slather it on pasta. It flavors the Herby Buttermilk Ranch Dip (page 116), the cocktail sauce for both the Fries with Eyes (page 213) and the Grilled Spot Prawn Cocktail (page 295), and the Lemon-Dill Relish for the Smoked Mackerel (page 263). It has the subtlety that raw garlic lacks, but it adds backbone. Most confit garlic recipes start gently, but I go hard on the initial heat to kill off unwanted germs. To peel a whole head of fresh garlic, rest a chef's knife with its blade flat on top of the head, then slam it with your palm to knock the cloves apart. Throw them in a metal bowl, turn another bowl of the same size upside down on top of it like a clamshell, and holding them at the seam, shake the hell out of them. The impact makes the peels fall off.

- 2 cups [250 g] peeled garlic cloves
- 2 cups [475 ml] extra-virgin olive oil
- 1 tsp peppercorns
- 3 fresh thyme sprigs
- 1 bay leaf

AROMATICS GO IN LATE, SO YOU DON'T FRY THEM AND MUDDLE THEIR FLAVOR.

In a medium saucepan over medium-high heat, bring the garlic and olive oil to a bubble, about 5 minutes. Knock the heat down to low and simmer for 15 minutes. Add the peppercorns, thyme, and bay leaf and simmer 15 minutes more.

Kill the heat and let the confit come to room temperature, then pour the mixture into an airtight container. It keeps, in the fridge, for up to 1 week. To use it, scoop the garlic and oil out together.

confit garlic

TIME
15 minutes active; 1 hour total

YIELD
3 cups [685 g]

1½ Tbsp red pepper flakes

1 Tbsp peppercorns

1 garlic clove

1 bay leaf

2 cups [475 ml] white balsamic vinegar

2 cups [400 g] sugar

3 large red onions, cut into ½ in [13 mm] thick slices

DON'T SLICE THE ONIONS TOO THIN, SO THEY RETAIN THEIR CRUNCH

On the Hen of the Woods or Hamburger Sandwich (page 91), Pickled Onions are part of the whole. But they're also the smallest member of the chorus. How do you make them sing loudly enough, so that everything's in harmony? With pickles, it's easy: Just remove the water that most recipes include. You're pretty much pouring vinegar simple syrup over the onions, and that's why they're so crispy-crunchy and candied. They're also fully injected with flavor. Bring them along to the Falafel Party (page 181) and the Taquito Party (page 364). They will also amp up the dressing for the Salt-Roasted Purple Potato Salad (page 238).

In a medium saucepan over medium-low heat, toast the red pepper flakes, peppercorns, garlic, and bay leaf until you can smell them, 1 to 2 minutes. Add the vinegar, increase the heat to high, and bring it to a boil. Add the sugar and stir to dissolve it. Put the onions in a heatproof container, then pour the hot liquid through a fine-mesh strainer over the top of them. Cool the onions to room temperature, then cover them and chill them overnight. They'll keep, in the fridge, for up to 1 month.

pickled onions

TIME
15 minutes active; overnight total

YIELD
About 4 cups [860 g]

1 cup [155 g] whole yellow mustard seeds

1 cup [240 ml] champagne, white balsamic, or apple cider vinegar

1 cup [200 g] packed dark brown sugar

1 Tbsp kosher salt

4 bay leaves

Good stadium mustard is tangy and spicy but a little sweet and earthy too. With all that going on, it's addictive. That's what you get with these pickled seeds. They're awesome on the Brussels Sprout Latkes (page 140). You'll want to sprinkle them on everything for the Country Toast Bar (page 262). You'll use 'em in the dressings for the Santa Maria Rib Eye and Mustard Greens (page 307) and the Salt-Roasted Purple Potato Salad (page 238). They make so many foods that much better: runny eggs, rare steak, roasted marrowbones. Whole pickled mustard seeds slammed on a buttery bun with a sausage right off the grill? Boom! That is it.

pickled mustard seeds

Rinse the mustard seeds in a fine-mesh strainer until the water runs clear. Transfer them to a medium bowl, cover them with 2 cups [475 ml] of cold water, and leave them on the countertop to steep overnight.

In a medium saucepan over medium-low heat, simmer the remaining ingredients, along with ½ cup [120 ml] of water, stirring to dissolve the sugar. Drain the seeds, then add them to the saucepan and bring them to a boil. Knock the heat down to a rumbling simmer and cook for 20 minutes. The seeds will plump. Let the mixture cool to room temperature, then pour into a jar, screw on the lid, and chill for 24 hours before using. The seeds will keep, in the fridge, for at least 1 month, and they only get better with time.

TIME
30 minutes active; 2 days total

YIELD
2 cups [495 g]

My pal Cheyenne, who shot the photography in this book, has a Greater Swiss Mountain Dog—a massive half-beast, half-Muppet named Bam Bam that you'll see in some of the photos in this book. I was dogsitting Bam Bam when the pears ripened on the tree in Cheyenne's yard. So I made a savory pear butter. Those pears were super ripe Anjous. You can use any really ripe pears for this recipe, but remember that moisture is key. That's why Asian pears work so well. They're sugary juice bombs. Just be forewarned: Fruit butter wants to stick. Your sole goal when cooking it is to avoid having to use a paint scraper to peel burnt pear butter off your pot. So, stir, stir, stir. This butter is deadly as the marinade base for the Korean BBQ Pear Butter Ribs (page 304) or served alongside a mess of Brussels Sprout Latkes (page 140).

pear butter

In a heavy-walled medium pot over medium-high heat, melt the butter. Add the onion, cover, and cook until fork-tender, about 10 minutes. Add the pears, honey, and salt. The pears will start to break down and release their juice. Bring the mixture to a boil. Knock the heat down to a simmer, cover, and cook it, stirring and scraping the pot sides and bottom with a rubber spatula every 5 minutes, until the pears break down, 30 to 45 minutes. Uncover the pot and continue cooking, stirring constantly to evaporate the water. You will know when that happens because the pear butter will stop bubbling and start sputtering. Kill the heat when your spatula can part the butter like Moses, 5 to 10 minutes. Add the lemon juice and stir to cool the pear butter, about 2 minutes.

Transfer the pear butter to a food processor and blitz it until chunky-smooth, then chill it in the fridge. It keeps, in the fridge in an airtight container, for up to 1 week.

1½ Tbsp unsalted butter

1 white onion, quartered and thinly sliced

2 lb [910 g] Asian or other very juicy, ripe pears, peeled, cored, and diced

2 Tbsp honey

½ tsp kosher salt

2 Tbsp fresh lemon juice, preferably Meyer

TIME
50 minutes

YIELD
6 cups [1.4 L]

2 cups [475 ml] white balsamic vinegar

1 cup [50 g] fresh parsley sprigs

5 fresh thyme sprigs

4 by 2 in [10 by 5 cm] piece kombu

4 bay leaves

Peel of 1 lemon, preferably Meyer

Here's a simple one: Jam a bunch of stuff into a jar, let it hang out, and then strain it. Use it for the Confit Tuna Salad with Sea Salt Lavash (page 126). Whip it into mayo. Marinate your tomatoes in it. It goes anywhere you want and adds a good, sweet zip. Just don't dig in too hard when you're peeling your lemon. You want as little pith as possible to avoid those bitter oils. Also, wash and dry your parsley well, especially if it's coming from the farmers' market. No one needs grit and caterpillars in their dressing.

Put all the ingredients in an airtight container, pushing the aromatics down into the vinegar. If you're using a jar, put plastic wrap over the mouth before screwing on the lid, so the vinegar doesn't touch the metal and corrode it. Stow it in a cool, dark place and leave for 1 week. Strain the mixture through a fine-mesh strainer into a clean bottle, and it's ready to go. You can store it in an airtight jar in the fridge indefinitely.

seasoned vinegar

TIME
5 minutes active; 1 week total

YIELD
About 2 cups [475 ml]

Here's your California dressing: a patchouli-wearing, hippie-dippie, broken vinaigrette whose sleeper ingredient is funky, deeply savory Bragg Liquid Aminos. You'll dress the Seasonal Herb Salad (page 278) and the Kumquat and Kale (page 229) with it, and anything left over is so good, it's practically drinkable. Play with it. Add shallots, Confit Garlic (page 47), anchovies, Pickled Onions (page 48), whatever you want, and then make more and more salad.

½ cup [120 ml] California extra-virgin olive oil

¼ cup [60 ml] fresh lemon juice, preferably Meyer

¼ cup [60 ml] Bragg Liquid Aminos

3 Tbsp Seasoned Vinegar (page 52)

2 Tbsp honey

Pinch of kosher salt

8 to 10 cranks black pepper

hippie vinaigrette

Whisk all the ingredients together in a medium bowl or shake them in a jar. The vinaigrette keeps, in the fridge in an airtight container, for up to 1 month.

TIME
10 minutes

YIELD
1¼ cups [300 ml]

1¼ lb [570 g] koji rice, preferably Cold Mountain Dried Rice Koji

¾ cup [150 g] Celtic salt

At Saison, I made all sorts of koji-fermented things: mirin, miso, sake, shōchū. But my favorite was shio koji, a heady marinade that starts with rice that has been steamed and inoculated with koji (*Aspergillus oryzae*), a mold that breaks down its proteins and carbs, fermenting it into this beautiful product with a brioche-like aroma. Unless you live near a big Japanese market, you'll have to order koji rice online. Cold Mountain Dried Rice Koji is my go-to. (They also make a prepared shio koji called Creamy Koji Sauce.)

Shio koji tenderizes protein overnight, turning a store-bought rib eye into something you'd mistake for a thirty-day dry-aged steak. You'll use it for the Shio Koji–Cured Jerky (page 115) and the Shio Koji–Roasted Goat Leg (page 282). I pickle veg and seafood in it. It's simple to make; it just takes time and precision. You want the sea salt to be exactly 10 percent the weight of the water and koji. And don't mess with the temperature here. When you buy it, the koji will be dormant. Making shio koji wakes it up. But you can kill it if your water is too hot, and if your water is too cold, it won't revive. Koji is alive; baby it right.

shio koji

Pour the rice into a large Cambro or mason jar. Pour the salt into a medium bowl. In a medium pot with a candy thermometer attached, heat 5 cups [1.2 L] of water to 140°F [60°C]. Measuring as you go, pour exactly 4⅓ cups [1.03 L or 930 g] of the water over the salt and whisk to dissolve. Pour the salt water over the koji. Secure the lid of your Cambro on three sides or cover the mouth of the mason jar with cheesecloth and screw on the lid rim only or wrap a rubber band around the neck to keep the cheesecloth in place. Leave it in a cool, dark place, stirring from top to bottom and scraping down the sides once a day, for 10 days. At the end of 10 days, the grains will have started to break down and the mixture will be thicker. Transfer the mixture to a blender and blend until it's uniformly smooth, then transfer it to the fridge. It keeps, in the fridge, for up to 6 months.

TIME
10 minutes active; 10 days total

YIELD
About 5½ cups [1.3 L]

sweet soy glaze

½ cup [120 ml] tamari

¼ cup [85 g] honey

½ cup [2.5 g] bonito flakes

1 by 1 in [2.5 by 2.5 cm] piece kombu

This sauce gets loads of deep flavor from bonito flakes and kombu, but it's a cinch to make. Use it on the Grilled Eggplant Yakitori (page 289) and the Albacore Pea Shoot Bowl (page 198). Slather it on tomatoes. Braise any kind of veg in it for extra umami love. Stir it into your stir-fries. Squeeze in lemon juice and swap it in place of ponzu sauce for dipping dumplings and tempura. Rip mushrooms in it and then slam those in the pan and sear them off for a steaky 'shroom situation.

In a small saucepan, bring the tamari, honey, and ½ cup [120 ml] of water to a boil. Pour the mixture into a heatproof container. Stir in the bonito flakes and kombu, then cover and let it marinate in the fridge for at least 12 hours. Strain the mixture through a fine-mesh strainer into a fresh container. It keeps, in the fridge, for up to 1 month.

TIME
5 minutes active; 12 hours total

YIELD
About 1 cup [240 ml]

coastal kraut

Kraut is healthy gut stuff. You'll throw it on the Smoked Tongue Reuben (page 94), use the brine for Fermented Hot Sauce (page 62), and incorporate both the brine and the kraut into the Asparagus Grain Bowl Benedict (page 146). Or just tie a bow on a jar of it and gift it to your friends.

A couple of kraut rules: First, you need a fermentation vessel (see page 33). Second, kraut is not where old veg goes to die. You want fresh, peak-season cabbage that's packed with moisture because the salt coaxes out all that liquid, and together they make up your brine. Third, the natural bacteria on our hands benefits us, but it's not what you want in your ferment. Glove your hands or wash 'em well. Use hot, soapy water and pat your hands dry, then rinse them again to remove stray soap that might kill the good bugs in your ferment.

Remove and discard the cabbage's loose outer leaves, then quarter it through its core and cut it into ⅛ in [3 mm] thick slices with a mandoline or sharp knife. Put the cabbage in a large bowl and mix in the cherry blossoms.

Working in batches as needed, use a spice grinder to grind the salt, caraway seeds, peppercorns, and juniper berries together. Massage the seasoned salt into the leaves to fully coat them, working the cabbage with your hands to break down its cells and release its liquid. Let the cabbage sit for 20 minutes, then massage the leaves again to crunch it up and make it easier to pack.

Cut the apples into ¼ in [6 mm] thick slices. Separating the slices as you go, mix the apples into the cabbage until they are evenly incorporated. Pack the kraut into your fermentation vessel, pressing down to remove air pockets and to get the brine to ooze up and cover the kraut. If you're using a mason jar or vinegar crock, push the kraut in with a muddler, and weight it down with fermentation weights so that the kraut is submerged below the brine. Cover the mouth of the mason jar with cheesecloth and screw on the lid rim only or wrap a rubber band around the neck to keep the cheesecloth in place; put the lid on the crock; or push the vacuum plate down in the E-Jen container (see page 33) and release the stopper from the airlock before covering it with the lid. Wipe down the inside of the fermentation vessel above the kraut. Let it rest in a cool, dry, dark place for 2 weeks. Transfer the kraut to mason jars or plastic quart containers, pour the brine over the top, and store it in your fridge. It keeps, in the fridge, for up to 6 weeks and will gain more depth over time.

3 lb [1.4 kg] green cabbage

¾ oz [20 g] salted cherry blossoms, rinsed and chopped

3 Tbsp Celtic salt

1 Tbsp whole caraway seeds

2 tsp white peppercorns

1¾ tsp juniper berries

2 Granny Smith apples, quartered and cored, about 17 oz [500 g]

ORDER SALTED CHERRY BLOSSOMS ONLINE

TIME
30 minutes active; 2 weeks total

YIELD
8 cups [2 kg]

SPECIAL GEAR
Fermentation vessel

4 lb [1.8 kg] Napa cabbage

5 large watermelon radishes, peeled and cut into ⅛ in [3 mm] thick slices, about 8¾ oz [250 g]

IF YOU CAN'T FIND WATERMELON RADISHES, JUST SLICE THE OTHER HALF OF THE DAIKON.

½ cup [80 g] kosher salt

2 large Asian pears, peeled, cored, and chopped, about 18½ oz [525 g]

½ daikon radish, peeled and chopped, about 12¼ oz [350 g]

8 oz [230 g] salted shrimp

¼ cup [60 g] grated fresh ginger

6 garlic cloves, peeled

¾ cup [75 g] Korean coarse red chili powder

3 Tbsp fish sauce, preferably Red Boat 40°N

1 Tbsp dark brown sugar

1 bunch green onions, halved lengthwise, then cut into thirds, about 3¼ oz [90 g]

KOREAN MARKETS SELL THE SALTED SHRIMP AND THE CHILI POWDER.

TIME
1½ hours active; 1 week total

YIELD
8 cups [1.9 L]

SPECIAL GEAR
Fermentation vessel

I eat buckets of kimchi. I have some every morning. It's like my cup of coffee. When it has just finished fermenting, I use it in the Jimmy Nardello Panzanella (page 168) and in the mayo for the Fish Stick Hand Roll Bar (page 358). If it's been sitting in the fridge for a while, slowly continuing to ferment in the cold, it's deep enough for stews like the Kimchioppino (page 337). You can drink the brine too. It brings spicy funk to the Kimchi Mary (page 316).

Called tongbaechu kimchi or pogi kimchi in Korean, this version leaves chunks of the cabbage intact, so you have options once you've made it: You can plate whole chunks, which is super beautiful; you can pull off leaves to use as wrappers; or you can chop the leaves as needed. And don't forget to wash your hands. Kimchi doesn't want your bacteria in its life.

whole nap cabbage

Remove the outer leaves of the cabbage, then cut it through the core into quarters. In a large bowl, mix the cabbage and watermelon radishes. Add the salt, massaging it into the vegetables and working it in between the leaves of the cabbage. Let it sit for 1 hour.

Put the cabbage mixture in a colander and rinse it in cold water three times, zhushing the cabbage and squeezing out excess water each round.

In a food processor or blender, blitz the pears, daikon radish, salted shrimp, ginger, and garlic until smooth.

In a large bowl, mix the chili powder, fish sauce, and brown sugar. Add the pear mixture and mix the paste well. Add the green onions and the cabbage mixture, then mix everything until it's fully incorporated, working the paste in between the leaves of the cabbage.

Fill your fermentation vessel with the kimchi, rolling the cabbage as needed to make it fit. If you're using a mason jar or vinegar crock, push it in with a muddler, and weight it down with fermentation weights so that the kimchi is submerged below the brine. Cover the mouth of the mason jar with cheesecloth and screw on the lid rim only or wrap a rubber band around the neck to keep the cheesecloth in place; put the lid on the crock; or push the vacuum plate down in the E-Jen container (see page 33) and release the stopper from the airlock before covering it with the lid. Stow it in a cool, dark place. It will be ready to eat in 24 hours, so you can pull some out, if you like, and store it in a mason jar in the fridge. Let the rest continue fermenting for up to 1 week, then store it in the fridge. It keeps, in the fridge, for up to 6 months.

2 red bell peppers

6 jalapeños

1 cup [250 g] Oven-Dried
Tomatoes (page 67)
with their oil

2 garlic cloves, chopped

2 tsp grated ginger

1½ cups [300 g] packed dark
brown sugar

6 Tbsp [90 ml] champagne
vinegar

Juice of 2 lemons,
preferably Meyer

2 Tbsp dark soy sauce

½ tsp fish sauce

½ tsp kosher salt

This jam is salsa-chunky, caramelly-charred, and hot-sweet. You'll use it in the Dungeness Crab Rice (page 218) and Dry-Fried Green Beans (page 352). It's killer with the Falafel Party (page 181) and Korean BBQ Pear Butter Ribs (page 304). You'll also want it to marinate chicken, slam onto roasted veg, stir into eggs, and pack on your next camping trip to throw on everything you're grilling.

I used to work with a line cook who always forgot to turn on a timer. He'd sprint across the kitchen, rip a pot off the flame at the perfect moment anyway, and declare, "Born to do it." He had a sixth sense. This jam isn't for people like that. It's meant to be coddled and stirred every five minutes, so use your timer.

chile jam

In a cast-iron pan over high heat, or directly on the burners of a gas stove set to high heat, char the bell peppers and jalapeños, rotating them, until you burn the living daylights out of them on all sides, about 10 minutes. Drop the peppers and jalapeños into a paper bag, close it up tight, and let them cool to room temperature, about 10 minutes. Peel the peppers and jalapeños by rubbing them with a paper towel to remove the charred skins. Discard the stems. Halve 3 of the jalapeños lengthwise and remove their seeds. This softens the heat so the sauce doesn't knock your head off.

Transfer the peppers and jalapeños to a food processor, then add the oven-dried tomatoes and their oil, garlic, and ginger and pulse until chunky. Pour the mixture into a Dutch oven. Stir in the brown sugar, vinegar, lemon juice, soy sauce, fish sauce, and salt and bring the mixture to a ripping boil. Knock the heat down to a simmer, stirring every couple of minutes, until almost all of the liquid is gone and a wooden spoon can part the mixture like Moses, about 1 hour. Let the jam cool to room temperature, then stow it in the fridge. It keeps, in the fridge in an airtight container, for up to 3 weeks.

TIME
1½ to 2 hours

YIELD
2 cups [700 g]

fermented hot sauce

4½ oz [130 g] dried ancho chiles

17⅔ oz [500 g] jalapeños (about 5 cups), cut into ¼ in [6 mm] thick slices

1 cup [240 ml] live-culture kraut juice, preferably from Coastal Kraut (page 56)

3½ oz [100 g] shallots, cut into ¼ in [6 mm] thick slices (about 1 cup)

3½ Tbsp [15 g] Szechuan peppercorns

3 Tbsp Celtic salt

3 Tbsp freshly ground black pepper

2 large garlic cloves, thinly sliced

1½ Tbsp whole yellow mustard seeds

1 Tbsp whole coriander seeds

¾ tsp whole cumin seeds

1 by 4½ in [2.5 by 11 cm] strip lemon peel

White soy sauce, for seasoning

TIME
20 minutes active; 6 to 8 days total

YIELD
About 4 cups [945 ml]

SPECIAL GEAR
Fermentation vessel

When Frost was about to be born, I switched from sous chef to running R & D at Saison. The hours were easier. That's when I developed this recipe. The meat course at the restaurant was a pared-down experience: a hunk of something like mountain ram, a tray of hunting knives, a biscuit, and this hot sauce. It starts with ancho chile broth and ends with white soy sauce, which serves three functions. It seasons the hot sauce, and because 500 grams of jalapeños are no joke, it dilutes it. Finally, the salt in the soy sauce puts a stop to the fermentation. That's key. You don't want this sauce blowing its lid in your fridge. You'll serve it with the Roasted Beef Tenderloin with Chanterelle Cornbread (page 253), mix it into the gloss for the Shrimp and Chicken Liver Grits (page 84), spike Herby Buttermilk Ranch Dip (page 116) with it, and use it all the many other places you want that delicious jolt.

In a cast-iron pan over medium heat, cook the ancho chiles until softened, 1 to 1½ minutes. Put them in a bowl, add 4 cups [945 ml] of water, cover, and let them rest at room temperature overnight.

Strain 2 cups [475 ml] of the ancho chile broth into an E-Jen container (see page 33), vinegar crock, or large mason jar. Add 15¾ oz [450 g] of the ancho chiles, reserving any remaining chiles and broth for another use, like making pizza dough (page 361). Add the jalapeños, kraut juice, shallots, peppercorns, salt, ground black pepper, garlic, mustard seeds, coriander seeds, cumin seeds, and lemon peel. Mix well, then cover the mouth of the mason jar with cheesecloth and screw on the lid rim only or wrap a rubber band around the neck to keep the cheesecloth in place; put the lid on the crock; or push the vacuum plate down in the E-Jen container and release the stopper from the airlock before covering it with the lid.

Leave the hot sauce in a cool, dark spot to bubble and ferment for 6 to 8 days. When the bubbles stop, put the hot sauce in a blender and rip it on high until smooth. Strain the hot sauce through a chinois into a bowl, pressing on and discarding any remaining solids. Measure your hot sauce, and then season it with the white soy sauce using a 3:1 ratio of hot sauce to soy sauce by volume. Mix it well to fully incorporate the soy sauce. It keeps, in the fridge in an airtight container, for up to 1 month.

When you're building flavor in recipes, you want every ingredient to have its own special touch before you add it to the final dish. This chicken stock brings the love to the Shrimp and Chicken Liver Grits (page 84), the Asparagus Grain Bowl Benedict (page 146), the Fried Artichokes with Artichoke Dip (page 164), the Head Cheese with Charred Onion Mustard (page 271), and anywhere else you need the most sublime version of a stock. Chicken feet and extra chicken backs boost the protein and collagen, because when it's cooled, I want my chicken stock to resemble Jell-O. It's all about a rich mouthfeel—and clarity. You're looking for a nice, clear broth that gets jiggly in the fridge, so skim it during simmering and gently strain it afterwards.

the best chicken stock

Let the chicken and chicken parts come to room temperature. Remove any giblets. If there's a neck, you can throw it in the stock with the other pieces. Pat the bird dry inside and out with paper towels and remove any stray guts.

Pat the backs and feet dry.

Break down the whole bird: With the breast facing up, remove any extra skin around the cavity. Cut the skin at one thigh joint and crack the joint to expose the bone. Cut the flesh on either side of the bone and remove the whole thigh. Repeat on the other side. Use the same technique to remove the wings. Set the bird on its butt and slice down on both sides between the backbone and breast. Slice the flesh on both sides of the butt to separate the backbone from the breast. Turn the breast flesh down and, forcing your knife blade between the halves of the breast, crack the breastbone to separate them. Sprinkle salt on the skin side of everything except the feet.

continued

1 whole chicken, about 3 lb [1.4 kg]

1 lb [455 g] chicken backs

1 lb [455 g] chicken feet

Kosher salt

2 Tbsp avocado oil

10 garlic cloves, peeled

2 Tbsp unsalted butter

3 Tbsp white soy sauce

3 by 6 in [7.5 by 15 cm] piece kombu

1 bay leaf

TIME
1 hour active;
7 hours total

YIELD
About 14 cups [3.3 L]

In a medium Dutch oven or heavy-walled pot over medium-high heat, heat the oil until it's close to smoking. Set the feet aside and, working in batches, tuck enough of the remaining parts of the chicken, skin-side down, into the pot to fill its bottom. Sear the chicken without moving it, letting it sizzle and pop, until the skin is crispy and caramelized, 4 to 6 minutes. Transfer it to a platter and repeat with the remaining chicken.

Keep the pot over medium-high heat and add the garlic and butter. Let the butter foam and the garlic brown a bit, 1 to 2 minutes. Tip the platter holding the chicken and carefully pour any liquid that's released from the meat into the pot, scraping the bottom of the pot with a wooden spoon to deglaze it.

Transfer the contents of the Dutch oven into a large stockpot, then add the seared chicken parts, chicken feet, white soy sauce, kombu, bay leaf, and 6 quarts [5.7 L] of water. Bring it to a boil, then knock the heat down to a simmer.

Set up a skimming station next to the stove with a spoon and a bowl of water to rinse it. Simmer the stock for 6 hours, skimming any foam from the surface every 30 minutes or so.

Kill the heat and rest the stock for 10 minutes, then gently strain it through a chinois. If you're not using the stock immediately, return it to the stockpot and place the stockpot in a sink full of ice water to cool it quickly. Once it's cool, stow the stock in an airtight container in the fridge. If fat solidifies at the top after chilling, remove and discard it. The stock keeps, in the fridge in an airtight container, for up to 3 days or frozen for up to 1 month.

CROWDING THE POT DROPS THE TEMP, SO THE CHICKEN DOESN'T BURN WHILE SEARING.

Bacon is in so many recipes in this book that you might as well learn how to make your own. The process of curing and smoking pork belly can seem dicey at first, but once it's complete and you see the result, you'll understand why it makes all the difference. You'll realize you're in control. That's a core lesson in cooking, so I'll say it again: You're in control. I brought that realization and the skill of making bacon with me to California, because all the fresh ingredients I get to use on this coast wouldn't be as compelling if they weren't abetted by the smoky, fatty boom of some melting lardons.

the best bacon

In a small bowl, mix the kosher salt, brown sugar, granulated sugar, black pepper, pink curing salt, and white pepper until they're well combined. Put each piece of pork belly in its own ziplock or resealable silicone bag. Divide the cure evenly among the bags, then seal the bags, pressing out all the air and shaking them around until the pork belly is evenly coated. Stow the pork belly in the fridge, flipping the bags once a day to ensure even curing, for 1 week.

Rinse the pork belly under cold water to remove the cure, then pat it dry.

Prep your smoker. If you're using a charcoal grill, bank your coals to one side. When the coals are glowing and no longer on fire, throw the hickory chunks on top of them. There's no need to presoak the wood chunks. For a gas grill, heat one side on high, place the hickory chunks in a smoker box, and place the smoker box over the flame. Decrease the heat to low once the wood starts smoking. Set a wire rack inside a sheet pan and put it near the smoker or grill.

Let the first blast of acrid smoke blow off, then arrange the pieces of pork belly on the cool side of the grill and close the lid. If you're using a charcoal grill, position the vents over the pork belly. Leave it to smoke, adding more coals as needed, until a meat thermometer inserted into the thickest part reads at least 160°F [71°C], about 1 hour. Transfer the bacon to the rack and let it cool to room temperature.

Use the bacon right away or stow it in an airtight container in the fridge and slice it as needed. It keeps, in the fridge, for up to 2 weeks or frozen for up to 2 months. To use the bacon from frozen, pull it out of the container and thaw it on a wire rack set inside a sheet pan in the fridge.

⅔ cup [110 g] kosher salt

2 Tbsp dark brown sugar

4 tsp granulated sugar

2 tsp freshly ground black pepper

1½ tsp pink curing salt

1 tsp freshly ground white pepper

3 lb [1.4 kg] skinless pork belly, cut crosswise into three equal pieces

Hickory chunks, for smoking

TIME
½ hour active;
1 week total

YIELD
Three 12 oz [340 g] slabs

SPECIAL GEAR
Grill or smoker
Lump charcoal

These aren't chewy and leathery like sun-dried tomatoes. They're jammy and still a bit juicy, with their flavor intensified after a long stretch in a just-hot oven. They amp up the love in the California PBLT (page 183), the Miso-Braised Gigante Beans (page 179), the Smoked Tongue Reuben (page 94), the Oyster Po'boys with Smoked Padrón Mayo (page 216), and the Falafel Party (page 181). But after you make them once, I guarantee you'll be making them on the regular to have in your fridge for throwing into a grain salad or stir-fry, on top of a soup, on franks and burgers, in BBQ sauce or shakshuka, and of course, in your next pasta. They go anywhere you want their rich, punchy, garlicky goodness.

2 lb [910 g] Early Girl or other medium tomatoes (about 8 tomatoes)

½ tsp kosher salt

6 to 8 cranks black pepper

8 garlic cloves, thinly sliced

12 fresh thyme sprigs

½ cup [120 ml] extra-virgin olive oil

Preheat the oven to 250°F [120°C]. Line a sheet pan with a silicone mat or parchment paper.

Core and halve the tomatoes crosswise. Lay them, cut-side up, on the prepared sheet pan and sprinkle them with the salt and pepper. Scatter the garlic and thyme over the tomatoes, then drizzle everything with ¼ cup [60 ml] of the olive oil. Bake until the tomatoes are curling at the edges and half-jammy, half-juicy, about 5 hours. Let the tomatoes cool until you can touch them, then peel and discard their skins and the thyme. Put the tomatoes and garlic in a jar and pour the remaining ¼ cup [60 ml] of olive oil on top. They'll keep, in the fridge, for up to 2 weeks.

oven-dried tomatoes

TIME
15 minutes active; 5 hours 15 minutes total

YIELD
About 3 cups [745 g]

¼ cup [32 g] lime peels
(from about 4 limes)

3 Tbsp Anaheim chili powder

1 Tbsp flaky salt,
such as Maldon

1 Tbsp garlic powder

1 tsp cayenne pepper

1 tsp freshly ground cumin

1 tsp smoked paprika

A chile and citrus salt, Tajín rocks your haunches, makes your mouth water, and draws out a ton of flavor. Branded in Mexico in the mid-1980s, it fast became integral to Californian Mexican food. Along with hot sauce, I keep it in my glove box. That's all I need to make gas station fried chicken taste the way it should.

This here is my homemade version. Since a little goes a long way, and you want to use it fresh, we aren't going to make a ton in each batch. You'll use it on the Grilled and Chilled Melon (page 309) and the chips for the Lingcod Ceviche (page 210), but if you're like me, you'll end up tapping it onto all kinds of foods. The recipe is a dump and stir with a caveat—you need to dehydrate the lime peels overnight because they are the key to Tajín's beauty. Peel the citrus in big, shallow strips, avoiding the bitter pith. Mix any leftover lime powder with salt and sprinkle it on grapefruit, fish, pork, or anywhere you want to bring up bright flavor.

tajín-style spice

In a dehydrator or on a sheet pan in a 150°F [65°C] oven (or your oven's lowest temperature setting), dry the lime peels for 12 hours, then blitz them in a food processor or spice grinder into a fine powder.

In a small bowl, mix 1 tablespoon of the lime powder with the remaining ingredients, breaking up the salt a bit with your fingers, until the spice mix is fully combined. It keeps, in a small jar in a cool, dry place, for up to 3 weeks.

TIME
**15 minutes active;
12 hours 15 minutes total**

YIELD
7 Tbsp [56 g]

SPECIAL GEAR
Dehydrator

furikake

4 sheets toasted, seasoned nori

4 Tbsp [35 g] toasted white sesame seeds

4 Tbsp [35 g] black sesame seeds

½ tsp sugar

¼ tsp kosher salt

⅛ tsp MSG

I like to snack. Who doesn't? But I'm happier when I can bring earth and brine to the party. Furikake does that job. It's the umami boost that makes the Furikake Popcorn (page 112) so addictive. It rocks condiments like the sauce for the Grilled Spot Prawn Cocktail (page 295). It adds dimension to desserts, like the Red Miso Caramel Apples (page 222). It's also easy to make. You want your nori fresh out of the package, so it grinds nicely. As for the MSG, don't sweat it. That flavor enhancer comes from glutamic acid, which occurs naturally in umami-rich foods like mushrooms, meat, and Parmesan. Some people are averse to it, though, so it's always good to mention it when you're serving a dish with this furikake in it.

In a food processor, pulse the nori until it's the size of crumbs. Transfer the nori to a small bowl.

In a coffee grinder, grind 2 tablespoons of the white sesame seeds into a powder. Add them to the nori, along with the remaining 2 tablespoons of whole white sesame seeds and the rest of the ingredients and mix well until the furikake is fully combined. It keeps, at room temperature in an airtight container, for up to 2 weeks.

TIME
10 minutes

YIELD
About 1 cup [80 g]

There are brands of this seasoning on the market, but when you make it yourself with fresh seeds and spices, you guarantee its potency, and its flavor is just dynamite. You'll sprinkle it on the tortillas for the Lox 'n' Tacs (page 148) and the nori for the Fish Stick Hand Roll Bar (page 358). Beyond that, you can use it to season everything in your life: steaks, eggs, grilled cheese sandwiches, mayo for veggie dip. You could even dust the lavash for the Confit Tuna Salad (page 126) with it for something extra. Sky's the limit.

In a small bowl, mix all the ingredients, breaking up the salt a bit with your fingers, until the seasoning is fully combined. It keeps, at room temperature in an airtight container, for up to 2 weeks.

2 Tbsp toasted white
  sesame seeds

2 Tbsp poppy seeds

2 Tbsp dried minced garlic

1 Tbsp dried minced onion

1 Tbsp black sesame seeds

1 Tbsp flaky salt,
  such as Maldon

everything seasoning

TIME
5 minutes

YIELD
9 Tbsp [72 g]

2 cups [185 g] masa harina,
plus more as needed

½ tsp kosher salt

homemade tortillas

Have you ever looked at the ingredients in packaged tortillas? It's a mind-boggling array of weirdo stabilizers and thickeners. You don't know what you're eating, and the flavor isn't good. On the Central Coast, when I'm in a hurry, I score a stack of just-made tortillas at my local Mexican market. Super fragrant, earthy, and tender, those tortillas are made with just three ingredients: masa harina, salt, and water. If I have the time, I get 'em even fresher by making them myself. All you need is a tortilla press (see page 31). These babies are the vessels for the Lox 'n' Tacs (page 148), the dippers for the Lingcod Ceviche (page 210), and the wrappers for the Taquito Party (page 364). You'll never go back to packaged.

In a medium bowl, mix the masa harina and salt. Slowly add 1½ cups [360 ml] of hot water from the tap, kneading with your hands until it's the consistency of playdough. If it's too tacky, add more masa harina, 1 tablespoon at a time. If it's too dense, add more hot water, 1 tablespoon at a time. Form the dough into 8 to 10 smooth balls. Cover the balls with a damp kitchen towel so they don't dry out.

Arrange one ball of dough between two pieces of plastic wrap in a tortilla press, then use the press to flatten the dough until it's ⅛ in [3 mm] thick. Don't make it too thin, or it will tear.

Get a flattop grill or skillet sizzling hot over medium-high heat. Carefully peel the tortilla off the plastic wrap, put it in the pan, and cook it until its edges start to dry and curl, about 1 minute. Flip the tortilla and cook the other side until it puffs and chars slightly, about 1 minute more. Transfer it to a tortilla warmer, aluminum foil, or a plate covered with a kitchen towel to keep it warm. Repeat with the remaining balls of masa. Stow any leftover tortillas in a ziplock or resealable silicone bag and squeeze out the air. They keep, in the fridge, for up to 1 week or in the freezer for up to 1 month. Thaw them in the fridge, then heat them in a skillet for 15 seconds to serve.

TIME
30 minutes

YIELD
8 to 10 tortillas

SPECIAL GEAR
Tortilla press

afternoon at dad's

At the end of day, we don't take ourselves too seriously at Dad's Luncheonette. We're making sandwiches on the side of the road. It just so happens that they're really good, and that's about making yourself available: to ingredients, to flavor, to joy. There's a sign on Dad's kitchen door. It reads: "Don't fuck it up and do the hard work." We take that to heart. We make the food this way because, guaranteed, you want to eat it this way. I've done all the legwork.

It's pretty easy: We're rocking flavor, but we're also practical about it. We're all line cooks, and a line cook's mindset is to be a scavenger. We show up like badgers and gather what we need to make our mise en place, both in our minds and at our stations. Line cooks are all about efficiency. At Dad's, we use that efficiency to make the cooking easier, so we have more time for ourselves.

We have our shit down because that's how we thrive. Hyper-seasonal and -local, succinct, and focused, Dad's lends itself to the lifestyle I'm striving for: Work really hard, do it the right way, be personable and available, and when the doors close, California awaits. Go enjoy it. You're not at work anymore.

The restaurant was built on the idea that, if you focus on what you're doing and hone your skills, you can have fun while you cook and also have a life. I made it this way so that I can spend time with my daughter, Frost. Dad's wouldn't exist without the kid, and that's the underlying ethos of the book. We're feeding the people we love, and we're having good times with them. It's a restaurant in a train car; we're making it happen in a metal box. If we can do it there, you can do it at home. These recipes show you how.

What we reach for when creating a simple sandwich is transferrable to a simple life. I'm looking for a lot of fun things to happen, but I'm also looking for a subtle, calm, chill vibe. I want to pace myself, because I've seen the top of the mountain, and I've seen the bottom, and they're pretty similar views. I'm aiming for the sweet spot in between.

The recipes in this chapter are all made to strike that balance. They're bridging the gap between high and low. We're prepping down-home shrimp and grits (page 84), but then we're folding in Chicken Liver Mousse (page 270) to make the corn porridge creamier, weightier, and more luxurious with a bigger umami flavor, and we're glazing the crustaceans in a mega reduction using cheap lager and a French method. The result is just short of too much, but sucking those shrimp heads, people can't get enough of it.

That's the way we do it at Dad's. We use excellent technique to make flavor-packed food that's gutsy yet super relatable. We take some left turns on the way. We're accessible, but we're far from commonplace. We know, for instance, that everything doesn't have to be seasoned with salt. Hit it with white soy sauce; it's got more depth. Instead of balancing out a dish with black pepper, what does it taste like with a little more acid, like from white balsamic? We want to explore the edges of that homey profile and open up taste buds to way more flavors.

So, enjoy your visit to Dad's. Give yourself a break here. Relax and don't stress over these recipes, because that's not at all what we want for you. We want you to learn some stuff you didn't know before, try some unfamiliar and, in my opinion, delicious flavors, and feel proud of yourself that you pulled something off. We know because we're living it: You shouldn't have to sweat so damned hard for your lunch.

dad's potato chips

2 lb [910 g] unpeeled russet potatoes

½ cup [40 g] nutritional yeast

2 tsp kosher salt

10 cups [2.4 L] canola oil

Chips are a must at Dad's. Given our high flow of patrons and the tight train car setup with a fryer jammed into one corner, we can't make burgers and hot, fresh fries simultaneously. There's also no space for the infrared lamp that would hold fries at a decent temperature. But we must have something potato-y and salty, so the next logical step is chips. Born of necessity, Dad's chips have sold out daily since we opened. Nowadays, we hand slice forty pounds of potatoes each morning, then rinse them over and over, because removing the starch is key to great chips. The chips also sparked the nutritional yeast love affair in the Dad's family. We used to buy one-pound bags of that seasoning until we started getting five-gallon buckets of it. I'm scared to see what's next.

Fill a medium bowl with cold water. Using a mandoline, cut the potatoes into ⅛ in [3 mm] thick slices right into the water. Jostle them with your hands, pulling them apart to unglue the starches, then discard the water. Rinse the potatoes twice more, then fill the bowl with fresh water and refrigerate the potatoes in the water for at least 1 hour.

Line a sheet pan with paper towels. Drain the potatoes into a colander, then spread them out on the prepared sheet pan and use more paper towels to pat them as dry as possible.

In a small bowl, mix the nutritional yeast and salt. Line a large bowl with paper towels. In a medium Dutch oven or heavy-walled pot with a candy thermometer attached, heat the oil to 375°F [190°C]. Working with one handful at a time, fry the chips, continuously moving them around with a slotted spoon or spider, until they are golden brown, 3 to 4 minutes. Transfer the chips to the paper towel–lined bowl and sprinkle them with some of the nutritional yeast mixture. Repeat with the remaining potatoes, bringing the oil back to temperature before adding each handful.

These chips go like gangbusters, but if you want to save some for later, they'll keep, in an airtight container, for a day or two. For extra protection, wrap the container tightly with plastic wrap.

TIME
**45 minutes active;
1 hour 45 minutes total**

YIELD
About 3 qt [2.8 L] chips

2 large leeks

4 Tbsp [60 ml] unrefined, virgin coconut oil

1 Tbsp Madras curry powder

Pinch of kosher salt

2 lb [910 g] carrots, peeled and cut into ¼ in [6 mm] thick slices, about 6 cups

7 oz [200 g] ginger, unpeeled and cut into ¼ in [6 mm] thick slices, about 1½ cups

5 lemongrass stalks, cut into ¼ in [6 mm] thick slices

½ white onion, coarsely chopped

1 cup [145 g] garlic cloves

2 jalapeños, split vertically down the middle but with the stem end still intact

Two 14 oz [415 ml] cans unsweetened Thai coconut milk

3 Tbsp white soy sauce, plus more as needed

4½ tsp dark brown sugar

Yogurt, preferably homemade (page 43), for garnish

Lime zest, for garnish

Fresh lime juice, for garnish

Toasted pumpkin seeds, for garnish

TIME
1 hour

YIELD
4 or 5 servings

This is the fan-favorite soup at Dad's. Sweet, savory, a little salty, a little sour, with a host of beautiful aromatics, it has a lot going on. But it's one of those recipes where I don't do everything from scratch. I make my own coconut milk for desserts, but not for soups, where it gets loose and watery. Canned coconut milk typically has guar gum in it, which holds it together when hot. As for the Madras curry powder, my favorite is from Sun Brand. Established in 1876, they've had time to dial in their spice blend. I could be brash and say I'll make curry powder myself, but I'm certainly not going to do it as well. Some things you leave to other professionals.

Trim off and discard the dark green and root ends of the leeks. Peel and discard the first two layers, then rinse the leeks well. Cut them into ¼ in [6 mm] thick slices, then drop them into a bowl of cold water, separating them into rings and agitating them to clean them thoroughly. Drain the sliced leeks in a colander. You should have about 2 cups [200 g].

In a medium Dutch oven over medium-high heat, melt 2 tablespoons of the coconut oil until it's just beginning to smoke. Add the leeks, curry powder, and salt and cook, stirring, until the leeks are just beginning to caramelize, 3 to 4 minutes. Add the carrots, mix well, and cook for 2 to 3 minutes more. The carrots should still be crunchy. Kill the heat.

In a medium saucepan over medium-high heat, melt the remaining 2 tablespoons of coconut oil until it's just beginning to smoke. Add the ginger, lemongrass, onion, garlic, and jalapeños and cook them, tossing occasionally, until they are fragrant and caramelized, 8 to 10 minutes. Add the coconut milk and bring it to a boil, then knock the heat down to a simmer. Add the white soy sauce and cook for 10 minutes more.

Strain the broth through a chinois into the carrot mixture, pressing on the solids. Bring the soup back up to a boil, then knock the heat down to a simmer and stir in the brown sugar. Add more white soy sauce, 1 teaspoon at a time, as needed and cook until the carrots are crunchy-tender but not soft, 10 to 15 minutes.

To serve, divide the soup among bowls and garnish each bowl with a dollop of yogurt, some lime zest, a squeeze of lime juice, and a handful of pumpkin seeds. If you have leftover soup, treat it like a stew the next day: Poach shrimp, fish, or tofu in it, and serve it over rice.

curried carrot soup

Puffed Rice Topping

Canola oil, for frying

1 cup [180 g] wild rice

½ cup [40 g] nutritional yeast

Pinch of kosher salt

What everyone doesn't want to admit is that life is better if you just make mac 'n' cheese. I was a latchkey kid. My brother and I would smoke dope, play video games, and eat Velveeta Shells & Cheese straight from the pot. That's why, at Dad's, where we boil ten pounds of elbows a day, we make mac 'n' cheese on the stove in a gooey béchamel. It's nostalgic for me. But people crave a golden, crunchy top. So, I puff California wild rice as a topper. It's my compromise for not throwing the thing in the oven. You still get crunch in every bite.

The trick to making béchamel that doesn't stick and burn is to start with warm milk. I learned this technique from a guy who worked for me. Sick of scrubbing scorched Dutch ovens, he just dropped the milk jug straight into the boiling pasta water, and that became a standard. At home, if you want, you can pour your milk into a stainless steel bowl set over the pasta water as it's heating up, and warm your milk that way. Then, when you stir the milk into your roux, it'll be warm enough to start cooking the cheese without scorching.

mac 'n' cheese with puffed rice topping

To make the puffed rice topping: Line a bowl with paper towels. In a medium Dutch oven or heavy-walled pot with a candy thermometer attached, heat 3 in [7.5 cm] of oil to 400°F [200°C]. Put the rice in a fine-mesh strainer, then carefully lower the strainer into the hot oil. The rice will start puffing right away. Give it a shake and a stir, then cook it until the bubbles fade, 1 to 1½ minutes. Drain the rice, shaking off any excess oil, then transfer it to the paper towel–lined bowl. Shake the bowl, pull out the paper towels, and season the rice with the nutritional yeast and salt. You can make the puffed rice topping ahead. It keeps, in an airtight container on your countertop, overnight.

TIME
45 minutes

YIELD
6 to 8 servings

To make the mac 'n' cheese: Add 2 tablespoons of the salt to 6 to 8 quarts [5.7 to 7.5 L] of water in a large pot, and bring it to a boil. Stir in the elbows, and cook them to al dente, about 6 minutes. Drain and shake them to dry.

In a medium Dutch oven over medium-high heat, melt the butter. Whisk in the flour until it's incorporated, about 30 seconds. Add the Gouda and warm milk, then turn the heat to medium, and whisk until the béchamel thickens, 3 to 4 minutes.

You WANT A BIG, BUBBLY, LAZY-BABY SAUCE, THICK ENOUGH TO WRITE YOUR NAME IN IT.

Add the remaining 1 tablespoon of salt, the pepper, and paprika. Add the elbows and stir until they're evenly coated. Spread the puffed rice over the top, scatter on the chives, and drop the pot on the table. This is a serve-immediately situation.

Mac 'n' Cheese

3 Tbsp kosher salt

1 lb [455 g] elbow macaroni

½ cup [113 g] unsalted butter, diced

½ cup [70 g] all-purpose flour

14 oz [400 g] aged smoked Gouda, diced

3 cups [710 ml] warm whole milk

40 good cranks black pepper

1 tsp smoked paprika

1 bunch fresh chives, chopped

Grits

1 cup [170 g] stone-ground grits

1 bay leaf

1 Tbsp white soy sauce

1 tsp freshly ground black pepper

½ tsp kosher salt

½ cup [120 g] Chicken Liver Mousse (page 270)

shrimp and chicken liver grits

When you cook in fine dining, your head is in the clouds, and your path veers away from the simple foods that once brought you joy. I forgot how raucous and fun a beer-drinking, shrimp-peeling hoedown can be. But I grew up going to the fire department oyster roast with my mom, and now that I flip burgers for a living, I've become nostalgic. So, here I've combined my professional experience with my seafood-slurping childhood by bringing French technique to shrimp and grits.

Stone-ground grits are earthy and textural. We put a heady crown on them by blending in Chicken Liver Mousse (page 270). Then we treat the shrimp to a glace—a thick sauce reduction—that we flavor with Old Bay and lager beer as a nod to California's working harbors. Work in steps: While your glace is cooking, get the grits on, then clean and sear your shrimp. Head-on shrimp are worth seeking out. As Frost said, when she learned to suck shrimp heads, "The juiciness! Woo, mama!"

To make the grits: The day before, in a medium pot, combine the grits with 4½ cups [1 L] of water and soak them overnight in the fridge.

To make the shrimp glace: In a Dutch oven over high heat, heat the umami oil. Turn on your vent hood, then add the fennel and shallots, cut-side down, and sear for 2 minutes. Add the garlic and sear for 1 minute. Add the serrano, cut-side down, and sear for 15 seconds. Add the shrimp shells and cook, stirring, until they're opaque, 1 to 2 minutes. Add the lager, Old Bay, and hot sauce and cook until the liquid is reduced by about half, 3 to 5 minutes. Add the chicken stock and tomatoes and bring the mixture to a boil. Knock the heat down to a simmer and cook until the flavor is deep and tasty,

TIME
2 hours active; overnight total

YIELD
4 to 6 servings

about 40 minutes. Throw in the basil and fennel fronds, and cook until they turn dull, 2 minutes. Kill the heat, then strain the stock through a chinois into a heatproof bowl, pressing on the solids.

Give the pot a quick wash, then pour the stock back in and bring it to a boil. Knock the heat down to a simmer and cook, skimming any floating schmutz, until it's reduced to about ¼ cup [60 ml] and a spoon can part it like Moses, about 1 hour.

Meanwhile, for the grits: Skim off any floating schmutz from the soaking water, then put the pot on the stove and bring it to a boil. Continue boiling until the grits thicken, 5 to 6 minutes, then stir them, cover the pot, and turn off the heat. Let the grits rest for 10 minutes. Add the bay leaf, white soy sauce, pepper, and salt, and simmer, uncovered, over low heat, stirring occasionally, until the grits coat the back of a spoon, 45 minutes to 1 hour. Cool them for 15 minutes, then stir in the chicken liver mousse.

To make the shrimp: In a 9 in [23 cm] cast-iron pan over medium-high heat, heat 1 tablespoon of the canola oil. Add the cipollinis and a pinch of salt and cook, stirring, until they're deeply browned, about 2 minutes. Add them to the grits, then return the pan to medium-high heat. Add half of the shrimp and a pinch of salt to the pan and sear the shrimp on one side until the color has crept halfway up their bodies, 1 to 2 minutes. Flip them, and sear them until cooked through, 1 to 2 minutes more. Add the shrimp to the grits, then cook the remaining shrimp, using the remaining canola oil and salt. Add the remaining shrimp to the grits. Return the pan to medium-high heat, then add the butter and garlic and cook, swirling the pan, for 30 seconds. Pour the garlic butter over the grits, then drizzle the shrimp glace all over the shrimp and grits and serve it in the pot.

Shrimp Glace

2 Tbsp Umami Oil (page 46) or canola oil

1 small fennel bulb, halved lengthwise

2 large shallots, quartered

8 garlic cloves, peeled

1 serrano chile, halved lengthwise

Reserved shells from 2 lb [910 g] shrimp

¾ cup [180 ml] lager

2 tsp Old Bay Seasoning

2 tsp hot sauce, preferably Fermented Hot Sauce (page 62)

6 cups [1.4 L] chicken stock, preferably The Best Chicken Stock (page 63)

2 plum tomatoes, halved

5 fresh basil sprigs

¼ cup [8 g] fennel fronds

Shrimp

2 Tbsp canola oil

4 cipollini onions, peeled, cut lengthwise into eighths, and separated into petals

3 pinches of kosher salt

2 lb [910 g] head-on shrimp, bodies peeled and deveined (see page 295), shells reserved

2 Tbsp unsalted butter

1 large garlic clove, chopped

smoked chicken with smoked chimichurri

Smoked Chicken

1 whole chicken, about 3 lb [1.4 kg], giblets removed

3 Tbsp freshly ground black pepper

2 Tbsp kosher salt

Almond, hickory, apple, or cherry wood chunks, for smoking

continued

Smoke, salt, lots of black pepper—that's the love that penetrates everything in this simple but wildly flavorful smoked chicken paired with a spicy relish made from vegetables smoked alongside it. The chimichurri is a dynamite dunker for the bird. The veg confits in the smoker and gets blitzed into a tangy, herby sauce with the kick to contrast the chicken.

I'm a fan of a barrel smoker. It's just a big, old steel drum with some rods welded inside for hanging birds. But use any kind of smoker you can get your hands on, or your grill. Just don't soak the wood chunks. It's not only unnecessary, but it also lowers the temperature. Make sure your top and bottom vents are clear, and keep coals on deck to feed your fire midway. You'll get a luxuriously smoked bird that's deeply bronzed and as moist as can be.

To make the smoked chicken: The day before, pat the chicken dry inside and out with a kitchen towel. Set a wire rack inside a sheet pan and arrange the chicken on top. Stow it in the fridge, uncovered, to rest overnight. Rub the pepper and salt all over the chicken, inside and out. Let the chicken come to room temperature.

Prep your smoker. If you're using a charcoal grill, bank your coals to one side. When the coals are glowing and no longer on fire, throw a big handful of almond, hickory, apple, or cherry wood chunks on top of them. For a gas grill, heat one side on high, place the wood in a smoker box, and place the smoker box over the flame. Decrease the heat to low once the wood starts smoking.

Let the first blast of acrid smoke blow off, then put the chicken on the grate on the cool side of the grill, and close the lid. If you're using a charcoal grill, position the vents over the chicken. Leave it to smoke, adding more coals as needed, until the chicken is burnished a deep golden brown, its juices run clear, and a thermometer inserted into the thickest part of the thigh reads at least 165°F [74°C], about 1 hour.

continued

TIME
1½ hours active; overnight total

YIELD
4 to 6 servings

SPECIAL GEAR
Grill or smoker
Lump charcoal

Smoked Chimichurri

3 jalapeños, stemmed and halved lengthwise

8 garlic cloves, peeled

3 whole shallots, peeled

3 Tbsp avocado oil

3 Tbsp extra-virgin olive oil

1 tsp kosher salt, plus more as needed

2 cups [80 g] coarsely chopped fresh parsley

1 cup [40 g] coarsely chopped fresh cilantro

4 fresh oregano sprigs, stems removed

6 cranks black pepper

½ cup [120 ml] red wine vinegar

½ tsp red pepper flakes

Zest of 3 lemons, preferably Meyer

Juice of 2 lemons, preferably Meyer

Meanwhile, to make the smoked chimichurri: Create a little cradle out of aluminum foil. Remove the seeds from two of the jalapeños, then put all the jalapeños, along with the garlic and shallots, inside the foil. Drizzle the mixture with 1 tablespoon each of the avocado and olive oils, then sprinkle it with the salt. When the bird has smoked for 35 minutes, arrange the cradle of aromatics next to it on the cool side of the grill.

When the chicken hits 165°F [74°C], transfer it to a cutting board and let it rest for 15 minutes while you finish the chimichurri.

Put the smoked aromatics in a blender or a food processor, then add the parsley, cilantro, oregano, the remaining 2 tablespoons each of avocado and olive oils, a few big pinches of salt, and the black pepper. Pulse it until the sauce has a uniform consistency but still has texture. Add the vinegar and red pepper flakes, then season with more salt and pulse it to combine. Add the lemon zest and juice and pulse it once more to fully incorporate everything. Carve your chicken and serve it on a platter with the chimichurri alongside.

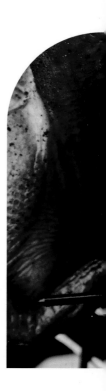

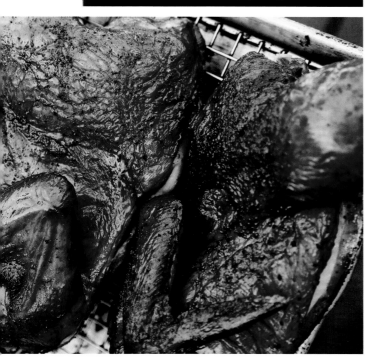

These sandwiches are the heart and soul of Dad's. They're informed by my Wonder Bread days growing up on the East Coast, but they're executed right here on the West Coast. When I came to Half Moon Bay, I was surfing with the egg farmer and kicking it with the local veg producers. How could I cook the beautiful ingredients my friends here were providing while being less stressed than I was in San Francisco? I knew the answer. Give the goodness to the people in the simplest format: between two slices of bread.

The music is in how you interweave the elements. We make it fresh and alive: tickly with pickled onions and a mustardy sauce but also savory with ghee-griddled mushrooms or charred beef. For the burger, we use an 80/20 meat-to-fat mix of chuck and top sirloin, and we smash it hard on the griddle. We want it juicy and crusty all at once.

As for the mushrooms, here's a secret: Dad's is a vegetarian restaurant that serves a hamburger. We have this thing that everyone wants, and then we have all this other stuff people don't know they want, and those are the vegetables. If you make them right, people come back for them. The mushrooms are grown in hoop houses near us. We char them until the moisture releases, and if you were farsighted, you'd barely know them from the beef patty. Flavor, backbone, texture, earth, punch—you get all that when you cook vegetables right.

To make the Dad sauce: In a food processor, a blender, or with an immersion blender in a container that's just wide enough for it to fit, blend the egg yolks, Worcestershire, mustard, honey, vinegar, salt, and pepper until they're fully combined. While blending constantly, slowly stream in the oil to emulsify the sauce into a mayo-like consistency. You'll have about 1½ cups [360 ml] of sauce. It keeps, in the fridge in an airtight container, for about 1 week, so you can spread it on franks and sammies, dip in raw veggies, dab it on eggs, whatever you like.

continued

hen of the woods or hamburger sandwich

Dad Sauce

2 egg yolks

2 Tbsp Worcestershire sauce

2 Tbsp spicy brown mustard

1 Tbsp honey

1 Tbsp apple cider vinegar

2 tsp kosher salt

2 tsp freshly ground black pepper

1 cup [240 ml] canola oil

continued

TIME
45 minutes

YIELD
1 sandwich

To make the toast: In a large skillet over medium-high heat, melt the ghee. Add the bread and toast it, without flipping, until golden and crunchy on one side only, 1 to 2 minutes. Set aside.

If you're making the mushroom option: Heat a grill pan or large skillet over medium-high heat. Season the mushroom with salt and pepper, then add it to the pan and drop in the ghee. When the ghee is melted, spoon it over the mushroom, basting it until it's golden brown and crisp, 2 to 3 minutes. Flip the mushroom and use a spatula to press it into the pan. Move the mushroom to the side of the pan and top it with the cheese. Crack the egg into the open space in the pan and cook it until the white is set and the cheese is melted, 1½ to 2 minutes. Flip the egg and kill the heat.

If you're making the burger option: Form the ground beef into a ball and season it with lots of salt and pepper. In a grill pan or large skillet, heat the oil until it's close to smoking, then add the beef, smashing it down into the pan. Cook the burger until it's charred on the bottom, 1½ to 2 minutes, then flip it. Move the burger to the side of the pan and top it with the cheese. Crack the egg into the open space in the pan and cook it until the white is set and the cheese is melted, 1½ to 2 minutes. Flip the egg and kill the heat.

To make the sandwich: Spread about 1 tablespoon of Dad sauce on the untoasted sides of the bread. Add the lettuce and some pickled onions. Top one slice with the mushroom or burger (whichever you've cooked). Top it with the egg. Close the sandwich and cut it in half to serve.

Toast

1 Tbsp ghee, preferably homemade (page 42)

2 slices good-quality white bread

Mushroom Option

3½ oz [100 g] hen of the woods mushroom

Kosher salt

Freshly ground black pepper

1½ Tbsp ghee, preferably homemade (page 42)

2 or 3 slices sharp Cheddar cheese

1 large egg

Burger Option

4 oz [115 g] grass-fed ground beef

Kosher salt

Freshly ground black pepper

1 Tbsp canola oil

2 or 3 slices sharp Cheddar cheese

1 large egg

Sandwich

1 Tbsp Dad Sauce, plus more as needed

2 lettuce leaves

Pickled Onions (page 48), for garnish

Tongue

1 cow's tongue,
about 2 lb [910 g]

4 garlic cloves, peeled

½ white onion

3 Tbsp white soy sauce

2 Tbsp whole coriander seeds

1 Tbsp peppercorns

1 Tbsp smoked paprika

1 Tbsp whole yellow
mustard seeds

2 tsp whole caraway seeds

2 tsp kosher salt

4 fresh thyme sprigs

4 whole allspice berries

Hickory chunks, for smoking

I used to be a picky eater. You couldn't pay me to eat tongue, brain, foot, or anything like that. But when I moved to San Francisco, there was a taqueria inside a Mexican supermarket, across the street from a bar in the Tenderloin, where I would go and get pissed. I'd stumble into the taqueria afterwards and always go for the white boy–bland order of carne asada. Then, one night, I got smart and ordered lengua. From that point on, offal cuts were all I was doing. Nose-to-tail eating became everything to me.

Tongue is one of the most tender, flavorful cuts ever. In all the taquerias up and down the Central Coast, in any good Jewish deli, wherever you get it, it's working folks' food, prepared by more working folks in a beautiful way—on a taco, on rye bread, whatever. This lean-over-the-table-and-get-filthy Reuben is here to celebrate that.

smoked tongue reuben

To make the tongue: Pat the tongue dry and cut off any weird hang-y bits. In a large stockpot, combine the tongue and the remaining ingredients, except the hickory chunks, with 6 quarts [5.7 L] of water and bring it up to a boil. Knock the heat down to a simmer, cover the pot with the lid cracked to let the steam out, and braise the tongue until a paring knife easily slides through the skin into the meat without any resistance, 1 to 1½ hours. Cool the tongue in the braising liquid until you can handle it, but it's still warm, about 20 minutes. Remove the tongue, and starting at the back, poke your finger in between the skin and the meat to separate them, then peel off and discard the skin. Strain the braising liquid through a fine-mesh strainer into a container large enough to fit the tongue; discard any solids. Add the tongue to the strained liquid, then stow it in the fridge to marinate overnight, so its proteins relax and it gains more flavor.

TIME
**2 hours active;
overnight total**

YIELD
4 hefty sandwiches

SPECIAL GEAR
**Grill or smoker
Lump charcoal**

Pull the tongue out of the liquid and wipe it down. If you're not making all the sandwiches right after smoking, reserve the liquid. After you smoke the tongue, you can store it in the liquid in the fridge and slice it as needed, warming the slices by gently heating them in some of the liquid in a small saucepan on the stove. The smoked tongue keeps, in the fridge in its liquid, for up to 4 days.

Prep your smoker. If you're using a charcoal grill, bank your coals to one side. When the coals are glowing and no longer on fire, throw a handful of hickory chunks on top of them. There's no need to soak the wood chunks. For a gas grill, heat one side on high, place the hickory chunks in a smoker box, and place the smoker box over the flame. Decrease the heat to low once the wood starts smoking. Set a wire rack inside a sheet pan and put it near the smoker or grill.

Let the first blast of acrid smoke blow off, then arrange the tongue on the cool side of the grill and close the lid. If you're using a charcoal grill, position the vents over the tongue. Leave the tongue to smoke, adding more coals as needed, until it's burnished a deep reddish-brown and you can see a smoke ring around its exterior when you cut into it, 45 minutes to 1 hour. Transfer the tongue to the rack and let it cool until you can handle it, then use a sharp knife to slice it crosswise, pastrami-thin.

To make the Russian dressing: In a medium bowl, mix all the ingredients together until they're fully combined. If you have leftover dressing, it keeps, in the fridge in an airtight container, for up to 3 days.

To make the sandwiches: Preheat the oven or toaster oven to 350°F [180°C].

Slice the bagels in half and spread ghee on all the cut sides. In a cast-iron pan over medium-high heat, toast the bagels on the cut sides only until golden, 2 to 3 minutes. Slather Russian dressing on the bottom half of each bagel, then divvy up the kraut, pile on the tongue, and put 2 slices of cheese on top of each. Close the sandwiches with the bagel tops and toast them in the oven or toaster oven until the cheese is melty. To cut them in half, wrap them in parchment paper first to hold them together, then use a sharp knife. Pass out bibs and dive in.

Russian Dressing

½ cup [110 g] The Best Mayonnaise (page 45) or Kewpie

¼ cup [65 g] Oven-Dried Tomatoes (page 67), minced

3 Tbsp minced dill pickles

1 Tbsp minced white onion

2 tsp Pickled Mustard Seeds (page 50)

1 tsp Worcestershire sauce

Kosher salt

Sandwiches

4 everything bagels

3 Tbsp ghee, preferably homemade (page 42)

1 cup [240 g] sauerkraut, preferably Coastal Kraut (page 56)

8 slices Swiss cheese

From left to right: Erik Andreassen, Mimi Peña, Luca Balbi, Anthony Keels, and me
Page 98: Alexis Liu

THE CREW AT ● DAD'S

Alexis Liu → My co-parent and co-owner, Alexis, found Dad's caboose one night after I had a horrible service at Saison, when I was questioning what I was doing with my life. Payroll, writing checks, branding, merchandise—she takes care of things that would otherwise make me lose my mind. On top of all that, she owns a café in San Francisco and a vintage store on the coast. Operating three businesses in California is enough to make anyone's hair fall out, but Alexis remains sane.

Erik Andreassen → Erik came to us after running himself thin cheffing at a restaurant in Santa Cruz. Another East Coast transplant, he resonated with our mission of slowing down and not being fully destroyed by restaurant life. At Dad's, he's all over the place, prepping, doing grill, working salads, expediting. Outside of Dad's, he's home with his own kid or out on his commercial fishing boat being a salty son of a gun.

Anthony Keels → Anthony started at the bar at Saison when I was still a sous chef. I pushed his buttons, he took it in good spirit, and we developed a collaborative relationship doing R & D on shrubs, infusions, and vinegars. He's a wizard when it comes to liquids and a savant about everything else. He can go from fringe music to fringe sherry in the same swath of conversation. He makes Dad's weekend cocktails, pitches in with the kitchen, and handles the front of house with grace.

Mimi Peña → The silent assassin, the bringer of peace, and a hardcore worker, Mimi is also a strong, independent, single mother. She has one kid in nursing school, two others at home, and she worked until she was eight months pregnant, not letting anybody do anything for her. She's a rock when you need a hug. She's quiet yet full of wisdom. She does all the prep, then stands in her window and wraps two hundred sandwiches a day, Dad's origami artist.

Luca Balbi → Luca showed up one rainy day, having run from high school to the restaurant for lunch and a job. He was a goofy, diminutive, fifteen-year-old kid, and we put him through the paces. Now twenty-two, he's a fully aware, incredible young man studying to be an investment banker. I can call him anytime I'm in a pinch, and he'll come to work, run errands, and do what needs to be done. If the crew at Dad's has done anything, at least we raised a good kid here.

Frost Quartz Liu Clark → I was a twentysomething kid whose only focus was destroying myself for someone else's restaurant. Frost showed me there was life beyond the stove. We started Dad's with her in a baby jail—a playpen carved out in a corner of the caboose—and now she's the smartest, most empathetic, most joyful and crazy, loudest, funniest one in the room. She speaks her mind, says how she feels, and isn't afraid to show it. At Dad's, she runs bags to customers, watches *Betty Boop* on her phone, and is an all-around terror and treat.

★ ✩ KIDS ❀ ☮
PLAIN MAC   7.50
GRILLED CHEESE
HAMBURGER   7.50
CHEESEBURGER 8.50
JUST A PATTY 6.50

HAMBURGER SANDWICH $14.5
MAITAKE MUSHROOM
SANDWICH $14.5
-BOTH COME WITH-
SOFT EGG MELTY CHEESE
PICKLED RED
OAK LETTUCE, ONIONS,
ON GRILLED ROSALIND BREAD
RECOMMENDED AS IS
HOMEMADE POTATO CHIPS 4.50
MADE FRESH DAILY
MOM'S HERB SALAD
MEYER

KID'S LUNCHEONETTE
PLAIN MAC & CHEESE   5.5
GRILLED CHEESE   6
MEAT + CHEESE SANDWICH 8
MEAT ONLY SANDWICH   7
JUST A PATTY   6

Graham Cracker Crust

1 cup [120 g] graham cracker crumbs

⅓ cup [65 g] sugar

⅓ cup [75 g] unsalted butter, melted

Earl Grey Filling

⅔ cup [130 g] sugar

¼ cup [35 g] cornstarch

3 large eggs

Pinch of kosher salt

1⅔ cups [400 ml] whole milk

½ cup [120 ml] heavy cream

⅓ cup [35 g] loose Earl Grey tea leaves

3 oz [85 g] white chocolate, coarsely chopped

Yogurt, preferably homemade (page 43), for garnish

Orange and lime zest, for garnish

TIME
45 minutes active;
3 hours 45 minutes total

YIELD
One 9 in [23 cm] pie

earl grey icebox pie

I gave up coffee and cigarettes when I gave up cooking in Michelin-starred restaurants. Earl Grey is my go-to cup now, but it's polarizing. People think they don't like the bergamot flavor, but really, what they don't like is oversteeped tea. In the States, we put a bag in water, forget about it until it's cold, then chug it when it's dark and bitter. But there's a right way to brew tea. The steeping time for this filling is dead-on for making a good cup of tea, then the tea leaves stay in the custard, flecking the pie. The recipe came from my personal challenge to get people on board with Earl Grey. It's the most requested dish at Dad's. Every week, people ask me, "When are you going to do that tea pie again?"

To make the graham cracker crust: In a medium bowl, mix the graham cracker crumbs and sugar. Add the melted butter and mix until the texture is like sand. Press the mixture evenly into the bottom and sides of a 9 in [23 cm] pie pan. Chill the crust for at least 15 minutes.

To make the Earl Grey filling: In a medium bowl, mix the sugar and cornstarch. In a second medium bowl, whisk together the eggs and salt. Whisk the eggs into the sugar mixture.

In a medium Dutch oven over medium-high heat, bring the milk, heavy cream, and tea to a boil. Kill the heat and let it steep for 2 minutes. Whisk one-third of the hot milk mixture into the sugar-egg mixture to temper it, then pour the sugar-egg mixture into the saucepan with the remaining hot milk mixture. Bring it to a simmer and continue simmering, whisking constantly, until it's thick enough to coat the back of a spoon, 5 to 10 minutes.

Pour the custard into a blender, add the white chocolate, and blend it on high until it's smooth, about 1 minute. Pour the filling into the chilled pie crust, then freeze the pie until it's set, about 3 hours. Let the pie rest at room temp for 5 minutes before slicing and serving it topped with yogurt and orange and lime zest. Leftover pie keeps, in the fridge covered, for up to 3 days.

This recipe is a riff on Greek donuts, which come in these fun little esoteric shapes. I replicate that weirdness by not measuring when frying and just scooping up batter with a soup spoon and dropping it in the oil. Traditionally, Greek donuts get doused in honey water, but I like these beignet-style, dusted in powdered sugar, with a little cinnamon for snap. Suit yourself, though, because there are so many ways to freestyle with them. Add chopped nuts or rose water to the batter or melt chocolate into the mascarpone. However you want to go off script, the best thing about these yeasty boys is there's not a ton of sugar in them, which makes them easy to eat. You can down a million and still keep going. Correction: "Two million," says Frost.

yeasty drop donuts

Maple Mascarpone

1 lb [455 g] mascarpone

¼ cup [60 ml] maple syrup

Donuts

Two ¼ oz [7 g] envelopes instant yeast

3 Tbsp granulated sugar

4 cups [560 g] all-purpose flour

½ tsp kosher salt

1 cup [240 ml] whole milk

1 tsp vanilla extract

Canola oil, for frying

Powdered sugar, for dusting

Ground cinnamon, for dusting

To make the maple mascarpone: In a food processor, a stand mixer fitted with a paddle attachment, or a medium bowl with a hand mixer or whisk, whip the mascarpone until it holds soft peaks. Add the maple syrup and whip until soft peaks form again.

To make the donuts: In a medium bowl, combine the yeast, 1 tablespoon of the granulated sugar, and ½ cup [120 ml] of warm water. Let the yeast bloom until it's slightly frothy and smelling bready, about 10 minutes.

In another medium bowl, mix the remaining 2 tablespoons of granulated sugar, flour, and salt.

You don't want the warm liquids too hot. Make them tea-chugging temperature

In a small saucepan over medium heat, warm the milk, vanilla, and 1½ cups [360 ml] of water for about 3 minutes. Add the milk mixture to the yeast mixture, then pour that into the flour mixture and whisk the living daylights out of the batter until there are no lumps. Cover the bowl tightly, and let the batter sit until it's doubled in size, about 30 minutes.

continued

TIME
45 minutes active;
1 hour 45 minutes total

YIELD
About 3 dozen donuts

Beat down the batter, knocking out the air with a spatula. Cover the bowl tightly, let it rise again for 30 minutes, then beat it down once more. It should be elastic and tacky. At this point, you can fry the donuts or stow the batter in the fridge overnight. Bring the batter back to room temperature before frying.

Set a wire rack inside a sheet pan. In a medium Dutch oven or heavy-walled pot with a candy thermometer attached, heat 3 in [7.5 cm] of oil to 375°F [190°C]. Quickly dip a soup spoon into the oil, then scoop up a spoonful of the batter, and carefully drop it in the oil. Fry the donut, moving it around and flipping it, until it's golden brown all the way around, about 1 minute per side. Transfer the donut to the wire rack. Repeat with the rest of the batter, frying four or five donuts at a time without crowding the pot. Dust the donuts with the powdered sugar and cinnamon, then serve them immediately with the maple mascarpone on the side for dipping. These don't keep well, but that's OK because folks will gobble them up.

rhubarb brownies

Shortly after Dad's first launched, I was tired, overworked, and didn't know what I wanted to serve for dessert that week. Somebody had dropped off a bunch of rhubarb, and I thought, "Screw it." I knew how to cook down rhubarb, I often made brownies, and I just wanted to get it done. Out of a low moment came something special.

People get bent out of shape about rhubarb. "What do I do with this red celery?" Here's a fudgy, shiny-topped brownie to get your feet kicking in the rhubarb pool. The fruitiness of the vegetable elevates the chocolate's intensity. And after you make the jam once, you'll want to make it again for PB & R sandwiches, to top yogurt or oatmeal, or to mix with mustard, spices, and tomato paste for a rhubarbecue sauce to slather on roast pork.

To make the rhubarb jam: Trim the tops and bottoms off the rhubarb. Starting at one end of a stalk, tuck a paring knife just beneath the skin, and peel it off in strips. Repeat to peel the rest of the rhubarb. Cut the rhubarb into ¼ in [6 mm] thick slices, then put it in a medium pot. Add the sugar, vanilla, and ¼ cup [60 ml] of water and bring the mixture to a boil. Knock the heat down to a simmer and cook it, stirring occasionally, until the liquid has evaporated and the jam has thickened, about 30 minutes. Cool the jam to room temp. You should have about 1½ cups [500 g].

To make the brownies: Preheat the oven to 350°F [180°C]. Spray a 9 by 13 in [23 by 33 cm] baking pan with pan spray, line it with parchment paper, and spray the paper.

In a medium bowl, use a rubber spatula to mix together the eggs, cocoa powder, vanilla, baking powder, and salt until they're smooth.

Make a double boiler: Add 2 in [5 cm] of water to a medium saucepan, set a medium stainless steel bowl over the top, combine the sugar and butter in the bowl, and stir over medium heat until they are melted together. Add this mixture to the egg mixture and mix it until it's smooth and uniform. Fold in the flour, chocolate chips, and rhubarb jam. Pour the batter into the prepared baking pan and bake it until the edges pull away from the pan but the center is still jiggly, 30 to 40 minutes. Cool the brownies to room temperature, then let your people devour them, slicing them to serve. Store leftover brownies at room temperature in the pan, wrapped tightly in plastic wrap. They keep like that for up to 5 days.

Rhubarb Jam

1 lb [455 g] rhubarb

1½ cups [300 g] sugar

1 vanilla bean, seeds scraped and pod discarded

Brownies

Pan spray, if needed

4 large eggs

1¼ cups [100 g] Dutch process cocoa powder

2 tsp vanilla extract

1 tsp baking powder

1 tsp kosher salt

2¼ cups [450 g] sugar

1 cup [226 g] unsalted butter

1½ cups [210 g] all-purpose flour

2 cups [360 g] dark chocolate chips, preferably 70% cacao

1½ cups [500 g] Rhubarb Jam

You want slick, shiny, fudgy brownies. If you don't use a double boiler, you'll get cakey brownies.

TIME
1½ hours

YIELD
One 9 by 13 in [23 by 33 cm] tray of brownies

road trip snacks

•

Now we're hitting the road, heading south on Highway 1. It's summertime. The hills are golden with mustard flowers. All through winter, we hunkered down. We gained some weight. Then spring came, and we shed our shells. Now it's time to get up and go. Let's see cool things, eat good food, hike, and swim in icy water. We're hugging the cliffside highway, redwoods on one side, the Pacific on the other. The kid and I always get hungry in the truck. When I'm feeling real road-trippy, I want a bag of Hot Cheetos. But we like to stay active, so instead of gas-station snacks, we pack fresh-made things that hit flavor head-on and fuel us for the next stretch of driving and peeing in a milk jug.

I learned how to eat in the car from the queen of all road trips. In her Black Dodge Caravan, my mom was not to be messed with. She sped hard down to North Carolina and Florida, and on one formative drive after my parents broke up all the way to Minnesota, skirting the Great Lakes. Mom would prep beef jerky. She'd dump buttered popcorn into a plastic bag, a salty, greasy, inhalable mess. She'd give us this Tupperware full of magical snacks, and now that I have a child of my own, I understand how practical that was, saving her money and getting us excited for twelve hours in the car. That and a VHS TV plugged into the cigarette lighter preserved her sanity while we watched *The Princess Bride*, grubbing on snacks.

My mom nailed the great American road trip. From her, I discovered early on that you can alter your life by getting in the car, and that's how I got to California. The day I was leaving, I was backing down the driveway when, lo and behold, out comes Mom with a Tupperware of road snacks for me ready to roll.

I took those lessons and applied them to my now. If Frost and I are driving for more than two hours, we're stacked with a cooler of tasty food to keep us going twice as long. We just sit in the breakdown lane, get sated, breathe in the sunset over the Pacific, then move along in our travels.

Road-trip snacks need to deliver a variety of textures and flavors. They have to be sweet, salty, acidic, umami, and also filling, so you can keep on going, whatever your destination. To help us maintain laser-focus, our cooler gives it all: Furikake Popcorn (page 112) and Shio Koji–Cured Jerky (page 115) that riff on my mom's road trip Tupperware; proteins like Confit Tuna Salad with Sea Salt Lavash (page 126); California Kimbap (page 122), a full meal in a nori wrap; Herby Buttermilk Ranch Dip (page 116) for dunking raw veg grabbed from the farmers' market on the way out of town; and for a sweet treat, CA Muddy Buddies (page 131), a riff on a recipe I stole from my bestemor, my Norwegian grandma on my mom's side. She was a maniac whose idea of a road snack was a nose-clearing, head-spinning Bloody Mary made with about a medicine dropper's worth of tomato juice.

There's nothing like lemonade on a summer road trip. On the coast, we have year-round access to the best lemons in the world. Originally from China, Meyer lemons are named for wild man Frank Meyer, who worked for the USDA. A plant explorer, he brought more than twenty-five hundred species to the States. He died in 1918, under mysterious circumstances on the Yangtze River, but not before getting this lemon-mandarin cross to California. Meyers are large, with an orange-ish hue, and they taste like lemon flowers drizzled in honey. Chamomile tea and wildflower honey make this lemonade even more floral. When you travel with a jar of it, bring a cooler of ice. The lemonade is full strength; the dilution happens when you pour it over ice.

8 Meyer lemons, plus Meyer lemon slices, for garnish

1 bag chamomile tea

½ cup [170 g] wildflower honey

perfect meyer lemonade

Roll the lemons under your palm to break the membranes and get the juices flowing. Cut them crosswise in half, then use a citrus squeezer to juice them into a pitcher.

In a medium saucepan, bring 1 cup [240 ml] of water to a boil, then kill the heat, add the chamomile tea bag, and steep the tea for 10 minutes.

Remove and discard the tea bag and bring the tea back to a simmer. Add the honey and stir it to dissolve. Kill the heat and let the tea come to room temperature.

Pour the cooled tea into the pitcher of lemon juice, add 3 cups [710 ml] of cold water, and give it a stir. Garnish the lemonade with the Meyer lemon slices. To serve it, fill glasses halfway with ice and pour the lemonade over the ice.

TIME
30 minutes

YIELD
About 6 cups [1.4 L]

2 Tbsp ghee, preferably homemade (page 42)

2 tsp toasted sesame oil

½ cup [115 g] popcorn kernels

1 tsp kosher salt

3 Tbsp unsalted butter, melted

½ cup [40 g] furikake, preferably homemade (page 70)

Pinch of sugar

I have strong feelings about popcorn, because after my parents split, on Popcorn Tuesdays, that's what we ate. My mom was a working woman, and sometimes she didn't want to cook for her stoner teens. So, she'd make a brown paper grocery bag full of popcorn, drizzle it with butter, sprinkle it with salt, and put it on the table. I don't know if she knew it was high in fiber and good for you, but we loved those nights. Normally, she would never let us watch TV while eating. But Popcorn Tuesday was party-vibe, no-holds-barred magical. I didn't have to complain about eating lima beans and other stuff I hated. It was just, "Hell, yeah, Mom is the best!"

She always reserved her own portion of popcorn, which she'd douse in Parmesan cheese. I thought that looked disgusting until I tried it. Savory, sweet, and deep, this popcorn mimics it. Now that I'm a parent, this is the easiest way for me to keep doing what I'm doing, such as cruising down Highway 1 with the kid in the back tearing through a big bag of the stuff.

In a medium Dutch oven, combine the ghee and sesame oil, then add the popcorn and salt, cover the pot, and turn the heat to medium. With oven mitts on, shake the pot back and forth on the burner. About 3 minutes in, you'll start to hear popping. Continue shaking the pot until the popping slows to 5-second intervals, 4 to 5 minutes more. Dump the popcorn into a large bowl, or a big paper bag if you're traveling, then drizzle it with the butter, sprinkle it with the furikake and sugar, and give it a good stir or shake to thoroughly coat it. Let everyone rip in. It keeps, in a paper bag at room temperature, overnight. It will be greasier and chewier the next day, but I like it even better that way.

TIME
15 minutes

YIELD
4 servings

furikake popcorn

Beef jerky is the ultimate road-trip craving. But instead of a twenty dollar, quarter-pound bag of some overprocessed brand you grab at a quick mart, for a fraction of the cost, you can make it yourself and perfume your kitchen with the heady aroma of drying beef. The recipe is minimalist. That's intentional. You're not throwing a bunch of spices on the beef. It's three ingredients and patience, and when you cook like that, magic can happen. Once you have it in your back pocket, you can spread it around. Need an easy gift for someone? Slam some beef in your dehydrator and turn out a batch of jerky. It's easiest if you go to an Asian market and buy presliced shabu-shabu meat. That, or ask your butcher to cut you some lean eye-of-round beef about ⅛ in [3 mm] thick.

In a medium bowl, mix all the ingredients. Cover the bowl and stow it in the fridge to marinate the beef for 12 hours.

Using gloved hands, scrape off any excess shio koji. Arrange the beef in a single layer on your dehydrator racks or on a fine-mesh grate set over a sheet pan in a 155°F [68°C] oven (or in your oven at its lowest temperature setting). Dry it for 10 hours for chewier jerky and 12 hours for crispy, crackly jerky. Let the jerky sit at room temp for 45 minutes, then store it in a mason jar or a ziplock or reusable silicone bag. It keeps, at room temperature, for up to 2 weeks, with the texture relaxing a bit over time. But really, it will last a few hours—unless you hide it from yourself and everyone else. It's that good.

shio koji-cured jerky

1 lb [455 g] thinly sliced, eye-of-round beef, cut into 2 in [5 cm] strips

5½ oz [155 ml] shio koji, preferably homemade (page 54)

2 tsp freshly ground black pepper

YOU CAN USE MORE OR LESS BEEF. JUST MAKE SURE THE SHIO KOJI'S WEIGHT IS 30% OF THE BEEF'S WEIGHT.

TIME
10 minutes active; 1 day total

YIELD
About 8 oz [230 g]

SPECIAL GEAR
Dehydrator

herby buttermilk ranch dip

1 cup [220 g] The Best Mayonnaise (page 45) or Kewpie

2 Tbsp buttermilk

Zest of 2 lemons, preferably Meyer

2 tsp fresh lemon juice, preferably Meyer

1 tsp Confit Garlic (page 47)

1 tsp hot sauce, preferably Fermented Hot Sauce (page 62)

½ tsp Oriental hot mustard powder

¼ tsp smoked paprika

10 cranks black pepper

Kosher salt

¼ cup [12 g] packed fresh chives

¼ cup [10 g] chopped fresh parsley

¼ cup [3 g] chopped fresh dill

Lots of whatever raw veg you want, for serving

Whatever veg is at the market when you're gearing up for a roadside picnic, this is the dipper they need. My preference is chicories: radicchio, dandelion, and definitely Belgian endive, which is nature's shovel. Also try tender celery stalks with their leaves, small radishes and turnips with their greens, slices of watermelon radish and carrots for color, blanched asparagus, raw snap peas and green beans, and jicama, if you're of the crunchy persuasion. You get to use all this veg to hammer a bunch of mayo into your face and feel good about it.

The recipe includes a smart way to process your chives. I call it the Chive Harness, and it requires a sharp knife. Otherwise, you'll bruise your herbs as you slice, and that muddies their taste. To ensure you're not whisking through a jungle, you add the herbs last, after you've built your base flavor. The hot mustard snaps you to it. The paprika adds a smoky edge. And the buttermilk brings the acid that takes the herb notes where you want them to be.

In a medium bowl, whisk the mayo and buttermilk together until you get soft peaks. Whisk in the lemon zest and juice, confit garlic, hot sauce, mustard powder, paprika, pepper, and salt to taste.

Fold a paper towel in half lengthwise, then in half again, and in half again so it's a strip. Even the ends of the chives by gently tapping them together on your cutting board. Roll the paper towel tightly around their middle. Place the heel of your palm on the towel and, curling your fingers, rest them on the chives. Chop the chives finely from the top, inching the towel and your hand down as you go. Discard the fibrous root ends. Whisk the chives, parsley, and dill into the dip. Serve it with the veg. It keeps, in the fridge in an airtight container, for up to 5 days.

TIME
15 minutes

YIELD
About 2 cups [475 ml]

shredded potato salad

I first ate this kind of potato salad at a San Francisco restaurant called Terra Cotta Warrior that specializes in northwest China's Shaanxi cuisine. It looked like a pile of matches. But I dove in and got this mélange of subtle textures and flavors: numbing and a little hot with nice crunch and salt rounded out with vinegar. That salad did something to me. I wanted to make it at Saison for the caviar course, but I never got the go-ahead. Now, I get to do it my way, swapping out the black vinegar a Chinese cook would use for malt vinegar. I grew up on East Coast boardwalks, so I'm a big fish and chips guy, and the flavor profile of malt vinegar is nostalgic for me. If you're wondering whether the potatoes are too raw, don't worry. We don't often eat crunchy blanched potatoes, but they're cooked enough.

Fill a large bowl with cold water and another large bowl with ice water. In a large stockpot, bring 12 cups [2.8 L] of water and ⅓ cup [55 g] of the salt to a boil.

Meanwhile, make your matchsticks. If you have a food processor with a julienning attachment, run the potatoes through it. Otherwise, using a sharp knife or mandoline, slice the potatoes into ¼ in [6 mm] thick slices. Pile the slices on top of each other, then cut them into ½ in [13 mm] wide matchsticks. Drop them into the bowl of cold water to release their starch and stop oxidation.

Drain the potatoes, then add them to the boiling salted water and cook them, stirring, until they're just a little floppy but still crisp, 1 to 2 minutes. Drain the potatoes in a colander, then plunge the colander into the ice bath. Stir the potatoes to cool them evenly, then drain and shake them dry. Place the potatoes in a serving bowl and top them with the garlic and the remaining 1 teaspoon of salt.

In a small sauté pan over medium-high heat, heat the umami oil and sesame oil for 1 minute. Moving the pan back and forth, add the peppercorns and fry them until you can smell them, about 45 seconds. Pour the hot oil through a fine-mesh strainer over the garlic and potatoes and mix well. Add the jalapeño, vinegar, and sesame seeds, and mix again.

You can serve this salad right away, but if you're taking it traveling, stow it in your cooler in a ziplock or resealable silicone bag with the air pressed out, or in a transportable bowl with plastic wrap pressed down on the spuds so they don't oxidize. The potato salad keeps, in the fridge, for up to 3 days.

⅓ cup [55 g] plus 1 tsp kosher salt

1 lb [455 g] baseball-size, waxy red or yellow potatoes

YOU WANT YOUR POTATOES TO BE THE SAME SIZE SO THAT YOUR MATCHSTICKS END UP A UNIFORM LENGTH.

3 garlic cloves, chopped

2 Tbsp Umami Oil (page 46)

1 Tbsp toasted sesame oil

1½ tsp Szechuan peppercorns

Three ¼ in [6 mm] thick jalapeño slices

YOU'RE GOING FOR SUBTLE SEASONING, SO YOU ONLY NEED A BIT OF JALAPEÑO.

1½ tsp malt vinegar, plus more as needed

1 tsp toasted white sesame seeds

TIME
30 minutes

YIELD
About 6 cups [1.4 L]

7 tsp toasted sesame oil

2 bunches green onions, tops and root ends trimmed

½ cup [120 ml] rice vinegar

½ cup [120 ml] mirin

1 large carrot

½ cup [150 g] plus 2 tsp kosher salt

4 bunches, about 14 oz [400 g] mature watercress, tough stems trimmed

1 cup [240 ml] shiro dashi

½ cup [2.5 g] bonito flakes

4 large eggs

4 tsp canola oil

4 medium king trumpet mushrooms

4 nori sheets

2 cups [360 g] cooked short-grain white rice, such as Calrose

Toasted white sesame seeds, for garnish

Kimbap, Korea's nori-rolled snack, is beautiful to look at and eat. When you make it right, it's a mosaic of mise en place, its colorful fillings all displayed in their own spots, bringing diverse flavors and textures. I came up with this one when I was eating a bulgogi kimbap from H Mart. Packed with grilled beef, it was so good but so filling that I thought, how can I make one equally unctuous but just slam it with vegetables? Trumpet mushrooms were the answer. They pack a hearty punch, but you won't have to pull over and nap afterwards.

A compact refuel, kimbap's portability relies on clean, tight rolling. I worked at a burrito shop in college, where I acquired sick skills in this department. The key to freestyle rolling: Keep your hands dry, so nothing sticks to you. But if these big boys are too unwieldy, roll 'em with a bamboo sushi mat.

california kimbap

In a 9 in [23 cm] cast-iron pan over medium-high heat, heat 3 teaspoons of the sesame oil. Add the green onions without crowding them, working in batches if needed, and cook them, flipping, until they're browned but not charred, 2 to 3 minutes per side. Drop them in a medium bowl and coat them evenly with 3 teaspoons of the sesame oil, the rice vinegar, and the mirin. Cool the green onions to room temp.

Using a mandoline or sharp knife, cut the carrot at a 45-degree angle into very thin slices. If you do it right, the slices will land on top of each other. Otherwise, stack them by hand, then cut lengthwise through the stacks to make matchsticks. In a small bowl, mix the carrots with 1 teaspoon of the salt and leave them to sweat out some moisture for 30 seconds. In a medium sauté pan over medium-high heat, heat the remaining 1 teaspoon of sesame oil. Add the carrots and sauté them for 30 seconds. Spread the carrots on a plate to cool.

Fill a large bowl with ice water. In a large pot, bring 4 quarts [3.8 L] of water and the ½ cup [150 g] of salt to a boil. Add the watercress and blanch it for 30 seconds, then plunge it into the ice bath.

continued

TIME
2 hours

YIELD
4 rolls

In small pot, bring the shiro dashi, bonito flakes, and 1 cup [240 ml] of water to a boil. Kill the heat.

Squeeze the watercress dry and place it in a medium bowl, then pour the hot dashi over it and stir to coat. Cool the watercress to room temp.

Whisk the eggs with the remaining 1 teaspoon of salt. In a 9 in [23 cm] skillet, heat 1 teaspoon of the canola oil over medium-high heat. Add the eggs, then knock the heat down to low. Swirl the eggs all over the pan, moving the pan as the omelet cooks and thickens, 2 to 3 minutes. Flip the omelet, kill the heat, and cool it in the pan.

Cut the mushrooms lengthwise into ¼ in [6 mm] thick slices. In a cast-iron pan over high heat, heat the remaining 3 teaspoons of canola oil. Press half the mushrooms into the pan and cook them until they're golden brown, 1½ to 2 minutes. Flip and cook them 1½ to 2 minutes more. Repeat with the remaining mushrooms.

IT'S ALL ABOUT SHOWCASING THE INGREDIENTS, SO NEATNESS COUNTS.

YOU WANT YOUR CRESS MOIST BUT NOT SO MUCH THAT IT SOAKS THE NORI.

Place 1 nori sheet, glossy-side down and with a shorter side facing you, on a bamboo mat, if you're using one. Press ½ cup [90 g] of the cooked rice evenly over the nori sheet, leaving 2 in [5 cm] at the top of the sheet bare. Lay one-quarter of the mushrooms in a horizontal line across the rice. Drain most of the marinade from 2 to 4 pieces of green onion and lay them next to the mushrooms, with their root sides at either end. Lay one-quarter of the carrot next to the green onions. Cut the omelet into ¼ in [6 mm] strips and lay one-quarter of it on top of the carrot. Pull one-quarter of the watercress from the dashi, gently squeeze it, and lay equal amounts of greens and stems on top of the mushrooms. Sprinkle sesame seeds all over.

Using your index fingers and thumbs, pick up the mat, or if you're not using a mat, pick up the nori sheet by the corners nearest you. Holding in the filling, hug the nori with the mat or the rest of your fingers, as you roll the kimbap away from you. Tighten as you go and press down at the end. The roll should stick together as moisture flows from the watercress, acting as a glue. Otherwise, dampen the edge by brushing it lightly with dashi. Repeat with the remaining fillings and nori sheets.

To prep the kimbap for travel, wrap each roll in wax paper or plastic wrap like a Tootsie Roll. To serve, cut slices through the wrapper with a sharp knife.

Tuna Salad

10 oz [285 g] fresh tuna

Kosher salt

2 cups [475 ml] extra-virgin olive oil

2 fresh thyme sprigs

½ in [13 mm] thick jalapeño slice

½ cup [110 g] The Best Mayonnaise (page 45) or Kewpie

2 tsp Seasoned Vinegar (page 52)

2 tsp gochujang

2 tsp white soy sauce

1 tsp dark soy sauce

4 celery stalks, thinly sliced

4 green onions, thinly sliced

I have my qualms about the standard deli tuna salad, so I make it the way I like it. I use less mayo and the freshest fish possible, dial up the flavor and technique, and then I have something to be proud of. I developed this recipe with Santa Cruz bluefin tuna that I caught myself, but you can get fresh albacore, yellowtail, or skipjack from your local fish counter. After you confit the fish and make the base dressing, play around with the veg. I'm giving you celery and green onions, but if you want a sweeter, spicier flavor, swap in a couple of carrots and a half-dozen small radishes cut into thin coins. This is your tuna salad; own it. Then stow it in a mason jar and tuck it in the fridge the night before your road trip. It's always better the second day. The lavash is an excellent dipper. The recipe makes plenty, so you'll have it around for scooping up Herby Buttermilk Ranch Dip (page 116) or adding more love to the Country Toast Bar (page 262).

confit tuna salad with sea salt lavash

To make the tuna salad: Season the fish all over with salt and let it come to room temp, about 15 minutes.

In a medium saucepan, submerge the tuna in the olive oil. Over medium-high heat, bring it just to where it's sheened with fluttery bubbles, about 3 minutes. Knock the heat down to low and cook for 4 minutes more. The tuna should be slightly firm but with some give. Drop in the thyme and jalapeño and kill the heat. Let the tuna rest until it's cool enough to pull out of the oil, about 5 minutes. Pat the tuna dry and crumble it into a medium bowl. Discard the oil.

In another medium bowl, whisk together the mayo, vinegar, gochujang, white soy sauce, and dark soy sauce. Fold in the celery and green onions. Gently fold half of this sauce into the tuna, adding more as needed. Stow the salad in the fridge for a while. It's best marinated overnight. If you have leftover dressing, it's great on anything: sandwiches, fried chicken, steamed veg, rice.

TIME
1 hour

YIELD
Enough for 2 hungry road trippers or 4 snackers

To make the lavash: Preheat the oven to 375°F [190°C]. Line a sheet pan with a silicone mat or parchment paper; if using parchment, lightly coat it with pan spray.

In a medium bowl with your hands or a wooden spoon, mix the flour, milk, eggs, sugar, sesame oil, olive oil, and kosher salt. Knead the dough until it's smooth, 2 to 3 minutes. Rest it for 10 minutes. On a floured surface with a floured rolling pin, roll the dough out until it's ⅛ in [3 mm] thick. Sprinkle with the sesame seeds and flaky salt, then use the rolling pin to roll them into the dough. Use a fork to poke holes all over the dough to allow steam to escape and the crackers to stay flat when baking. Cut out whatever shapes you want, either wabi-sabi or uniform. Just make them all about the same size so they bake evenly.

Arrange the crackers on the prepared sheet pan, making sure they aren't touching. The dough will shrink a bit as it bakes. Brush them with olive oil. Bake them for 10 minutes, then rotate the pan and bake them until the crackers are slightly puffy and golden brown, about 10 minutes more. Cool to room temp. Use the crackers to scoop up the tuna salad. The crackers keep, in an airtight container at room temperature, for up to 3 days.

Lavash

Pan spray, if needed

4 cups [560 g] all-purpose flour, plus more for dusting

¾ cup [180 ml] whole milk

2 large eggs

3 Tbsp sugar

3 Tbsp toasted sesame oil

2 Tbsp extra-virgin olive oil, plus more for brushing

1½ tsp kosher salt

Black sesame seeds, for garnish

Flaky salt, such as Maldon, for garnish

Cookies

2 cups [400 g] packed dark brown sugar

1½ cups [300 g] granulated sugar

1 Tbsp kosher salt

2 tsp baking soda

2 cups [452 g] unsalted butter, roughly diced, at room temperature

4 large eggs

3 Tbsp sweet white miso

2½ Tbsp vanilla extract

2½ Tbsp rose water

1½ cups [210 g] whole shelled pistachios

1 cup [180 g] white chocolate chips

5 cups [700 g] all-purpose flour

Pan spray, if needed

Glaze

2 cups [240 g] powdered sugar

3 Tbsp fresh lime juice

1 tsp rose water

Lime zest, for garnish

TIME
**45 minutes active;
2 hours 45 minutes total**

YIELD
28 cookies

This recipe came from a mistake. I ordered a bottle of rose water, got delivered a case, and was like, "Man, I have no clue what to do with all this." Dad's Luncheonette is a train car, so people expect it to be simple. What's simpler than cookies? This big-ass, glazed cookie with lime zest pops visually and smells rad. The dough needs to be cold when you bake it so that the butter resolidifies. Otherwise, it spreads in the oven. Do it right, and you get a crunchy bottom with a chewy interior. You know the age-old debate: Which cookie is better, crunchy or soft? The answer is both.

These are one of Frost's favorite road-trip treats. They're inspired by Curry Leaf, the Indian spot down the street from my house when I lived in San Francisco. They flavored their rice pudding with rose water and lime and covered it in crushed pistachios. It was so good that I riffed on it when I got my excess of rose water and now, two years later, we're a quarter of the way through the case.

white chocolate, pistachio, and rose cookies

To make the cookies: In a stand mixer fitted with the paddle attachment, or in a large bowl with a fork, mix the brown sugar, granulated sugar, salt, and baking soda until uniform. Adding the butter a few chunks at a time, cream the butter into the sugar mixture until it's fully incorporated.

In a medium bowl, mix the eggs, miso, vanilla, and rose water. Add this mixture to the sugar mixture and slowly fold it in, scraping down the bowl as you go, until it's uniform and the consistency of wet sand. Fold in the pistachios and white chocolate chips. With the machine running on the lowest setting, or mixing by hand with a spatula, add the flour ½ cup [70 g] at a time until the dough is uniform.

Arrange a big piece of plastic wrap on a work surface, then drop one-third of the dough on top and form it into a log about 2 in [5 cm] in diameter. Wrap the log tight, twisting the ends of the plastic to tighten it. Repeat with the remaining

IF YOU NEED TO SHAVE YOUR
SLICES DOWN, THAT'S AN
EXCUSE TO EAT RAW DOUGH.
OR PRESS THE SHAVINGS
BACK INTO THE LOG.

dough. Refrigerate it for at least 2 hours and up to 2 days or freeze it for up to 1 month. The dough can be baked cold or frozen.

When you're ready to bake, arrange a rack in the center position of the oven and preheat the oven to 350° [180°C]. Line a sheet pan with a silicone mat or parchment paper; if using parchment, lightly coat it with pan spray.

Cut the chilled dough into ¾ in [2 cm] thick slices, or 85 grams by weight, and arrange the dough slices on the prepared sheet pan. Bake the cookies on the center rack of the oven f or 9 minutes, then rotate the pan, and bake for 9 minutes more, until they're golden brown. Let them cool to room temp.

To make the glaze: In a medium bowl, mix the powdered sugar, lime juice, and rose water together until fully combined and smooth. Stream some glaze all over as many cookies as you've baked, like they're a Jackson Pollock painting. Microplane some lime zest over the top. Let the glaze set for 5 minutes. The glaze keeps, in the fridge in an airtight container, for up to 1 week. Just whisk it to loosen it up before you drizzle it.

Glazed cookies will keep in an airtight container on the countertop for 2 days. The glaze tends to droop a bit, so just don't stack them on top of each other.

CA muddy buddies

This recipe takes me back to trips with my mom, when she would load up the car with kid food. We don't need to totally reinvent the wheel on some timeless things. Chex is good, chocolate is good, powdered sugar is good. Throw it all in a bag and grab it to go. It's not diet food; it's road food, and we're going.

But we're also making a classic even better. When I was working in DC, the pastry chef vacuum sealed white chocolate for petit fours and forgot it at the bottom of the sous vide machine. When we found it after service, it was super dark. We threw it in an ice bath, and it was delicious.

You'll use the same technique in your home oven, pushing that chocolate darker and darker. Cook times will vary, depending on your oven, but take my word for it: This is a technique that is so close to burning, it should scare you. With tahini, nut butter, and Chex—regular wheat or the rice version for gluten-free humans—the transformed chocolate turns muddy buddies into something ungodly addictive. They'll ruin your day—in the best way.

Preheat the oven to 300°F [150°C]. Line a sheet pan with a silicone mat.

Spread the chocolate chips in a single layer on the prepared sheet pan and bake for 10 minutes. With a rubber spatula, fold the darkening edges of the chocolate over and into the center of the sheet pan and smooth out the chocolate. Continue baking the chocolate, folding, flipping, and spreading it every 10 minutes, until it looks like dark chocolate and is slick with cocoa fat, 45 minutes to 1 hour. You can use the chocolate right away or let it cool and harden, then break it into pieces to use.

In a Dutch oven over medium heat, melt the butter. Add the chocolate, almond butter, tahini, and vanilla. Melt it all together, stirring with a rubber spatula, until it's smooth and uniform, 6 to 8 minutes.

Put the Chex in a large bowl, then pour the chocolate mixture on top and use a rubber spatula to fold it in and fully coat the Chex. Add the powdered sugar, shaking the bowl to evenly coat the muddy buddies.

Spread the muddy buddies on a sheet pan to cool, then bag them up, and they're ready to roll. They'll keep, at room temperature in an airtight container, for up to 6 days or in the freezer for up to 3 weeks.

8 oz [230 g] white chocolate chips

¼ cup [55 g] unsalted butter

½ cup [170 g] almond butter

¼ cup [55 g] tahini

1 tsp vanilla extract

8 cups [470 g] wheat Chex or 8 cups [425 g] rice Chex

1 cup [120 g] powdered sugar

BE CAREFUL OF SPLASHING. IT'LL MELT YOUR SKIN.

BROKEN CHEX ARE FINE. THEY GET BLOBBED BACK TOGETHER BY POWDERED SUGAR.

TIME
1 hour 40 minutes

YIELD
About 8 cups [830 g]

post-break breakfast

●

Surfing is one of the things that keeps me sane. When I'm alone in the water, I can feel close to something indescribable. But I get even more from being in the water with friends, sharing success or letdown. There are mitigating factors: sandbars, wind swell, ground swell. Some days we get there and say, "No one's going to surf today. It's garbage." So instead, we just hang out, crack jokes at each other's expense, laugh. There are also days when, wow, I'm scared, and I know everyone else is too. But we are going to learn from it, and hopefully no one gets hurt. Other days, it's perfect and we get to be children floating around, picking off waves, basking in it all. Any which way, being in the water is a blessing. You're with your buddies, and it's good.

Afterwards, we're famished. All the little Central Coast beach towns have their town break, the spot where the waves are. They have their history and their surfing legends. They also have their surfside shacks where you can scarf down a meal after playing in the ocean. One of them, Ruddell's Smokehouse, a Cayucos legend for smoked fish tacos, was the inspiration for Dad's Luncheonette and, in a way, for this book. It closed for good in 2022, after more than two decades of service. These small surf towns are precious, but they're changing. So, we're celebrating them here, exploring their rare and genuine vibe the way it's meant to be taken—from the waves first, followed by breakfast.

When we're surfing, we want to eat hearty but healthy foods to start the day. This chapter includes riffs on the snacks you'd grab from that old-school health food store near the water, like gingery Pre-Surf Fire Cider (page 136) and Goji and Hemp Overnight Oats (page 137). It's got favorites from the local greasy spoon that

have been cleaned up and brightened, like Brussels Sprout Latkes (page 140), the potato version's leaner, meaner cousin, and Lox 'n' Tacs (page 148), built up with salmon you cured yourself, crème fraîche you fermented, and masa you pressed to make everything-spiced tortillas.

For years, I was an anti-breakfast guy. My ADHD left me with a sense of wild excitement, and I just wanted to get out the door each day. But after surviving on cold brews and morning cigarettes for too long, my body said, "No. We're not doing this anymore. I need to be taken care of." Now on the mornings when I'm not surfing, I have a routine. I set my alarm for 6 a.m. and put it in another room, so I have to get up to turn it off. Then there's no going back to bed. I do thirty minutes of breathing exercises, sit in the sauna in my garage for thirty minutes, then dunk in an icy cold plunge for as long as I can handle it. That jolts me into life. Recently I've started to meditate too. That's just sitting with myself, setting myself up for the day, and recognizing that today will be beautiful but it will also have hardships, and I can face them. Then I take a hot shower and make Frost and me breakfast.

Even if you've never surfed, there's a ton of flavor and nutrition in this chapter, because it's the top of your day, and if you don't hit the mark, you'll be lagging. Maybe you've been in the ocean; maybe you've had a long workweek on dry land. Whatever you've done, you've done a lot, and there's more to go. One of the greatest acts of self-care you can show yourself is to slow down every morning and feed yourself before you continue.

pre-surf fire cider

- 2 cups [475 ml] unfiltered raw apple cider vinegar
- ½ cup [65 g] unpeeled, chopped fresh ginger
- ½ cup [80 g] peeled, chopped fresh horseradish root
- ½ cup [75 g] garlic cloves, peeled and smashed
- ¼ cup [40 g] peeled, chopped turmeric
- 3 Tbsp honey, plus more as needed
- 2 serrano chiles, halved lengthwise
- Peel of 1 lemon, preferably Meyer, pith removed
- Peel of 1 navel orange, pith removed
- Peel of 1 grapefruit, pith removed
- ½ tsp black peppercorns
- ½ tsp pink peppercorns
- ¼ tsp fine salt, such as Maldon

This is a digestive, immune-boosting ripper. I go nuts for it. I chug a hefty pour before surfing because it gets me loose. It will get you going in the morning, and you're going to use it to make the Ghee-Roasted Oysters with Fire Cider Mignonette (page 301), but you can also slam it into cold water, pour it over ice, make a tea with it, whisk it into salad dressing, or if you're feeling real frisky, blend it into a Bloody Mary. But beware: It's not the easy sipper you're looking for; it's a shot of nature's high-octane fuel.

In a large mason jar, combine all the ingredients. Use a wooden spoon to push the solids down to submerge them in the vinegar. Crank a lid on the jar, give it a good shake, and store it somewhere dark and cool for 4 weeks. Pour the cider through a fine-mesh strainer lined with cheesecloth into a clean mason jar. Discard the solids. Taste the cider and add more honey, as needed, 1 teaspoon at a time, until it's perfect for you. The cider keeps, in the fridge, for a few months.

TIME
15 minutes active;
1 month total

YIELD
About 2 cups [475 ml]

Here's some delicious, healthy slop for all you Marxists and hippies. The milk comes from young coconuts, which you can find at larger markets and Asian stores, or online already shed of their hairy, outer husks. Young coconut milk is wildly rich and floral. I serve it to Frost inside its shell with a slice of lime. All that's missing is the drink umbrella.

Use the coconut milk to hit the golden ratio, which is one-to-one liquid to oats, aided and abetted by a bunch of nutritious mix-ins and garnishes. I top mine with a honking spoonful of nut butter and some flavor-concentrated satsuma mandarin slices that I dry in my dehydrator. Those are also great, by the way, to throw on desserts like the Earl Grey Icebox Pie (page 100). But don't stop there. This recipe is meant to be messed with. Add cinnamon, allspice, turmeric, or grated ginger. Sprinkle on fresh berries or drizzle it with fresh orange or lime juice. Take it in any direction you want. Then pack it into mason jars and head for the beach.

10 satsuma mandarins, peeled and sectioned

2 young coconuts, about 15¾ oz [450 g]

2 cups [200 g] rolled oats

1 cup [195 g] packed grated, skin-on Fuji apple (1 or 2 apples)

3 Tbsp dried goji berries

3 Tbsp hemp hearts

1 Tbsp maple syrup, plus more as needed

2 tsp chia seeds

Nut butter, if you want

Flaky salt, such as Maldon, if you want

goji and hemp overnight oats

Arrange the satsumas in a single layer on your dehydrator racks or on a fine-mesh grate over a sheet pan in a 155°F [68°C] oven (or your oven's lowest temperature setting). Dry the satsumas until they're chewy and concentrated but not brittle, 8 to 12 hours. Cool them to room temperature. You'll have more than you need, but they're awesome for snacking. They keep, in a ziplock or resealable silicone bag with the air squeezed out, for a month.

Put 1 coconut in a large bowl to catch drips, then use a cleaver to hack around the top and make a hole large enough to fit your hand inside. Pour the coconut water into a blender, then use a spoon to scoop out the coconut flesh and add that to the blender too. Repeat with the other coconut. Blitz it on high until a smooth, white milk forms, 1 to 2 minutes.

continued

TIME
50 minutes active; overnight total

YIELD
4 to 6 servings

SPECIAL GEAR
Cleaver or breaking knife Dehydrator

In a large bowl, mix 2 cups [475 ml] of the coconut milk with the oats, apple, goji berries, hemp hearts, maple syrup, and chia seeds until everything is fully combined. Cover the bowl or, if you're taking it on the go the next morning, portion the oats into individual mason jars and screw on the lids. Stow the oats in the fridge to chill and soak up the coconut milk overnight. Reserve the rest of the coconut milk for loosening the oats the next morning. It will keep, in an airtight container in the fridge, for up to 5 days.

The next morning, check the oats for thickness and flavor. Add more coconut milk and maple syrup, as needed. If it isn't already in mason jars, portion the oats into bowls, and top each with some dried satsumas, nut butter, and flaky salt, if you want.

coastal

Feta Dip

8 oz [230 g] sour cream

4 oz [115 g] aged feta, crumbled

Brussels Sprout Latkes

1½ lb [680 g] large Brussels sprouts

3 large shallots, halved lengthwise

1 Tbsp avocado oil

1 Tbsp extra-virgin olive oil

8 to 10 cranks black pepper

Kosher salt

2 large eggs

½ cup [70 g] all-purpose flour

1 tsp baking powder

4 Tbsp [60 ml] canola oil

Pear Butter (page 51), for serving

Pickled Mustard Seeds (page 50), for serving

BIG BOY BRUSSELS ARE EASIER TO MANDOLINE; USE THEIR STEMS AS A HANDLE WHILE YOU'RE SHAVING THEM.

TIME
1 hour

YIELD
6 latkes

Sometimes I want pancakes after surfing, but I know that after I eat them, I'll crash. If I need to stay active, I go for these latkes. Who says latkes have to be potato? Brussels bring the cruciferousness that feels great in your body and contrasts so well with sweet, creamy, and tart condiments. The best thing about this recipe is, once you go this far, you can keep on going. This feta dip is my homage to Pescadero goat farmer Dee Harley (see page 143). But you could score a jar of chili crisp, whip that into sour cream, and serve the latkes with that and a pile of green onions. Or add Coastal Kraut (page 56) and green apples to the batter. Or fry the latkes in the oil leftover from the Charred Broccolini with Melted Anchovy and Garlic (page 231). Do your thing.

To make the feta dip: In a small bowl, mix the sour cream and feta until they're well combined. The dip keeps, in the fridge in an airtight container, for up to 1 week, and it's addictive with raw veg or chips.

To make the Brussels sprout latkes: Use a mandoline to shave the sprouts ⅛ in [3 mm] thick into a large bowl; discard their stems. Repeat with the shallots. Toss the sprouts and shallots to combine, pulling apart the sprout strands and shallot half-moons with your fingers.

Line a sheet pan with a silicone mat or parchment paper. Set a wire rack inside a second sheet pan and put it near the stove.

In a cast-iron pan, heat the avocado oil and olive oil over medium-high heat. Add the sprouts, shallots, pepper, and 2 pinches of salt. Cook, stirring and moving the pan around, to sweat out the moisture, about 4 minutes. Spread the sprout mixture on the prepared sheet pan and stow it in the fridge to chill for 15 minutes.

Transfer the sprout mixture to a large bowl, add the eggs, flour, baking powder, and 1 teaspoon of salt. Using your hands, massage everything together to make a stiff batter. It should hold together in a ball when squeezed.

In a cast-iron pan over medium-high heat, heat 2 tablespoons of the canola oil. Using your hands, form a palm-size latke that is about ½ in [13 mm] thick. Add it to the pan and repeat to make two more latkes. Cook them, flipping once, until crisp and caramelized, 1 to 1½ minutes per side. Set the latkes on the wire rack and season them with salt. Repeat with the remaining canola oil and latke batter. Serve the latkes warm with the feta dip, pear butter, and pickled mustard seeds on the side.

brussels sprout latkes

DEE HARLEY, HARLEY GOAT FARM

At Harley Goat Farm in Pescadero, Dee Harley raises beautiful American Alpine goats. More than thirty years ago, she got her first herd, and they helped her clean up a derelict pile of garbage that is now lush pasture, where just-born kids race around in spring, guarded by Anatolian sheepdogs. Dee cares for her goats, and in turn, they give her what she calls "white gold": feta. Dee's team takes four days to make feta and a year to age it in buckets where it's saturated with salt brine and stored in a cooler. In all Dee's cheeses—fresh ricotta; sweet, densely textured chèvre; tangy, citrusy fromage blanc—the secret ingredient is the ocean. "The foggy breeze grows the grass," says Dee. "They say vineyards have terroir. Well, we have it here. You can taste it." But the way the goats live is important, too, as are the people who work with them. "You have to be mellow," she says. "You can't be annoyed or hungover. The goats pick up on it, and they don't forget." The people who make the cheese don't forget, either. When you're working with it and feeling it every day, you can put your hand on it and know when it's right, says Dee. That's a real connection between people, goats, and cheese, and Dee keeps the quality of life just right so that things on the farm don't go haywire. She learned the hard way, growing too big years ago, and she scaled back for everyone's sake. "We get on this thing of more, more, more. You think you're supposed to live like that, but really, if you're doing this, it's about having fun and evolving." When she needs a reminder of what's important, she says, "I can always look at the goats. They tell me." That level of sensitivity is why Dee is legendary on the Central Coast—that and some damn fine cheese.

Rye Berry Salad

1 Tbsp Umami Oil (page 46)

2 oz [55 g] bacon, preferably The Best Bacon (page 65), cut into ½ in [13 mm] pieces

1 shallot, cut into paper-thin slices

1 cup [170 g] rye berries

1 bay leaf

1 Tbsp white soy sauce

1 grapefruit

¼ cup [60 g] chopped sauerkraut, preferably Coastal Kraut (page 56)

1½ tsp apple cider vinegar

asparagus grain bowl benedict

TIME

2 hours

YIELD

2 servings

Here's a brunch made to show off your kitchen skills. They grow beautiful asparagus in the California Delta. Peeling those spears, then cooking them in a broth made with the peels, makes their flavor intense and their texture super tender. The technique only works with fat, juicy spears. Don't buy those pencil-thin ones. The asparagus gets draped over a rye berry salad. I love working with that grain. You don't have to soak rye berries, they have a nice bite, and their molasses-y flavor rings my bell.

Poached eggs and béarnaise are the dish's crowning achievements, but they give me flashbacks to my early restaurant days. When you're a line cook working brunch, those two can ruin your day, so you learn trade secrets. You run your eggs through a fine-mesh strainer to remove loose whites that can screw your poaching. You get to know the two things that break a béarnaise: impatience and heat. Stay loose and pay attention because it's a dance. If the sauce isn't thickening, it might be too hot. Pull it off the heat for 15 to 20 seconds; try again. Take your time, and the reward is right there in the bowl.

To make the rye berry salad: In a medium Dutch oven over high heat, heat the umami oil. Add the bacon and when it starts to render, 2 to 3 minutes, knock the heat down to medium. Stir in the shallots, and let them melt, 3 to 4 minutes. Add the rye berries, stirring to coat them, and toast them until golden, 1 to 2 minutes. Add 2½ cups [600 ml] of water, the bay leaf, and white soy sauce. Bring the mixture to a boil, then knock the heat down to a simmer, cover it with the lid cracked to let out the steam, and cook until the rye berries have a springy bite and the water is absorbed, 1 to 1½ hours. If your water evaporates before the berries are done, add 2 tablespoons of water, as needed. Remove the bay leaf and drain the rye berries, then transfer them to a bowl and let them come to room temp. You can make the rye berries ahead of time. They'll keep, in the fridge in an airtight container, for up to 3 days. Bring them to room temp before using them.

Meanwhile, use a sharp paring knife to supreme the grapefruit, cutting off the top and bottom of the fruit, then running your knife down the sides of the fruit, following its contour to remove the skin, pith, and outer membrane. Free the segments by slicing on either side of the membrane that separates the segments. Fold the grapefruit segments, sauerkraut, and apple cider vinegar into the rye berries.

To make the asparagus: Wet a kitchen or paper towel. Fill a large bowl with ice water and rest another bowl on top.

Snap the woody ends off the asparagus spears, then use a vegetable peeler to peel each spear starting just beneath the crown and reserving the peels. Rest the spears under the wet towel, so they don't oxidize.

In a 9 in [23 cm] sauté pan over medium-high heat, wilt the asparagus peels in ½ cup [120 ml] of water until you can smell them, about 1 minute. Discard the peels, add the olive oil, salt, and asparagus spears, and cook until they're just bendy and vibrant green, 2 to 3 minutes. Cool the asparagus spears in the bowl over the ice bath.

To make the béarnaise: In a small pot over medium heat, bring the champagne vinegar, tarragon, and peppercorns to a simmer. Continue simmering the mixture until it's reduced by half, 5 to 10 minutes. Remove it from the heat and let it cool to room temperature.

Meanwhile, in a medium pot, bring 4 cups [945 ml] of water to a boil. Knock the heat down to a simmer, then place a large metal bowl over the pot, making sure the bowl doesn't touch the water. Add the reduced vinegar mixture, the egg yolks, and salt and cook, whisking, until the mixture starts to turn pale and thicken, 30 seconds to 1 minute. Whisking continuously, slowly drizzle in the melted ghee until the sauce is smooth and thick. Remove the sauce from the heat and cover it to keep it warm. Turn the heat under the pot of warm water to medium and bring it to an undulating simmer.

To make the eggs: Crack 1 egg into a fine-mesh strainer, letting the loose whites drip away, then transfer the egg to an individual ramekin or small bowl. Repeat for the remaining 3 eggs. Add the apple cider vinegar to the pot of simmering water, then use a large kitchen spoon to stir the water around the perimeter of the pot to create a vortex. Drop 1 egg into the pot and poach it, while stirring, until it comes together and tightens, about 2 minutes. Use a slotted spoon to scoop the poached egg from the water and gently transfer it to a plate or bowl. Repeat with the remaining 3 eggs.

To make the grain bowls: Divide the rye berries between two bowls, then top each with half the chervil, watercress, green onion, and asparagus. Add 2 poached eggs to each bowl and drizzle 3 tablespoons of béarnaise, more if you want, over the top.

Asparagus

10 thick asparagus spears

1 Tbsp extra-virgin olive oil

1 tsp kosher salt

Béarnaise

½ cup [120 ml] champagne vinegar

4 fresh tarragon sprigs

10 peppercorns

2 egg yolks

Pinch of kosher salt

1 cup [200 g] ghee, preferably homemade (page 42), or unsalted butter, melted

Eggs

4 large eggs

2 Tbsp apple cider vinegar

Grain Bowls

½ cup [20 g] roughly chopped fresh chervil or ¼ cup [10 g] roughly chopped fresh parsley and ¼ cup [10 g] roughly chopped fresh tarragon

½ cup [20 g] roughly chopped watercress, tough stems removed

1 green onion, chopped

lox 'n' tacs

I'm a taco freak, just like everybody else in California. Thanks to Mexican cooking and Jewish cooking, these tacos bring the party. They're fish tacos but not fish tacos. They're little, self-saucing towers of flavor. You fold and bite, the yolk bursts, you bite again, and they're done.

If you catch the salmon yourself, like I try to do when they're running, awesome. If not, buy it wild and fresh, and remove the pin bones with kitchen tweezers. If you can't get it fresh, get the highest quality frozen salmon available, and thaw it in the fridge. A center-cut fillet from the middle of the body gives you the biggest, most uniform slices.

To cure the salmon: In a medium bowl, mix the salt, shiso, granulated sugar, brown sugar, and pepper. Coat the skin side of the salmon with the cure, then place the salmon, skin-side down, in a glass container or on a quarter sheet pan lined with aluminum foil. Liberally coat the top and sides of the salmon with the cure. Wrap plastic wrap around a second glass container that fits into the first, then place it on top of the salmon, weighting it down with soup cans or other heavy objects. Stow the fish in the fridge to cure for 12 hours, then flip it over, put the weights back on top, and leave it to cure for 12 hours more. It will deepen in color and firm up considerably.

Rinse the salmon in ice-cold water, rubbing off the cure. Pat it dry. It keeps, in the fridge in an airtight container, for up to 6 days.

When you're ready to make your tacos, grab your sharpest knife and cut the salmon, on the bias, into ¼ in [6 mm] thick pieces, slicing off the skin at the end of each cut.

continued

Cured Salmon

1 cup [160 g] kosher salt

½ cup [20 g] chopped shiso

6 Tbsp [75 g] granulated sugar

¼ cup [50 g] packed dark brown sugar

¾ tsp freshly ground white pepper

1 lb [455 g] skin-on, center-cut, pin-boned salmon fillet

continued

TIME
1 hour active; 1 day total

YIELD
8 tacos

SPECIAL GEAR
Tortilla press

Everything Tortillas
Homemade Tortillas (page 72)

Everything Seasoning
(page 71)

Red Onion and Dill Salad
1 small red onion, thinly sliced

1 cup [12 g] fresh dill sprigs,
tough stems removed

Sunny-Side-Up Eggs
1 Tbsp ghee, preferably
homemade (page 42)

8 large eggs

Tacos
Crème fraîche, preferably
homemade (page 44),
for serving

To make the everything tortillas: Make the masa balls following the Homemade Tortilla (page 72) recipe, but sprinkle ½ teaspoon of everything seasoning on top of each ball before pressing it. Cook the tortillas according to the recipe.

To make the red onion and dill salad: In a small bowl, mix the onion and dill.

To make the eggs: In a medium sauté pan over medium-high heat, melt ½ tablespoon of the ghee, then crack 4 eggs into the pan and cook them until brown around the edges, about 2 minutes. Lower the heat to medium, add 2 tablespoons of water, cover the pan, and cook until the whites set, about 1 minute more. Transfer the eggs to a plate, then repeat with the remaining eggs and ghee.

A steam bath creates pillowy whites and custardy yolks.

To make the tacos: Slap an egg on a tortilla, dress it with some salmon, schmear on crème fraîche, and top it with the salad. Repeat with the remaining ingredients.

At dawn, I take a bucket and pry mussels off the rocks at Martins Beach. Half the year, there's a quarantine. But November through April, I can take up to ten pounds of these delicious mollusks. I smoke the mussels, fold them and their liquor into beaten eggs, and set the custard in a steamer to gently cook. My homage to great Asian custards—Korean gyeranjjim, Japanese chawanmushi—this is a soothing dish that reminds me how far I've come from my earlier custard-making days. At Benu, I made ginko chawanmushi without ever tasting it. Then I messed one up, ate it so that no one would know, and learned how amazing it was.

Put the mussels in a pie tin or cast-iron pan.

Prep your smoker. This is a good one for a stovetop smoker. If you're using a charcoal grill, bank your coals to one side. When the coals are glowing and no longer on fire, throw a handful of wood chunks on top of them. There's no need to soak the wood chunks. For a gas grill, heat one side on high, place the wood chunks in a smoker box, and place the smoker box over the flame. Decrease the heat to low once the wood starts smoking.

Let the first blast of acrid smoke blow off, then place the pan of mussels on the cool side of the grill and close the lid. If you're using a charcoal grill, position the vents over the mussels. Leave them to smoke until they open, release their liquor, and turn a deep orange, 15 to 20 minutes. Remove the mussels from their shells and retain the liquor.

In a 6 in [15 cm] heat-safe vessel, beat the eggs, then stir in the white soy sauce and mussel liquor. Fold in the mussels. Add 2 in [5 cm] of water to a steamer pot or a pot fitted with a steamer basket, cover it, and bring it to a boil over medium-high heat. Put the custard inside the basket and steam it until it firms up around the edges but is still a bit jiggly in the center, 10 to 15 minutes. Drizzle the custard with the sesame oil, then garnish it with the bonito flakes, green onions, and sesame seeds. Serve it with fermented hot sauce on the side.

STONEWARE IS A BEAUTIFUL CHOICE HERE.

smoked mussel custard

1 lb [455 g] mussels, scrubbed and debearded (see page 338)

Apple or cherry wood chunks, for smoking

6 large eggs

1 tsp white soy sauce

2 tsp toasted sesame oil

¼ cup [1.25 g] bonito flakes

4 green onions, thinly sliced

2 tsp toasted white sesame seeds

Fermented Hot Sauce (page 62) or chili crisp, for serving

TIME
45 minutes

YIELD
3 or 4 servings

SPECIAL GEAR
Grill or smoker
Lump charcoal

1 Tbsp ghee, preferably homemade (page 42)

4 oz [115 g] hen of the woods mushroom, broken into pieces

2 shallots, thinly sliced

2 garlic cloves, thinly sliced

12 oz [340 g] baby spinach

1 tsp kosher salt

4 or 5 cranks black pepper

3 duck eggs

3 Tbsp Chile Jam (page 60)

5 oz [140 g] triple-cream Brie, broken into pieces or left whole

⅓ cup [35 g] sliced green onions

½ tsp red pepper flakes, if you want

This is a one-cutting board, one-pan recipe, a cast-iron job that came to me in a moment when I just needed to get something in my face and get out the door. There's a gas station in Pacifica that sells duck eggs. They always have them on the checkout counter, and truthfully, I don't go there for gas or anything else, just duck eggs. The woman who runs the place told me that they come from her ex-husband's flock, and the deal is, he gets to keep the ducks, but she gets the profit from the eggs. I don't really know what kind of deal that is, but those eggs came in handy one morning when I had a nearly empty fridge and had to get a bunch of stuff done, including surfing. Duck eggs are so large that they're almost funny. This recipe is a great way to show off a big, rich, clownlike duck egg, any time of day.

duck egg brie bake

Preheat the oven to 350°F [180°C].

In a 9 in [23 cm] cast-iron pan over medium-high heat, melt the ghee. Add the mushrooms and fry them, flipping once, until they're golden brown, 4 to 5 minutes. Add the shallots and garlic and cook, tossing and stirring, until they start to caramelize, 2 to 3 minutes. Add the spinach, sprinkle it with the salt and pepper and, using tongs, turn it to wilt it and release its liquid, 4 to 5 minutes. Crack the duck eggs on top, dollop on the chile jam and Brie, and bake until the egg whites are set and the yolks are custardy, 10 to 12 minutes. Scatter on the green onions and the red pepper flakes, if you want, and bring it to the table.

TIME
30 minutes

YIELD
2 servings

coastal

bacon-gouda dutch baby

4 large eggs

½ cup [70 g] all-purpose flour

½ cup [120 ml] whole milk

2 Tbsp unsalted butter, melted

1 Tbsp nutritional yeast

1 tsp kosher salt

1 tsp freshly ground black pepper

8 oz [230 g] bacon, preferably The Best Bacon (page 65), cut into ¼ in [6 mm] lardons

½ cup [80 g] sliced shallots

2½ oz [70 g] aged smoked Gouda, shaved with a vegetable peeler

Baby arugula, for garnish

Sliced fresh chives, for garnish

Lemon, preferably Meyer, for garnish

As long as your pan is piping hot when you pour the batter in, Dutch babies are nearly impossible to screw up. The baby does its little performance, puffing up dramatically in the oven and then deflating once you take it out. It's half quiche, half custard.

Once you learn the basic batter, you can do whatever the hell you want with it. Nutritional yeast gives this savory version a nutty hint, and the caramelized shallots and bacon will have your house smelling insane. Throw fried eggs in the middle of this baby and revel in yolky, cheesy glory. Toss on some crab or avocado. If you want a sweet batter, kill the nutritional yeast and savory add-ins, and drop in 3 tablespoons of sugar. For Frost and her pals, I use strawberry milk, blueberries, vanilla, and orange zest. I put powdered sugar and maple syrup all over the top, serve strawberry milk on the side, and everyone gets all riled up, then we play hide-and-seek. "And I wrestle everybody," says Frost. She's not lying.

Preheat the oven to 450°F [230°C].

In a blender, combine the eggs, flour, milk, butter, nutritional yeast, salt, and pepper and blitz until fully incorporated.

Heat a 9 in [23 cm] cast-iron pan over medium-high heat. Throw in the bacon and turn the heat down to medium. Cook the lardons, breaking them apart with a wooden spoon, until they're halfway rendered, 4 to 5 minutes. Pour off all but 2 tablespoons of the bacon fat, reserving the extra for another use, then toss in the shallots and cook them until they're caramelized, 4 to 5 minutes.

Pour the batter into the hot pan with the bacon and shallots, and bake it until puffy and bronzed, 15 to 20 minutes. Garnish the baby hot out of the oven with the Gouda, handfuls of arugula and chives, and a squeeze of lemon. Serve it immediately.

TIME
30 minutes

YIELD
2 to 4 servings

Ice cream, baby! Get your calories back after burning them surfing. Even if you didn't work out, you deserve it. The world is a vampire sucking you dry. Have a sundae; feel good about it.

You'll top it with caramel made from the kind of IPA Californians love: deep, dank, and basement-y. The hoppy notes play with the toasty caramelized sugar. The pecans are like ones you'd make for holidays. Throw the extras on cheese platters, sprinkle them on pies and cakes, or tie ribbons around jars of them for gifts.

The ice cream is based on a traditional crème anglaise. Salt brings out the sweetness and denatures the egg proteins, so they cook evenly. There's no stabilizer in this ice cream, so don't over churn it lest it get grainy. If you don't yet own an ice cream maker, I suggest Yaylabs' version, which is shaped like a soccer ball. You kick it around the yard to churn the ice cream, so you get your workout in after all.

after-surf sundae

To make the ice cream: In a medium bowl, whisk together the sugar and cornstarch.

In a second medium bowl, whisk together the eggs, vanilla seeds, and salt. Pour this mixture into the sugar mixture and whisk to form a smooth slurry, about 2 minutes.

Fill a large bowl with ice water.

In a medium saucepan over medium heat, heat the milk and heavy cream, whisking occasionally, until it's uncomfortable to put your finger in, about 5 minutes. While whisking, ladle the hot milk mixture, one ladle at a time, into the egg slurry, adding enough hot liquid (three or four ladles) to bring the slurry to a similar temperature as the milk mixture. Then pour the egg slurry into the milk mixture. While whisking continuously, cook it until it's smooth and thick and bubbles start to burp to the top, 4 to 5 minutes. Carefully place the pot in the ice bath, without allowing any water to get in the pot, and let the crème anglaise cool to room temperature. Transfer the crème anglaise to an airtight container, then stow it in the fridge to chill for 1 hour. Churn and freeze it in your ice cream machine per the maker's instructions. You'll have about 1 quart [945 ml] of ice cream.

continued

Vanilla Ice Cream

¾ cup plus 2 Tbsp [180 g] sugar

⅓ cup [45 g] cornstarch

4 large eggs

2 vanilla beans, seeds scraped and pods discarded

Pinch of kosher salt

2½ cups [600 ml] whole milk

¾ cup [180 ml] heavy cream

continued

TIME
2 hours active; about 10 hours total, depending on your ice cream maker

YIELD
2 monster sundaes or 4 reasonable ones

SPECIAL GEAR
Ice cream maker

To make the candied pecans: Preheat the oven to 250°F [120°C].

In a medium bowl, whisk together the sugar, salt, and pepper. Line a sheet pan with a silicone mat or parchment paper; if using parchment, lightly coat it with pan spray.

In a second medium bowl, whisk together the egg white, bourbon, vanilla, and 1 teaspoon of water until it's frothy. Add the pecans and toss to evenly coat them, then fold in the sugar mixture and toss again until the pecans are nice and sandy. Spread the pecans on the prepared sheet pan and bake them, stirring every 10 minutes, until they're crispy and toasted, about 45 minutes. You'll have about 4 cups [560 g].

To make the caramel: In a medium saucepan over medium-high heat, stir the sugar into ¼ cup [60 ml] of water, then bring it to a boil. Continue boiling it, without stirring, until its color deepens to a dark amber, about 5 minutes. Carefully stir in the heavy cream, butter, and salt, then pull it off the heat. While whisking, stream in the IPA. Place the saucepan over medium-low heat, and cook the caramel, stirring constantly with a rubber spatula, until it thickens, 8 to 10 minutes. Let it cool for 4 to 5 minutes before drizzling it over the ice cream. If you're not using it right away, you can pour it into a heatproof jar and leave it on your countertop for up to 3 days. Set the jar in a water bath over low heat to gently rewarm it.

To make a sundae, using an ice cream scoop, drop as many scoops of ice cream as you want into a small serving bowl, drizzle on as much caramel as you like, and top with plenty of pecans.

Candied Pecans
1 cup [200 g] sugar
½ tsp kosher salt
½ tsp freshly ground black pepper
Pan spray, if needed
1 egg white
1 tsp bourbon
1 tsp vanilla extract
1 lb [455 g] pecans

IPA Caramel
1 cup [200 g] sugar
¼ cup [60 ml] heavy cream
2 Tbsp unsalted butter
¼ tsp kosher salt
¼ cup [60 ml] West Coast IPA

visit to the seaside farmers

Central California is an ag powerhouse. Here on the coast, the Salinas Valley, near Monterey Bay, is known as The Salad Bowl of the World. It produces 70 percent of the planet's lettuce and plenty of other crops too. Around Half Moon Bay, artichokes, Brussels sprouts, and butter beans are grown by multigenerational families whose kids sell vegetables on the side of the road. The land between my bungalow and the beach is a protected reserve now, but you can still see the irrigation infrastructure from the pea fields that used to be there. My neighbor is a horse named Lexia that I feed apples and carrots to by way of hello. And though Half Moon Bay is changing, and nowadays, it seems that every third car is a Tesla, Latino farmers still dance their horses in the streets.

A lot of the agriculture on the Central Coast is conventional, but there's also an up-and-coming generation of younger, open-minded farmers. Rather than spraying chemicals and killing things in the process, farmers like my friends at Brisa Ranch (see page 173) are mom-and-pop'ing it out here. Working within the sustainable constraints of cover crops and compost, they're shepherding the land as they develop a gentler way of producing food. I've walked fields with the soil experts who are helping them fix their land. Those guys grab handfuls of earth and can tell if it is alive with beneficial microbes or not. This new crop of farmers didn't create the ecological problems on their land, but they're working to fix them.

As someone who buys intentionally for my restaurant, I feel good supporting that. This chapter is written with gratitude to the farms that I work with and the fruits of their damned hard labor. We are spoiled on the Central Coast. We take for granted the kind of produce you might not find in other places: fire engine–red Jimmy Nardello peppers that bring their sweet flavor to a panzanella (page 168); garbanzo beans pulled fresh from their pods for grinding raw into falafel (page 181); monstrous Treviso radicchio that works like a scoop in a hand salad with jammy Mission figs (page 169); perfect artichokes for frying and serving with artichoke mayo (page 164). I've suggested substitutions, to help you work with what's at farms or markets near you.

If anything, these recipes spread the love for the growing seasons: the moment in summer that the corn is ripe for roasting and tossing in a salad with cucumbers and a whole lot of funky cheese (page 170) or the time of year when the big, creamy beans are bursting at their seams, just right for a first-of-the-season braise (page 179).

Fried Artichokes

3 lemons, preferably Meyer

10 medium artichokes (see headnote)

12 cups [2.8 L] chicken stock, preferably The Best Chicken Stock (page 63)

8 oz [230 g] slab bacon, preferably The Best Bacon (page 65), cut into 1 in [2.5 cm] cubes

6 garlic cloves, peeled

2 large shallots, cut into ½ in [13 mm] thick slices

40 cranks black pepper

Pinch of kosher salt

Canola oil, for frying

Flaky salt, such as Maldon

1 bunch fresh chives, thinly sliced, for garnish

To do justice to Central Coast farming, you must cook artichokes. Gigantic, spiky thistles, with a hairy "choke," they're intimidating. But work them down to their tender center, and you're rewarded with juicy umami bombs.

Michelin-starred restaurants make vegetables sing by having them harmonize with themselves. In a single dish, you use the same veg over and over, pushing its flavor to the limit. Here, the artichoke's braising liquid amps up the dip's goodness. It's artichokes dipped in artichokes. Serve 'em at cocktail hour with ice-cold Cynar and soda water.

Use common sense when you're trimming artichokes. If you can only get monster-size ones, buy half as many and cut them into eighths when you get to that step. If they're babies, just cut them in half and pull out the choke. You'll have delicious braising liquid left over from this recipe. Cook rice or other grains in it; braise sunchokes in it, smashing them on a sheet pan and roasting them; or simply sip it like a cup of tea.

fried artichokes with artichoke dip

To make the fried artichokes: First, braise them. Cut a square piece of parchment paper a bit bigger than your braising pot. Fold it into quarters, then fold it in half to create a triangle with the gathered corner at the tip. Fold it in half two more times to make a narrower triangle. Lay the triangle with its tip centered inside a large Dutch oven. Crimp the other end of the parchment where it meets the inside edge of the pot. Cut along the crimp. Cut off the tip of the triangle. Open it up. You should have a round parchment cloche with a center hole.

Set a wire rack inside a sheet pan and put it near the stove.

Cut 2 of the lemons in half and squeeze the juice into a big bowl of water, then drop the lemon halves in. Cut off the stems and the top two-thirds of each artichoke. Cut the artichokes lengthwise in half, then scrape out the chokes with a sharp-tipped spoon. Halve the

ARTICHOKE STEMS CAN BE TOUGH AS A #2 PENCIL. EATING THEM REMINDS ME OF TAKING THE SATs. NOT FUN.

TIME
2 hours

YIELD
6 to 8 servings

artichokes again, dropping them into the lemon water as you go, so they don't oxidize.

Pour the chicken stock into the Dutch oven. Cut the remaining lemon into ½ in [13 mm] thick slices and remove any seeds. Add the lemon slices, along with the bacon, garlic, shallots, pepper, and salt, to the Dutch oven. Use a spider or slotted spoon to scoop the artichokes from the lemon water, then add them to the Dutch oven. If the liquid isn't just covering the artichokes, add water to cover. Lay the cloche on top of the liquid and press it down so some of the liquid floods the hole. This keeps it in constant contact with the braise. Bring it to a boil, then knock the heat down to a simmer, cover the pot with the lid cracked to let some steam out, and cook the artichokes until they're tender, 20 to 30 minutes.

Kill the heat and let the braise cool until you can handle the artichokes, about 15 minutes. Use a spider or slotted spoon to scoop the artichokes from the braising liquid, then pat them dry and set them on the wire rack. Let the braising liquid cool until you can skim off and discard the fat. Strain the liquid into an airtight container and measure out ¼ cup [60 ml] of the braising liquid and reserve it for the artichoke dip. The leftover braising liquid keeps, in the fridge in an airtight container, for up to 4 days or in the freezer for up to 1 month.

To make the artichoke dip: In a blender, a food processor, or with an immersion blender in a container that's just wide enough for it to fit, blend together the egg, egg yolk, vinegar, sugar, mustard, lemon juice, and salt. With the blender running, slowly stream in the umami oil until the mixture comes together and is smooth and thick. Stir in the reserved braising liquid to loosen the mixture for dipping. The dip keeps, in the fridge in an airtight container, for up to 1 week.

In a medium Dutch oven or heavy-walled pot with a candy thermometer attached, heat 3 in [7.5 cm] of canola oil to 350°F [180°C]. Carefully add 6 to 8 braised artichoke quarters to the hot oil and, moving them around and flipping them at least once, fry them until they're golden and crispy, 1 to 1½ minutes. Use a slotted spoon to transfer the fried artichokes back to the wire rack to drain. Repeat to fry the remaining artichokes, bringing the oil back up to temp each time. To serve, pile the artichokes on a platter, finish them with flaky salt and loads of sliced chives, and serve them with the dip on the side.

Artichoke Dip

1 large egg

1 egg yolk

2 tsp apple cider vinegar

2 tsp sugar

1 tsp whole-grain mustard

1 tsp fresh lemon juice, preferably Meyer

1 tsp kosher salt

1 cup [240 ml] Umami Oil (page 46)

¼ cup [60 ml] artichoke braising liquid

The farmer who sells me summer squash at the farmers' market wraps each one in newspaper before she hands it over. "I don't want them bruised or sad," she says. That's wisdom. Summer squash are filled with so much water, you have to treat them with care. Avoid the big, waterlogged monsters. Go for the smaller, crisper, more flavorful ones.

Then make this special salad to show off summer. Plan ahead: The dressing, a cherry blossom vinaigrette, is thickened with kombu. It hugs the salad like a coat, but it should sit overnight first. You need to shop at a Japanese market or online for some of the ingredients, including the cherry blossoms and leaves. But if you haven't cooked with punchy umeboshi or briny, floral sakura, you're in for fun. At these proportions, this is a salad for a crowd. It's an awesome palate cleanser for fire-cooked meats like the Korean BBQ Pear Butter Ribs (page 304) or the Smoked Chicken with Smoked Chimichurri (page 87).

To make the cherry blossom vinaigrette: In a pint jar, combine the vinegar, umeboshi, bonito flakes, white soy sauce, cherry blossoms, sugar, and kombu. Screw on the lid and give the jar a good shake, then let it sit at room temperature overnight to thicken and infuse. Strain it through a fine-mesh strainer, and discard the solids. Leftover vinaigrette keeps, in an airtight container in the fridge, for 1 month. Make mayo, marinate fish, and dress other salads with it.

To make the summer squash and plum salad: Cut off and discard the tops and bottoms from the squash. With your mandoline set at ⅛ in [3 mm], shave the pattypans sideways into a large serving bowl to make thin disks. Shave the zucchinis lengthwise into the bowl to make long, noodley ribbons. Shave the plums into the bowl, turning them as you shave down to their pits. Mix the salad well with your hands.

Use half of the vinaigrette to dress the salad, adding more, 1 teaspoon at a time, as needed. Mix the salad gently with your hands, then fold in the shiso leaves. Garnish it with the cherry leaves and serve it right away.

summer squash and plum salad

Cherry Blossom Vinaigrette

1 cup [240 ml] white balsamic vinegar

¼ cup [50 g] umeboshi plums (about 10 plums), pitted

¼ cup [1.25 g] bonito flakes

2 Tbsp white soy sauce

¼ oz [7 g] salted sakura blossoms (cherry blossoms), rinsed and squeezed dry

2¼ tsp sugar

3 by 2 in [7.5 by 5 cm] piece kombu, cut into 1 in [2.5 cm] pieces

Summer Squash and Plum Salad

5 medium pattypan squashes

4 medium zucchinis

5 greengage or other variety of firm plums

10 shiso leaves, torn or left whole

8 salted cherry leaves (also called pickled sakura leaves), rinsed, squeezed dry, and torn into ½ in [13 mm] pieces

TIME
30 minutes active; overnight total

YIELD
6 to 8 servings

4 Tbsp [60 ml] extra-virgin
olive oil

8 oz [230 g] Jimmy Nardello or
other long, sweet peppers,
stemmed and cut into ¼ in
[6 mm] thick rings

1 lb [455 g] Sungold cherry
tomatoes, halved

1 Persian cucumber, quartered
lengthwise and cut into ¼ in
[6 mm] thick slices

1 large shallot,
very thinly sliced

¼ cup [60 g] chopped kimchi,
preferably Whole Napa
Cabbage Kimchi (page 58)

¼ cup [60 ml] kimchi brine,
preferably from Whole Napa
Cabbage Kimchi (page 58)

Juice of 1 lemon,
preferably Meyer

5 or 6 cranks black pepper

Pinch of kosher salt

1 garlic clove, peeled

4 oz [115 g] sourdough bread,
cut into ¼ by ½ in [6 by
13 mm] batons

1 Tbsp torn fresh lemon basil
leaves

1 cup [40 g] torn fresh Opal or
Genovese basil leaves

TIME
25 minutes active;
4 to 24 hours total

YIELD
2 to 4 servings

There's not much to a panzanella but fresh veg, a dressing, and beautiful, oily, crunchy-boy bread. It's all about marinating the veg before you add the croutons and serve it. Probiotic marinades knock the socks off vinegar-based ones. You get deep flavor and nice heat, and everything stays alive. The tomatoes start to bleed. The croutons crackle and then soak up the salad's velvety juices.

But the real heroes of this salad are the Jimmy Nardellos. I like a pepper that has a first and last name. The story goes that they're named after the son of the couple who brought the seeds with them when they emigrated from Italy. They look like willowy, red witches' fingers, and they get deeper and sweeter when you roast them. In California, their appearance tells you spring is here. If you can't find them, any long, sweet variety—Hungarian wax peppers, Cubanelles—will work. I also like a mix of different basils in this salad. Go for whatever two types are blasting you with aroma at the market. Just don't use Thai basil; it's too lemongrassy for this salad.

jimmy nardello panzanella

In a 9 in [23 cm] cast-iron pan over high heat, heat 2 table-spoons of the oil until it's smoking. Throw in the peppers and let them hard-sear until nicely charred on one side, 3 to 4 minutes. Put them in a bowl, then add the tomatoes, cucumber, shallot, kimchi, kimchi brine, lemon juice, pepper, and salt. Mix well to coat and blend the veg. Cover the salad and stow in the fridge for at least 3 hours and up to overnight to marry the flavors.

In a small sauté pan over medium-high heat, heat the remaining 2 tablespoons of olive oil, then add the garlic, and when it's brown on one side, discard it and add the bread, tossing to coat it in the oil. Toast it on one side until golden, 30 seconds to 1 minute, then flip it and toast the other side, 30 seconds to 1 minute. Add the lemon basil, and toast it for 15 seconds. Put the croutons and toasted lemon basil in a bowl to cool, 2 to 3 minutes, then add them to the salad, along with the Opal basil, and give the salad a big stir. Let the croutons soak up the flavors for 5 minutes, then dig in. If you think you are going to have leftover salad, don't add all the croutons at once. The salad keeps, in an airtight container in the fridge, overnight. Add the remaining croutons to it the next day. And here's an idea: Try blitzing any leftover salad, along with the croutons, in the blender, and drink it like gazpacho.

fig, feta, and radicchio hand salad

In summer in California, Black Mission figs are big and luscious. I made this salad just for them. A little cooking brings out the radicchio's sugars and mellows its bitterness. If you find long Treviso radicchio, use those leaves to grab this salad and eat it out of hand. Smaller Chioggia radicchio—the kind you mainly find in supermarkets—works, too, if you eat the salad with a fork. But this is also called a hand salad because of our Rule of the Road #6 (see page 29). You tear ingredients with your hands.

There's so much flavor wrapping the figs: sweet plum, bitter radicchio, acidic grapefruit, earthy pine nuts. But the key to the balance is brine-aged feta. For the love of God, do not buy dry feta "crumbles." Convenience food like that lives with purpose somewhere. "But not here," says Frost. She's right.

Get a 9 in [23 cm] cast-iron pan ripping hot over high heat, then sear the radicchio whole until charred on each side, 4 to 5 minutes per side. Put it on a plate and chill it in the fridge.

Meanwhile, use a sharp paring knife to supreme the grapefruit, cutting off the top and bottom of the fruit, then running your knife down the sides of the fruit, following its contour to remove the skin, pith, and outer membrane. Free the segments by slicing on either side of the membrane that separates the segments. Put the segments in a large bowl, then squeeze the juice from the membrane into the bowl and discard the membrane.

Halve the plums, remove and discard the pits, and rip the plums into eighths into the bowl with the grapefruit. Remove the stems from the figs and rip them into quarters into the bowl. Toss in the shallot. Separate the radicchio into individual leaves and add them to the bowl. Add the oil and toss until the salad is well coated with grapefruit juice and oil.

Cover the salad and stow it in the fridge to marinate and mellow for at least 4 hours and up to overnight.

Right before serving, in a cast-iron pan over medium heat, toast the pine nuts until they're fragrant and charred in places, about 1 minute. Let them cool, then toss them in the salad, along with the feta broken into small chunks. The salad is best served right away, but leftovers keep, in the fridge in an airtight container, overnight.

1 big head Treviso radicchio or 2 heads Chioggia radicchio

1 red grapefruit

3 ripe, juicy plums, preferably Santa Rosa

8 oz [230 g] Black Mission figs (5 to 8 figs)

1 shallot, very thinly sliced

1 Tbsp extra-virgin olive oil

½ cup [60 g] pine nuts

4 oz [115 g] brine-aged feta

TIME
30 minutes active; 5 to 24 hours total

YIELD
4 servings

roasted corn and smoked blue cheese salad

1 Tbsp extra-virgin olive oil

1 Tbsp ghee, preferably homemade (page 42)

2 large shallots, cut into ⅛ in [3 mm] thick rings

Kosher salt

Kernels from 4 ears of corn

6 to 8 cranks black pepper, more if you want

Juice of ½ lemon, preferably Meyer

2 tsp chopped umeboshi plums

2 cups [335 g] Sungold cherry tomatoes

2 cups [300 g] watermelon gherkins or chopped lemon or Persian cucumbers

6 oz [170 g] smoked blue cheese, preferably Rogue Creamery Smokey Blue

1 cup [15 g] tender dandelion greens

1 cup [12 g] packed fresh basil leaves, preferably Opal

At my grandparents' farm in the summer, we'd be out all day shooting BB guns and breaking the windows of abandoned barns. But just before dinner, Grandma would be in her porch rocking chair with a bushel of ears. "Go wash your filthy hands," she'd say, "and help me shuck this corn."

California's peak-season corn is as sweet as candy. Playing with textures, this salad mixes raw and roasted kernels in a pickly marinade. The Sungolds give it a sweet-tart kick, and the watermelon gherkins—tiny, football-shaped cukes—bring crunch. Add creamy cheese and bitter greens, and we're reaching for all the spokes on the flavor wheel.

Don't mix this salad too far ahead. You want the flavors together but separate. Throw the herbs in right before serving. If you want herbs to last, treat them like gold. Wrap them in a dry paper towel inside a moist paper towel, then stow them in a ziplock or resealable silicone bag in the fridge and don't put anything heavy on top. Before they go in the dish, get a little rough with them. Give them a tear.

In a 9 in [23 cm] cast-iron pan over high heat, heat the oil and ghee. Add the shallots and cook them until they're deep brown, 3 to 5 minutes. Sprinkle them with 2 big pinches of salt, then toss in half of the corn kernels. Cover the pan, so the corn doesn't fly out at you, and let it caramelize, stirring once or twice, until it's browned in spots and fragrant, about 5 minutes. Add the pepper.

With a slotted spoon, transfer the corn mixture to a bowl, then add the raw corn, along with the lemon juice and umeboshi, and toss to fully coat everything. Cover it and stow it in the fridge while you prep the rest of your veg.

Halve the tomatoes and gherkins lengthwise, then put them in a serving bowl and sprinkle with a big pinch of salt. Crumble in the blue cheese. Add the corn mixture, mixing so that everything's well combined. Right before serving, roughly tear and fold in the dandelion greens and basil leaves (either torn or whole), then season the salad with more salt and pepper.

TIME
30 minutes

YIELD
6 to 8 servings

CRISTÓBAL CRUZ HERNÁNDEZ AND VERÓNICA AND COLE MAZARIEGOS-ANASTASSIOU, BRISA RANCH

Cristóbal, Verónica, and Cole farm a gorgeous, yet extreme, fifteen acres on the San Francisco Peninsula in Pescadero. Located on Highway 1, Brisa Ranch is named after the relentless Pacific breeze that brings the ocean mist to nourish and quench their crops. "We've been tested a lot," says Verónica, "but this land has afforded us so much learning and growing." I've worked with them since 2018. They were just getting started, with an acre and a half, and Cole showed up at Dad's with a load of squashes, when what I really needed was potatoes for our chips. So, they ramped up production for us, and now Dad's gets one hundred pounds of certified-organic Désirée reds from them every week, plus peppers, artichokes, apples, tomatoes, and so much more. They grow heirloom fruit and veg without irrigation or chemicals, and they take deep care of the land. "We're taking from the soil to grow food, so it's our duty to give back to it," says Cole.

They also take care of their community. The three of them met at nearby Pie Ranch, a regenerative farm and education center, where they taught youth farming and food systems. They've since founded the first California chapter of the National Young Farmers Coalition, and Verónica works with the California Farmer Justice Collaborative. In 2020, when wildfire was licking across Highway 1, Cole stayed to protect his own and surrounding properties. He enlisted us to cook for his neighbors who were fighting the fires. I would meet him at the highway patrol's roadblock with a bunch of grub. Like other young farmers, the three of them are making it work through their hustle, doing farmers' markets, selling to restaurants like ours, and running a CSA. Dad's is a pickup spot for their members, who get a gorgeous box of produce each week for their fee. I'm proud as hell to be a part of that.

Here's what to eat when you're looking for a bowl of pure comfort. These beans are so buttery and savory, they almost have a cheesy flavor. The key is to make a beurre monté, emulsifying butter in broth to get yourself a super silky sauce. Always remember that two things break an emulsion: heat and impatience. Add your butter slowly. Baby each piece, treating it to a nice, warm broth bath. When you can part the seas with your spatula, you've made your beurre monté.

As for the beans, the salt in their overnight soak keeps their skins tight, so when you cook them, they won't burst. You get to enjoy beans that are taut on the outside and creamy within. The kombu helps the beans get tender and their skins stay toothsome, but it's also an anti-gas agent. That's a courtesy when you're serving a big pot of beans.

In a large bowl, combine the beans and 1½ teaspoons of the salt. Add enough water to cover the beans by 1 in [2.5 cm] and soak them at room temperature overnight. Stir and drain the beans.

Cut off and discard the dark green and root ends from the leeks, then peel off and discard the first two layers, and rinse the leeks well. Cut them into ¼ in [6 mm] thick rings, then drop them into a bowl of cold water, separating the rings and zhushing them to clean them thoroughly. Drain the leeks in a colander.

Cut 3 tablespoons of the butter into very small cubes and stow it in the fridge to keep cold.

In a medium Dutch oven over medium-high heat, melt the remaining 1 tablespoon of butter and 1 tablespoon of the umami oil until the butter stops frothing, 1 to 1½ minutes. Add the garlic and rattle it around the pot until it just gets colored, 2 to 3 minutes. Add the leeks, the remaining 1 teaspoon of salt, and 10 cranks of pepper and cook until the leeks are bright green, 2 to 3 minutes.

continued

miso-braised gigante beans

Ingredients

1 lb [455 g] dried gigante beans or another big, white bean, such as large limas or Royal Coronas

2½ tsp kosher salt

2 large leeks

4 Tbsp [55 g] unsalted butter

1½ Tbsp Umami Oil (page 46)

10 garlic cloves, peeled

20 cranks black pepper

2 Tbsp white soy sauce

1 bay leaf

2 Tbsp red miso

4 by 2 in [10 by 5 cm] piece kombu

2 cups [40 g] loosely packed red kale or spinach leaves

¼ cup [65 g] Oven-Dried Tomatoes (page 67), chopped

6 green onions, sliced

Juice of ½ lemon, preferably Meyer

Country bread, for serving, if you want

TIME
45 minutes active; overnight total

YIELD
4 to 6 servings

Add the beans, white soy sauce, and bay leaf. Add enough water to cover the beans by 1 in [2.5 cm], then bring it to a boil, stirring occasionally. Knock the heat down to a simmer.

Place a fine-mesh strainer in the pot, add the miso to it, and, scraping with a wooden spoon, strain the miso into the pot. Add the kombu and cover it with the lid slightly cracked to let the steam out. Braise the beans until all their graininess is gone and they're super creamy, about 1 hour. Kill the heat, then fish out the kombu and bay leaf.

In a large sauté pan over medium-high heat, heat the remaining ½ tablespoon of umami oil until it's just smoking, then add the kale and sauté it, tossing it, until it stops hissing and caramelizes, 2 to 3 minutes. Turn the heat down to low, then add the bean mixture to the kale. Slowly bring the heat back up to medium so the beans bubble, and the broth reduces by half, 5 to 10 minutes. Knock the heat down to low, then add the cold cubed butter, three or four pieces at a time, and stir to completely incorporate it until the broth tightens and starts to pull away from the edges of the pan, 2 to 4 minutes. Kill the heat and stir in the oven-dried tomatoes. Scatter the green onions over the top, then squeeze on the lemon juice, and add the remaining 10 cranks of pepper. Serve the beans in the pan with country bread on the side, if you want.

My eating goals have changed as I've gotten older. I can't scarf a mess of fried chicken anymore and think my body will feel OK. So, I look for other protein sources. Veg-forward is where I'm headed, though truth be told, this recipe harkens back to my college days. Morgantown, West Virginia, was not known for international cuisine, but I lived above a late-night joint where you could go hammered at 4 a.m. and eat any number of things in a pita. They'd give it to you with bacon and eggs, chicken teriyaki and pineapple, whatever. I was flirting with being vegetarian then, so I capped off those nights with a loaded falafel.

When I moved to San Francisco, I started going to this place called Old Jerusalem that does an incredible falafel with pine nuts and sumac. I wanted to recreate their specialty at home for me and the kid. Then I thought back to college, and figured, hell, let's just make this a party. This falafel spread comes with a spicy carrot salad and a punchy yogurt dressing, and it welcomes all those flavor-packed Go-Tos from chapter 1 (see page 39). Add whatever else you like to the platter: fresh radishes and tomatoes, dill pickles, green onions.

In California, I can get fresh garbanzos. Crack the pod open, and these tender, green legumes pop out, but you need almost a whole bushel of pods to get three cups. Dried garbanzos are easier to find, and they work just as well after soaking. Just don't use canned. They don't taste as good or bind as well. I grind my garbanzos in a meat grinder because I like that sausage-y texture, but a food processor does the trick too.

falafel party

Carrot Salad

5 medium carrots, peeled and quartered lengthwise

2 Tbsp toasted sesame oil

1 Tbsp Madras curry powder

Pinch of kosher salt

Yogurt Dressing

1 cup [240 g] yogurt, preferably homemade (page 43)

1 Tbsp tahini

2 tsp freshly ground black pepper

1 tsp sumac

Zest and juice of 1 lemon, preferably Meyer

Pinch of kosher salt

continued

To make the carrot salad: Place a half sheet pan in the oven and preheat the oven to 400°F [200°C].

In a medium bowl, mix the carrots, sesame oil, curry powder, and salt until evenly coated.

Spread the carrots in an even layer on the hot sheet pan and roast them, stirring every so often, until they're fork-tender and slightly charred, 35 to 40 minutes.

To make the yogurt dressing: In a small bowl, stir all the ingredients together.

continued

TIME
1 hour active; overnight total

YIELD
6 to 8 servings

SPECIAL GEAR
Meat grinder, if using

Falafel

3 cups [540 g] dried garbanzo beans, soaked overnight and drained

1 white onion, chopped

5 garlic cloves, chopped

1 bunch fresh parsley, chopped

1 bunch fresh cilantro, chopped

1 bunch fresh mint, stems discarded and leaves chopped

½ cup [70 g] toasted white sesame seeds

1½ Tbsp freshly ground cumin

1½ Tbsp freshly ground coriander

1 Tbsp baking powder

1 tsp kosher salt, plus more as needed

Canola oil, for frying

Your choice of Fermented Hot Sauce (page 62), Coastal Kraut (page 56), Whole Napa Cabbage Kimchi (page 58), Pickled Onions (page 48), Oven-Dried Tomatoes (page 67), and Chile Jam (page 60), for serving

Pita or cooked rice, for serving

To make the falafel: In a large bowl, mix the beans, onion, garlic, parsley, cilantro, and mint until fully combined. Using a medium die on your meat grinder, or pulsing in your food processor, grind the mixture until it's finely ground but not pasty. Return it to the bowl, then add the sesame seeds, cumin, coriander, baking powder, and salt and mix the dough with your hands until everything is combined and a handful holds its shape when you grab it.

Using two spoons or your hands, form as many tightly packed, golf ball–size falafel as the dough will make. You should get about four dozen.

Line a large bowl with paper towels.

In a medium Dutch oven or heavy-walled pot with a candy thermometer attached, heat 3 in [7.5 cm] of oil to 375°F [190°C]. Working in batches of four, carefully add the falafel to the hot oil and fry them, moving them around and flipping them, until they're golden brown on the outside but still tender inside, 2 to 3 minutes. Put the falafel in the paper towel–lined bowl and season them with salt. Bring the oil back to temperature between batches.

Serve the falafel arranged on a big platter with the carrot salad, the yogurt dressing, and all the condiments you want, plus pita or rice on the side.

The technique for the patties in these sandwiches keeps the moisture inside the bacon while giving you plenty of surface area for crispy crunch. It's like a smash burger made of bacon. I discovered the method at a place called Hodad's in Ocean Beach on a dissolute trip to San Diego during college, staying in hostels, bumming around, and smoking reefer. So here's a nod to Southern California.

But we excel at tomatoes on the Central Coast, and the sweet, tomato-on-tomato tang pulls the juicy pineapple, crisp lettuce, and a heinous pile of bacon together in these sandwiches. You'll have leftover mayo. Thin it out with white balsamic and lemon juice for dressing; add basil and chives and dunk vegetables or a slice of pizza into it; or load it up with Tabasco for swiping fried clams.

Keep the braising liquid too. In the fridge, the fat will rise to the top. It's gold. Fry bacon and eggs in it or use it for Confit Garlic (page 47). Use the liquid to braise artichokes; fortify it with The Best Chicken Stock (page 63) for ramen broth; or cook it down and glaze bone-in pork chops.

To make the oven-dried tomato mayo: In a food processor, in a blender, or with an immersion blender in a container just wide enough to fit it, blend the egg yolks, egg, vinegar, and salt. With the food processor or blender running, drizzle in the canola oil and the oil from the oven-dried tomatoes. When the mayo is silky and thick, about 5 minutes, add the oven-dried tomatoes and blend well. Season with salt. You'll have about 3 cups [710 ml], and it keeps, in the fridge in an airtight container, for up to 1 week.

continued

california pblt

Oven-Dried Tomato Mayo

2 egg yolks

1 whole large egg

2 Tbsp white balsamic vinegar

1 tsp kosher salt, plus more as needed

1½ cups [360 ml] canola oil

½ cup [120 ml] oil from Oven-Dried Tomatoes (page 67)

½ cup [125 g] Oven-Dried Tomatoes (page 67)

continued

TIME
45 minutes active; 1½ hours total

YIELD
3 sandwiches

SPECIAL GEAR
Meat grinder, if using

To make the bacon patties: In a medium Dutch oven, bring the bacon, onion, cider, and 4 cups [945 ml] of water to a boil. Knock the heat down to a simmer, cover it with the lid slightly cracked to let the steam out, and cook it for 1 hour. Scoop the bacon out and let it cool until you can handle it, then squeeze it to remove excess moisture. Using a medium die on your meat grinder, or pulsing in your food processor, grind the bacon until it's well shredded. Pressing with your hands, form the bacon into three patties.

In a 9 in [23 cm] cast-iron pan over medium-high heat, heat the ghee until it's starting to smoke, about 2 minutes. Knock the heat down to medium, then fry the patties, one at a time, until they are super crusty and caramelized, 3 to 4 minutes per side. Do not clean the pan.

To make the sandwiches: Cut off and discard the top and bottom of the pineapple. Running your knife down the outside of the fruit, remove all the skin and brown bumps. Cut it vertically in half to expose the core, then cut out the core and slice half of the pineapple into ¼ in [6 mm] thick slices. Reserve the other half for snacking or tossing onto your overnight oats (page 137).

Place the pan you cooked the bacon patties in over medium heat, then add the pineapple slices and sear them until they're caramelized, 1 to 2 minutes per side.

FRESH PINEAPPLE IS GREAT TREATED LIKE GRILLED AND CHILLED MELON (PAGE 309).

Spread 1 tablespoon of the mayo on each slice of bread. Lay 1 or 2 lettuce leaves on 3 of the slices. Lay the bacon patties on top of the lettuce. Add 1 or 2 tomato slices, then squeeze on 1 teaspoon of lemon juice. Add 2 or 3 pineapple slices and top the sandwiches with the remaining bread. Serve them big and whole.

Bacon Patties

1 lb [455 g] slab bacon, preferably The Best Bacon (page 65)

½ large white onion

1 cup [240 ml] hard cider

1 Tbsp ghee, preferably homemade (page 42)

Sandwiches

1 small pineapple, about 1 lb [455 g]

6 slices country bread

1 big beefsteak tomato, cut into ¼ in [6 mm] thick slices

½ lemon, preferably Meyer

3 to 6 large butter lettuce leaves

fishing and foraging on the coast

The Central Coast offers loads of biodiversity, from the windswept sagebrush and berry bramble at the tippy top of the Southern Coast Ranges through the descent into lush forest with its wild fennel, water spinach, and mushrooms, to the shoreline's seaweeds and mollusks, and into the Pacific Ocean where creatures live in reef crevices amid a jungle of kelp. As someone who fishes and forages, I like to utilize these things, but always with respect and restraint. If California's fires and droughts and mudslides and floods have taught us anything, it's that this rugged place is delicate too. You can't take too much from it, so we learn to coax the most flavor out of the minimum take.

Starting with all the coastal First Nations people—the Ohlone, Esselen, Salinan, and Chumash, whose descendants are stewards of the land and sea here today—folks have fished and foraged this coast for millennia. There's such a variety of experiences to be had by walking out the door and connecting with these ecosystems. You get a sense of how small you are, and that can be grounding.

Fishing and foraging on the Central Coast takes me back to my childhood. I grew up, rising early, wiping crud from my eyes, an East Coast kid walking dank trails to hidden fishing holes and curling up in a blanket in the wheelhouse of a boat on the Chesapeake. I lost some of that pursuing my profession. In Michelin-starred kitchens, despite the products I was cooking, I wasn't in touch with the natural world. I'd feel that connection in the people we got fish or mushrooms from, but I didn't realize I needed it so badly until I stepped back from fine dining and reconnected with myself, and that took me right back outside, to the Central Coast mountains and ocean.

Grabbing a morel off the forest floor and doing something outrageous to it like chicken-frying it and dousing it in red-eye gravy (page 202); hooking a lingcod for ceviche (page 210); breaking down a Dungeness for a bowl of crab rice (page 218); sprinkling a caramel apple with some seaweed (page 222), and sharing these experiences with my daughter, I feel hopeful and joyous. So, in this chapter, we get into the nitty-gritty. We're pulling up bootstraps and grabbing sea lettuce from the surf, crawling in the dirt for porcini, getting our hands stinking with fish. I hope these recipes give you elemental, effective, and delicious ways to connect with the ingredients, even when you pick them up from the market. It's high-touch, high-reward cooking.

Smoked Berry Syrup

1 lb [455 g] huckleberries, ollalieberries, or blackberries

2 Tbsp sugar

2 pinches of kosher salt

Cherry wood chunks, for smoking

Old Fashioned

2 oz [60 ml] cask-strength rye, preferably Willett 4-Year

1 oz [30 ml] Smoked Berry Syrup

2 dashes Angostura bitters

1 lemon peel, preferably Meyer

1 orange peel

TIME
45 minutes

YIELD
1 cocktail

SPECIAL GEAR
Grill or smoker
Lump charcoal

smoked huckleberry old fashioned

Here's a drink for the end of a long, damp day of foraging. My man Anthony Keels (see page 97) conjured it in praise of California's wild huckleberries, a staple food of Indigenous folks and a favorite of foragers. In the fall in the Santa Cruz Mountains, you're going to run into them. They look like blueberries and taste like blackberries, and because they can't be cultivated, we pick them ourselves. Then we have a mess on our hands because huckleberries stain.

A good substitute is the ollalieberry that family farms such as Linn's of Cambria grow. But you can't really get those outside of the Central Coast, so you can also just use blackberries. The point is, you're making a dark, smoked berry syrup to swap in for the muddled fruit in an old fashioned.

To make the smoked berry syrup: With a pair of kitchen gloves on, in a medium bowl, pick the berries over and give them a rinse, removing stems, small rocks, and other grit. Squash and smash the berries with your hands, then mix them with the sugar and salt.

Prep your smoker. This is a good one for a stovetop smoker. If you're using a charcoal grill, bank your coals to one side. When the coals are glowing and no longer on fire, throw a handful of cherry wood chunks on them. There's no need to soak the wood chunks. For a gas grill, heat one side on high, place the wood chunks in a smoker box, and place the smoker box over the flame. Decrease the heat to low once the wood chips start smoking.

Fill a large bowl with ice and set the bowl of berries in the bowl. Let the first blast of acrid smoke blow off the grill, then arrange the bowls on the cool side of the grill, and close the lid. If you're using a charcoal grill, position the vents over the berries. Leave them to smoke for 30 minutes, then strain the berries through a chinois into a bowl, pressing on the solids. Use a funnel to transfer the syrup into a bottle. It keeps, in the fridge, for up to 1 month. You will have about 10 oz [300 ml], enough to make about 10 drinks.

To make the old fashioned: Fill a mixing glass halfway with ice, then add the rye, smoked berry syrup, bitters, and lemon peel and stir for 30 seconds. Strain the drink into an ice-filled rocks glass and garnish with the orange peel.

At Saison, I often used products flown in from Japan. But while walking the coast with foragers like Spencer Marley (see page 195), I realized this stuff is right in our backyard. California is edible, from the shrubs on the roadside to the weeds in the ocean. It's there, not to be ransacked but harvested sparingly. The kombu base for this soup imparts flavor, nutrients, and mouthfeel. The wakame expands when soaked, so you don't need a lot. Subtlety is key.

This recipe is grounded in fundamentals: Taste while cooking; pay attention; use care. At Saison, we tasted the kombu tea for this soup almost every minute until we got it where we wanted it, then we iced it down immediately. At home, there's no chef yelling at you, and dinner doesn't cost $800 a pop. But stay on top of things, so the tea, and then the soup, don't boil, and you'll get something pure, silky, and harmonious.

To make the kombu tea: In a medium bowl, sink the kombu into 8 cups [1.9 L] of water, then refrigerate it overnight.

To make the wakame-infused sake: In a pint jar, push the wakame into the sake, give it a stir, and refrigerate it overnight. Pour the sake through a fine-mesh strainer into another pint jar; discard the wakame. The sake keeps, in the fridge in an airtight container, for up to 2 weeks.

To make the miso soup: Remove the kombu from the tea; discard the kombu. Strain the tea into a medium stockpot set over medium heat, then gently bring it up to a simmer. Simmer for 10 minutes, cooking off some of the green flavor. Add the tofu, shiitakes, wakame, 2 tablespoons of the wakame-infused sake, and the sesame oil. Simmer for 10 minutes more, then kill the heat.

Place a fine-mesh strainer in the pot, add the miso to it, and, scraping with a wooden spoon, strain the miso into the pot. Add the white soy sauce, then taste and add more as needed.

Immediately ladle the soup into serving bowls and top it with the green onions and sesame seeds before serving.

seaweed-shiitake miso soup

Kombu Tea
6 by 3 in [15 by 7.5 cm] piece kombu

Wakame-Infused Sake
1 Tbsp dried wakame seaweed

1 cup [240 ml] Junmai or Junmai Daiginjo sake

Miso Soup
8 oz [230 g] extra-firm tofu, cut into 1 in [2.5 cm] cubes

5 oz [140 g] medium shiitake mushrooms, halved and hard stem bulbs removed

½ oz [14 g] dried wakame seaweed

1 tsp toasted sesame oil

¼ cup [25 g] sweet white miso

1 Tbsp white soy sauce, plus more as needed

4 green onions, thinly sliced

2 tsp toasted white sesame seeds

CHEAP CUP SAKE WORKS JUST FINE IN THIS RECIPE.

TIME
30 minutes active; overnight total

YIELD
4 to 6 servings

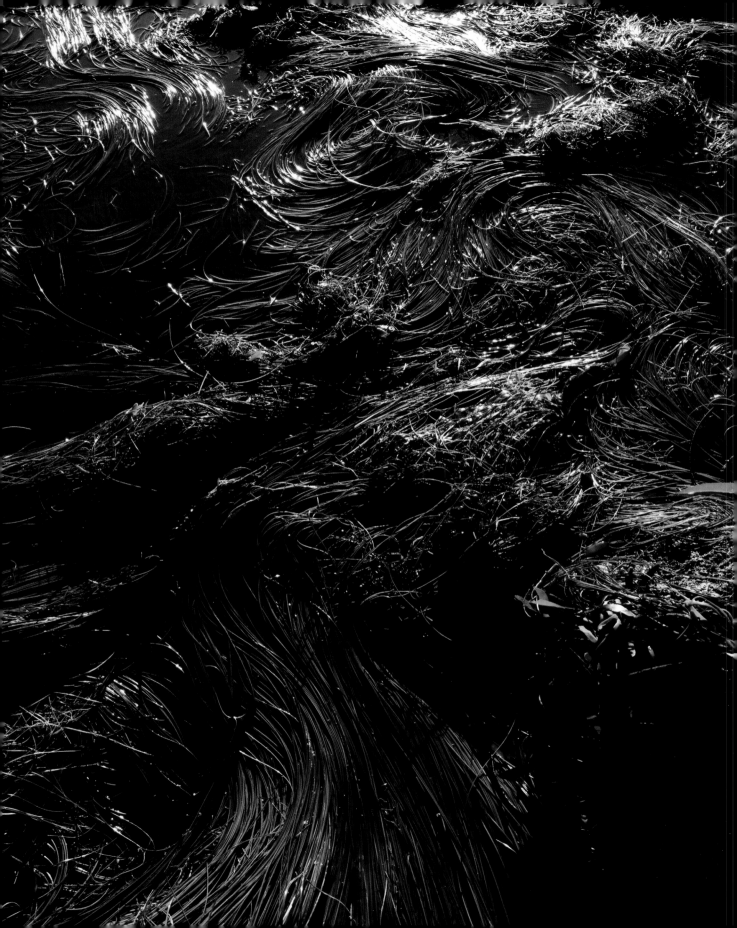

SPENCER MARLEY, MARLEY FAMILY SEAWEEDS

Spencer is a lifelong waterman. He's been a commercial albacore and salmon fisherman, an oyster farm manager, a merchant marine, and an oil spill remediator. Nowadays, you can book an afternoon splash with him through the tide pools at Estero Bluffs, grabbing kombu and wakame and sea grapes to eat, plus a species nicknamed Turkish towel you can dry for a body scrubber. He will tell you, "Seaweed is my chill." As a guide to all things ocean algae, he's so generous with his knowledge. He'll let you in on the best time to scavenge kombu, which is high tide, when the waves knock the kelp clear off the rocks, and you can grab a blade that's fresh and saline. He'll explain how nori is made by cultivating kombu spores, grinding them to a paste, running that through a roller, spraying it with oil and spices, and baking it in a 600°F [316°C] oven. He'll tell you about the Chinese abalone hunters in the 1800s who recognized the sea lettuce they found on the Central Coast as a delicacy from home. They practiced a smart, hard-core proto-aquaculture, giving the sea lettuce room to spread by torching other seaweeds and sterilizing the rocks. He'll advise you to pull a screen from your Airbnb's window for drying your harvest. Then he'll set up a camp stove on a kickboard he's made himself, fill a pot with sweet wakame, frilly Gracilaria, and sea grapes that pop when you bite them, along with some noodles, and make you seaweed ramen on the beach. He'll instill in you a love and epic respect for the Pacific's wild, delicious weeds.

Rice

1 cup [180 g] wild rice

2 Tbsp ghee, preferably homemade (page 42)

1 Tbsp Sweet Soy Glaze (page 55)

Tuna

1 Tbsp ghee, preferably homemade (page 42)

8 to 10 oz [230 to 285 g] fresh albacore tuna, patted dry and brought to room temperature

Pea Shoot Salad

3 Tbsp fine salt, such as Maldon

¼ cup [50 g] snap peas

1 cup [85 g] pea shoots, left long or cut into bite-size lengths

2 green onions, thinly sliced on the bias

1 tsp fresh lemon juice, preferably Meyer

2 Tbsp Sweet Soy Glaze (page 55), plus more for serving

Black sesame seeds, for garnish

The Best Mayonnaise (page 45) or Kewpie, for garnish, if you want

Hot sauce, preferably Fermented Hot Sauce (page 62), for garnish

TIME
30 minutes active time; 1 hour 15 minutes total

YIELD
2 servings

Albacore tuna is fatty and rich. These layered bowls treat this gorgeous fish like a surprise. But they also fit my philosophy of flavor, with each element complementing everything else without taking over. You get crisp salad, lemony acid, a sweet-salty glaze, the grounding, almost dirty flavor of wild rice and sesame, and that umami-packed tuna all harmonizing, like a sea shanty.

Here's a sea shanty theme: Embrace danger. Use a ripping-hot pan to sear the tuna, and if you don't want to tear it to bits, use your thinnest, sharpest knife to cut it. But be prepared. If you listen to me, you'll have Sweet Soy Glaze (page 55) hanging out in the fridge when you need it, so it's at the right level of unctuousness to honor the fish.

albacore pea shoot bowl

To make the rice: Rinse the rice in a fine-mesh strainer until the water runs clear.

In a medium saucepan, bring the rice, ghee, and 3 cups [710 ml] of water to a boil. Knock the heat down to a simmer, cover the pot with the lid cracked to let the steam out, and cook the rice, stirring it a couple times, until it's tender with some burst grains, about 45 minutes. Strain off any excess water, return the rice to the pot, and stir in the sweet soy glaze.

To make the tuna: Set a wire rack inside a sheet pan.

In a 9 in [23 cm] cast-iron pan over medium-high heat, melt the ghee until it's just smoking, about 2 minutes. Add the tuna and sear it until it's golden brown, 45 seconds to 1 minute. Flip it onto a plate, then ease it back into the pan, and sear it on the other side, 45 seconds to 1 minute. Put it on the wire rack and stow in the fridge.

To make the salad: Fill a large bowl with ice water.

In a medium pot, bring 3 cups [710 ml] of water and the salt to a boil. Add the snap peas and blanch them until they're beaming green, 1 to 1½ minutes. Immediately drain them and plunge them into the ice bath, zhushing them to cool them down. Drain the snap peas, pat them dry, and slice them into thin strips. Put them in a medium bowl, add the pea shoots, green onions, and lemon juice, and toss to combine.

To make the bowls: Divide the rice between two serving bowls. Cut the tuna into ¼ in [6 mm] thick slices, then divide it between the bowls, laying it on top of the rice. Brush the tuna in each bowl with 1 tablespoon of the sweet soy glaze. Divide the pea shoot salad atop the tuna. Scatter on some sesame seeds. Dollop on mayo, if you want, and serve the bowls with hot sauce and more glaze on the side.

There are different versions of a French ravigote. Mine is a broken pork vinaigrette, outrageously flavorful but balanced in acid, fat, savory, and sweet notes. When I was learning to cook, I'd make it with bacon for finishing fried sweetbreads. Here, we're using uncured pork jowl, or guanciale, which brings all the fatty, porcine goodness without the smoky cure that might overwhelm the mushrooms it dresses. I used porcini to develop this dish because my dog, Boone, and I had spent the day in the Monterey woods with Anthony Gerbino (see page 206), and we foraged a ton of porcinis. It isn't easy to find fresh porcini, in the ground or in stores. King trumpets are more available, and they're dynamite in this dish too. It's the best kind of recipe: fast, easy, but a bit fancy too.

To make the mushrooms: If you are using porcinis, you'll need to clean them. Use a pastry brush to remove any duff on the caps and in the gills, cut off the base at the dirt line, and starting on the cut end, peel the skin from the stem with a paring knife. King trumpets don't need as much cleaning. Whichever type you use, halve the mushrooms lengthwise and score them with crosshatches down both sides. Set them aside.

To make the ravigote: In a large sauté pan over medium heat, heat the avocado oil and olive oil. Add the guanciale and cook it until its fat starts rendering and it's caramelized but not too crisp, about 5 minutes. Remove 1 tablespoon of the fat from the pan and set it aside for cooking the mushrooms. Add the shallots and garlic to the pan and sweat them until they've released their liquid and are translucent but not browned, 2 to 3 minutes. Kill the heat, add the thyme and let it frizzle for a few seconds, then add the vinegar, honey, pickled mustard seeds, pepper, and white soy sauce. Return the pan to medium heat and cook the ravigote for 2 minutes to marry the flavors. Kill the heat again and put a lid on the pan to keep it warm.

Spread the arugula on a platter and squeeze the lemon all over it.

Heat a 9 in [23 cm] cast-iron pan over high heat, then add ½ tablespoon of the reserved guanciale fat, half the mushrooms, and a pinch of salt. Cook the mushrooms until well-seared, 2 to 3 minutes on each side. Place them on top of the arugula. Repeat with the remaining ½ tablespoon of fat, mushrooms, and another pinch of salt. Warm the ravigote gently, if needed, then stir the chives and parsley into it, pour it over the mushrooms, and serve.

Mushrooms

1 lb [455 g] porcini or king trumpet mushrooms

1 Tbsp guanciale fat

Kosher salt

Ravigote

1 tsp avocado oil

1 tsp extra-virgin olive oil

4 oz [115 g] guanciale, cut into small cubes

2 shallots, minced

2 garlic cloves, cut into paper-thin slices

1 thyme sprig

¼ cup [60 ml] sherry vinegar

2 Tbsp honey

2 Tbsp Pickled Mustard Seeds (page 50)

2 tsp freshly ground black pepper

2 tsp white soy sauce

1 Tbsp chopped fresh chives

1 Tbsp chopped fresh parsley

2 cups [40 g] baby arugula

½ lemon, preferably Meyer

TIME
30 minutes

YIELD
2 or 3 servings

Morels

1 lb [455 g] fresh morels or 3 oz [85 g] dried morels

6 tsp kosher salt

Morels thrive in high-altitude fires, which California has suffered plenty of lately. On the Central Coast, though, the honeycombed caps also see June gloom out the door. Sunshine is on the way. The worst is over, for now.

In spring, look for firm morels that smell of forest. Out of season, reconstitute dried, whole morels in warm water. Either way, they're pricey. What do you do with a $59 per pound mushroom? You chicken-fry it, blanket it in an audacious sauce, and eat it with a plastic fork in the back of a caboose. That is how we do it off-hours at Dad's.

Red-eye gravy is traditionally made with country ham drippings. We're using bacon drippings, but we'll drape the finished dish with country ham for good measure. Like the Virginian that I am, I salt-cured hams at Saison. Most weren't ready before I quit, but I branded my name into them with the fire poker, so they'd know who made them.

To make the morels: Set a wire rack inside a sheet pan. If you are using fresh morels, remove any stems with a sharp knife. Fill a medium bowl with 2 cups [475 ml] of water and 2 teaspoons of the salt, then add the morels, agitating them to jostle duff from the crevices. Drain the morels, rinse the bowl, and repeat two more times until the water runs clear. If you are using dried morels, soak them in unsalted warm water until they're tender, about 20 minutes. Fresh or dried, shake the water off the morels in a fine-mesh strainer, then transfer them to the wire rack and put them in the fridge to dry.

chicken-fried morels with red-eye gravy

TIME
1 hour

YIELD
2 to 4 servings

To make the red-eye gravy: In a 9 in [23 cm] cast-iron pan over medium-high heat, cook the bacon until it's crispy and most of the fat is rendered, 3 to 4 minutes. Remove the bacon from the pan and place the pan back over medium heat. Stir in the flour for 30 seconds, then add the coffee and give it a stir. Knock the heat down to a simmer and cook it for 5 minutes. Stir in the maple syrup, black pepper, and cayenne, then cook the gravy until it coats the back of a spoon, 3 to 5 minutes more. Kill the heat, and cover the gravy to keep it warm.

To make the chicken-fry: In a small bowl, whisk together the flour, Old Bay, salt, chili powder, paprika, and black pepper.

In another small bowl, whisk the eggs.

Line a medium bowl with paper towels.

In a medium Dutch oven or heavy-walled pot with a candy thermometer attached, heat 3 in [7.5 cm] of canola oil to 350°F [180°C]. Working with a few morels at a time, dredge them in the flour mixture, followed by the eggs, and then flour again, shaking off any excess between each dredge. Carefully drop the morels in the hot oil and fry them, moving them around and flipping them, until they're golden brown all over, 2 to 3 minutes. Transfer the morels to the paper towel–lined bowl and give them a shake to dislodge any oil. Repeat to fry the remaining morels, bringing the oil back to temperature each time. Transfer the morels to a serving bowl, pour on the gravy, and drape the country ham over the top to serve them.

Red-Eye Gravy

3 oz [85 g] slab bacon, preferably The Best Bacon (page 65), cut into ¼ in [6 mm] cubes

1 Tbsp all-purpose flour

1 cup [240 ml] strong brewed coffee

1 Tbsp maple syrup

10 cranks black pepper

Pinch of cayenne pepper

Chicken-Fry

1 cup [140 g] all-purpose flour

2 tsp Old Bay Seasoning

1 tsp kosher salt

1 tsp chili powder

1 tsp smoked paprika

½ tsp freshly ground black pepper

3 large eggs

Canola oil, for frying

2 oz [55 g] thinly sliced country ham, cut into strips, for garnish

ANTHONY GERBINO, MUSHROOM HUNTER

If you think all of California is warm and sunny, you haven't been to the Monterey Peninsula. Here, chilly fog rolls into the bay and up through redwood and pine forest. The mushrooms love it. I was schooled there by a legendary forager and chef named Anthony Gerbino, who leads mushroom hunts and dinners for the Big Sur Foragers Festival, which takes place in January, right after the Santa Cruz Fungus Fair. A man who would break his leg falling off a cliffside retaining wall in pursuit of a mushroom is a guy who will find you some fungus. The dude had to be airlifted out of a ravine, and he was arrested in the process, because he might have been trespassing. But he served his haul that night at Julia's, the vegetarian restaurant he used to own in a strip mall in Pacific Grove. Anthony made that place into a mushroom mecca. In the bathroom, there's a replica of a nine-thousand-year-old Algerian cave painting of a half man–half mushroom shaman. If you ask Anthony what the inspiration was for that mural, he'll say, "Tripping on psilocybin." Morels, chanterelles, and matsutakes remain add-ons to any dish there. They'll chicken-fry baby blue oyster and lion's mane mushrooms, make faux orange chicken with oyster mushrooms, and drape French toast in candy cap mushroom crème anglaise. Many of the mushrooms Julia's serves are foraged, and foraging is a blast. But do not get sassy. Go with someone who knows what they're doing. If you're on the Peninsula in winter, sign up for one of Julia's mushrooming trips led by the sharp-eyed experts of the Fungus Federation of Santa Cruz. My dog, Boone, and I have cruised to spots with Anthony in Monterey, and everywhere we walked there were porcinis. The ones already peeking out of the earth are at the end of their life cycle and ready to drop spores, but Anthony showed me how to find mushrooms buried under the duff. These were porcinis still at their peak—fist-size, firm, intensely aromatic, and growing right there in the forest bordering multimillion-dollar houses. No one in those houses had a clue.

coastal

Lingcod Ceviche

1 lb [455 g] fresh white-fleshed fish fillets, such as lingcod, cod, or halibut, cut into ¾ in [2 cm] cubes

Kosher salt

2 serrano chiles

1 Tbsp avocado oil

1 Tbsp extra-virgin olive oil

8 oz [230 g] Sungold cherry tomatoes, halved

8 oz [230 g] gooseberries, halved

2 fresh cayenne chiles, minced

1 shallot, thinly sliced

3 limes

6 cranks chile pequin or black pepper

2 green onions, thinly sliced

2 avocados, sliced, for serving

continued

lingcod ceviche

My Hobie pedal kayak is like the love child of a bicycle and a boat, and fishing on it is the scariest thing I do. I'm sitting six inches above the Pacific, and there are two things I'm thinking about: fish and, if necessary, swimming. It's just me and the squid fishermen at 4 a.m. I'm wearing a headlamp, cresting the mouth of Half Moon Bay, in the darkness next to thirty-five-foot commercial boats, and thinking to myself: I can do this. When I'm fully committed, I catch fish.

Behind Mushroom Rock, close to Mavericks, the site of California's biggest wave, I hooked a six-pound lingcod. A species nicknamed "buckethead," it came from 150 feet deep, with a massive mouth and a belly full of crabs. But when I filleted it, its flesh was flaky and mild. You won't find lingcod outside of the West Coast, so use any white-fleshed fish for this ceviche. Just don't use frozen fillets. You want it super fresh, so ask your fishmonger for something quality enough to eat marinated raw. Then you can go crazy with the other ingredients. If you can't find the gooseberries, no worries; just double up on the Sungolds. But go for a variety of textures, colors, and sensations, and people will remember it.

To make the lingcod ceviche: Put the fish in a medium bowl, then season it with 2 or 3 pinches of salt and stow it in the fridge to chill.

Put the serrano chiles in a small bowl, then coat them with the avocado oil, the olive oil, and a pinch of salt. In a 9 in [23 cm] cast-iron pan over high heat, pan-roast the serrano chiles until they're soft and charred all over, 2 to 3 minutes. When they're cool enough to touch, seed one serrano, and mince both. Put them in a serving bowl, then add the tomatoes, gooseberries, cayenne chiles, and shallot and mix to fully incorporate them.

continued

TIME
45 minutes active; 1½ hours total

YIELD
4 to 6 servings

Tortilla chips

Homemade Tortillas (page 72),
for serving

Canola oil, for frying

Tajín-Style Spice (page 68), for
garnish

Zest the limes into a small bowl. Set aside.

Using the heel of your palm, roll the limes on a hard surface to break down the pulp.

Halve them, then use your hands to squeeze the juice onto the vegetables. Add the chile pequin and a pinch of salt, then mix well. Rest the veg at room temperature for 30 minutes, then mix the fish into the vegetables and put the ceviche in the fridge to chill for at least 15 minutes and up to 1 hour, depending on how marinated you like your fish.

To make the tortilla chips: Follow the recipe for homemade tortillas, then rip them into big pieces.

Line a medium bowl with paper towels.

In a medium Dutch oven or heavy-walled pot with a candy thermometer attached, heat 3 in [7.5 cm] of canola oil to 350°F [180°C]. Carefully drop a tortilla's worth of chips into the hot oil, making sure not to crowd the oil, and fry them, moving them around and flipping them, until they're golden, about 2 minutes. Transfer the chips to the paper towel–lined bowl, then generously dust them with Tajín-style spice. Repeat to fry the remaining chips.

Season the ceviche with salt and pepper, then garnish it with the lime zest and green onions and serve it with the tortilla chips and avocado on the side.

HAND - SQUEEZING GIVES YOU SOME PULP FOR NICE TEXTURE.

fries
with
eyes

I first ate smelts at Duarte's Tavern, a Portuguese place in Pascadero that's been serving folks since 1894. I had no idea what I was snacking on. Turns out I grew up swimming with them. When they were running, my dad would hook his rod with smelts because stripers and bluefish chase them. My brother and I would go out on boogie boards and jump in the water with these big bait balls.

As primary food, smelts are precious to the ocean, and some species have been overfished. Seafood Watch greenlights smelts from the Great Lakes, so source those if you can. In California, night smelts are more abundant than others, but we only take a fraction of the twenty-five-pound limit. Headlamps on, we toss a net into ripping shore breaks. It's dangerous to catch smelts. But frying them is easy.

Their intense flavor merits a couple of tangy dips. For the mayo, splurge on Red Boat fish sauce. It's rounder and less pungent than others, so the dip won't knock you out. The cocktail sauce that goes with the Grilled Spot Prawn Cocktail (page 295) is super nice with these too.

To make the fish sauce mayo: In a small bowl, whisk all the ingredients together until they're fully combined. You'll have a little over 1 cup [240 g]. It keeps, in the fridge in an airtight container, for up to 3 days. It also makes a funky, spicy dipper for crudités or can be whisked with olive oil to dress Caesar salad.

continued

Fish Sauce Mayo

1 cup [220 g] The Best Mayonnaise (page 45) or Kewpie

1 Tbsp fresh lime juice

2 tsp fish sauce, preferably Red Boat 40°N

2 tsp chopped fresh ginger

1 tsp freshly ground white pepper

continued

TIME
45 minutes active;
2 hours 45 minutes total

YIELD
4 to 6 servings

To make the smelts: In a medium bowl, whisk the flour, ground ginger, mustard powder, kosher salt, and white pepper until fully combined.

Line a sheet pan with paper towels.

In a medium Dutch oven or heavy-walled pot with a candy thermometer attached, heat 3 in [7.5 cm] of canola oil to 350°F [180°C]. Working with a dozen or so smelts at a time, toss the fish in the seasoned flour, giving them a shake to remove excess, then carefully drop them in the hot oil and fry them, moving them around and flipping them, until they're golden brown, their bellies are hard, and the bubbles in the oil have subsided, 2 to 4 minutes. Use a spider or slotted spoon to transfer the fish to the paper towel–lined sheet pan. Repeat to fry the remaining smelts, bringing the oil back to temperature each time. Once all the smelts are fried, carefully drop the Thai basil leaves into the oil and fry them until they're translucent and brittle, 3 to 4 minutes. You can also just serve the Thai basil fresh alongside the smelts, for wrapping the fish as you eat them.

Finish the smelts with flaky salt and serve them and the basil on a platter with the lime slices, fish sauce mayo, and coastal cocktail sauce on the side, if you want.

Smelts

1 cup [140 g] all-purpose flour

2 tsp ground fresh ginger

2 tsp Oriental hot mustard powder

1 tsp kosher salt

1 tsp freshly ground white pepper

Canola oil, for frying

1½ lb [680 g] whole smelts

1 cup [12 g] packed fresh Thai basil leaves

Flaky salt, such as Maldon

Lime slices, for serving

Coastal Cocktail Sauce (page 295), for serving, if you want

Smoked Padrón Mayo

6 oz [170 g] Padrón peppers, stemmed, about 6 peppers

1 garlic clove, peeled

1½ tsp extra-virgin olive oil

Apple wood chunks, for smoking

1½ cups [330 g] The Best Mayonnaise (page 45) or Kewpie

I gained thirty pounds during my year at Louisiana's McNeese State University before I transferred schools. I spent my time there eating crawfish under the bridge, slamming she-crab gumbo, and going with the Lake Charles homies to holes-in-the-wall for oyster po'boys and sweet tea. West Coast oyster culture is so incredible, but you generally get oysters on the half shell with a beautiful mignonette. We do love that sharp vinegariness. But I like bringing some of the dirty South to the Central Coast. Neal Maloney (see page 296) grows these gorgeous Pacific Golds in Morro Bay, and the showstopper is frying them up and throwing them onto a gooey, crunchy, Podunk sub. Whatever fresh oysters you can get are fine, just skip the little Kumamotos. Buy them big, keep them cold, and take your time shucking. If the oysters you can get aren't as large as you want them, just buy a few extra.

oyster po'boys with smoked padrón mayo

To make the smoked Padrón mayo: Put the Padrón peppers and garlic into a small metal bowl or on a small, aluminim foil–lined tray, then coat them in the olive oil.

Prep your smoker. This works well on a stovetop smoker. If you're using a charcoal grill, bank your coals to one side. When the coals are glowing and no longer on fire, throw the apple wood chunks on top of them. There's no need to soak the wood chunks. For a gas grill, heat one side on high, place the wood chunks in a smoker box, and place the smoker box over the flame. Decrease the heat to low once the wood starts smoking.

Let the first blast of acrid smoke blow off, then arrange the bowl of peppers and garlic on the cool side of the grill, and close the lid. If you're using a charcoal grill, position the vents over the veg, and leave them to smoke until the peppers are delicately caramelized, wilted, and aromatic, and they start to give up their juices, 15 to 20 minutes.

TIME
1 hour

YIELD
2 po'boys

SPECIAL GEAR
Grill or smoker
Lump charcoal

Cool the peppers and garlic to room temperature, then put them in a blender or a food processor and blitz them until they're smooth. Transfer the mixture to a medium bowl, then fold in the mayonnaise until it's fully combined. You'll have about 2 cups [475 ml] of smoked Padrón mayo. It keeps, in the fridge in an airtight container, for up to 1 week. Slam it on a hamburger, dip veg in it, or use it anywhere you want mayo with a kick.

To make the fried oysters: Shuck the oysters, reserving half their liquor.

Put the reserved liquor in a medium bowl, then add the eggs and beat to fully combine them. Drop the oysters into the egg mixture and stow the bowl in the fridge to chill for 15 minutes.

In a medium bowl, mix the cornmeal, flour, Old Bay, salt, pepper, and smoked paprika. Spread the seasoned cornmeal in a 9 in [23 cm] pie pan or shallow bowl.

Line a plate with paper towels.

In a medium Dutch oven or heavy-walled pot with a candy thermometer attached, heat 3 in [7.5 cm] of canola oil to 375°F [190°C]. One by one, let the excess egg wash drip off the oysters, then spread them out in the seasoned cornmeal. Spoon the seasoned cornmeal on top of the oysters to evenly coat them. Working in batches of four, carefully drop the oysters in the hot oil and fry them, moving them around and flipping them at least once, until they're golden brown and crispy-crunchy, 1 to 2 minutes. Bring the oil back to temperature between batches. Use a spider or slotted spoon to transfer the oysters to the paper towel–lined plate.

To make the po'boys: Divvy up all the ingredients between the French bread, slathering on the mayo, adding the tomatoes, piling the iceberg high, and throwing the oysters on top of all that, then tie on your bib and tear in.

Fried Oysters

16 to 20 meaty oysters

2 large eggs

2 cups [280 g] cornmeal

2 Tbsp all-purpose flour

2 tsp Old Bay Seasoning

2 tsp kosher salt

2 tsp freshly ground black pepper

1 tsp smoked paprika

Canola oil, for frying

Po'boys

1 loaf French bread, split lengthwise and halved crosswise

¼ cup [60 g] Smoked Padrón Mayo, plus more as needed

½ cup [125 g] Oven-Dried Tomatoes (page 67)

2 cups [145 g] thinly shaved iceberg lettuce

Crabs

2 live 2 lb [910 g] Dungeness
crabs

2 lemons, preferably Meyer

1 Tbsp white balsamic vinegar

Kosher salt

continued

Crab season is huge in Half Moon Bay. We get screwed out of it often because of domoic acid, a toxin that builds up in the crustaceans from algae blooms, which are getting more frequent due to climate change and agricultural runoff. The pleasure of catching and eating Dungeness crab is just one small reason to be better stewards of the planet.

When the harvest is on, there's this buzz about town, weird knots to learn, and a giant ocean to deal with. On a fifty-foot boat, you feel small as a sea flea, packing fish heads into pots and heaving them overboard. They soak in the water for twelve to twenty-four hours, depending on restrictions around whale migration. Then you pull the crabs in with a fifteen-foot gaff. The ocean wants to swallow you, the captain wants to push you harder, and the crabs want to bite you, but you don't often feel so alive.

Back home with my catch, I always make crab rice. This is not fried rice; it's delicate, fragrant, and light. Asian pear elevates the crab's sweetness. Chrysanthemum greens, available at Asian markets, accentuate the depth of flavor of a beast from the ocean floor. If you don't want to kill a crab, or if Dungeness isn't available, lump crabmeat is all good.

dungeness crab rice

TIME
1½ hours for live crab;
30 minutes for lump
crabmeat

YIELD
4 servings

To make the crabs: Ask your fishmonger to dispatch the Dungeness or other live crabs, in the most humane way, or put them in the freezer for 15 to 20 minutes to knock them unconscious. Working with one crab at a time, flip the crab onto its back with the pinchers facing you and shove the tip of your sharpest knife into its body at the tip of the triangular piece that forms its abdomen. Force your knife blade downward through the head and between the eyes. Turn the crab around, pull up the triangular abdomen, stick your knife under the base of the triangle between the top shell and the body, and yank the crab free of its top shell. Cut it in half, pull the gills off, and clean the guts out.

continued

Fill a large bowl with ice water.

Fill a large stockpot with 6 qt [5.7 L] of water, squeeze the lemons into the water, and then drop the lemons in. Add the vinegar and a large pinch of salt and bring it to a boil. Carefully drop the crabs in and bring it back to a boil. Then start your timer. Cook the crab for 8 to 12 minutes, depending on how well-cooked you like your crab. If you shy away from it on the rawer side, go the full 12. Using tongs, immediately plunge the crabs into the ice bath. When they're ice-cold, shake them dry, and pick the meat out of them right away.

To make the rice: In a medium Dutch oven over medium-high heat, heat the sesame oil. Reserve a handful of shallots for garnish and add the rest, along with the garlic and ginger. Cook, stirring with a wooden spoon and adding a few drops of water to release any stuck bits that might burn, until the veg are deeply caramelized, 6 to 8 minutes. Add the Asian pear and cook, stirring, until it has some color, 2 to 3 minutes more. Add the rice and white soy sauce and stir to incorporate everything. Kill the heat, then gently fold in the crab. Garnish the rice with the reserved shallot, the green onions, and the greens. Drop the pot on the table with the condiments on the side.

Rice

1 Tbsp sesame oil

5 shallots, cut into paper-thin slices on a mandoline

3 garlic cloves, chopped

1 Tbsp chopped fresh ginger

½ cup [55 g] peeled, diced Asian pear

4 cups [720 g] cooked short-grain white rice

2 Tbsp white soy sauce

1 lb [455 g] fresh Dungeness or lump crabmeat

6 green onions, thinly sliced

1 cup [70 g] roughly chopped chrysanthemum greens, baby spinach, tatsoi, or bok choy

Hot sauce, preferably Fermented Hot Sauce (page 62), for serving

Chile Jam (page 60), for serving

Sweet Soy Glaze (page 55), for serving

4 or 5 medium Granny Smith apples

4 or 5 skewers

1 cup [200 g] packed dark brown sugar

¾ cup plus 2 Tbsp [210 ml] heavy cream

½ cup [120 ml] light corn syrup

2 Tbsp unsalted butter

¼ tsp kosher salt

¼ cup [68 g] red miso

¼ tsp vanilla extract

¾ cup [60 g] furikake, preferably homemade (page 70)

TIME
45 minutes

YIELD
4 or 5 apples

I like the meditation of making caramel. It starts off blonde and tall, the sugars boil up, and it slowly compacts and darkens as the butter's fat caramelizes and the cream evaporates. When you make it right, you nail a taffy consistency perfect for dipping apples.

I wanted to celebrate fall in California by doing some weird stuff to a clichéd treat. With red miso blended into the caramel and a funky, nutty furikake topping, these apples are gooey and sharp, but with the sweetness balanced by savory notes.

You need skewers for dipping the apples, and kids love food on a stick, but the adult way to eat them is to rest the apple on a cutting board, hold the skewer to steady it, and cut a slice. When Frost tasted one of these, she went bonkers. She was out of her mind. I learned to not give my kindergartener a caramel apple right before bedtime.

Remove the apples' stems, and push a skewer through the stem end of each of the apples. Place a mug of hot water and a pastry brush next to the stove.

In a medium Dutch oven over medium heat, heat the brown sugar, heavy cream, corn syrup, butter, and salt, stirring with a wooden spoon, until the butter is melted, about 5 minutes. Attach a candy thermometer to the side of the pot, making sure it doesn't touch the bottom. Dipping the pastry brush in the water and frequently painting the edges of the pot to wipe off stray sugar that will otherwise burn, cook the mixture, without stirring, until it hits 240°F [116°C], 10 to 15 minutes. It should be the consistency of taffy.

Pull out the thermometer and drop it in the cup of water so the caramel doesn't stick. Add the red miso and vanilla to the caramel and stir gently. Kill the heat, then let it rest for 5 minutes.

Put the furikake in a small bowl. Tilting the pot so the caramel pools on one side, dip and spin an apple, turn it upside down over the pot, and allow the excess to drip down and drape the fruit. You want the caramel to set, so don't coat it too thickly. Hold the apple upside down for 20 to 30 seconds, then immediately dip it in the furikake, spinning it to coat it all over. Repeat with the remaining apples.

Eat the apples immediately or cool them on a silicone mat or parchment paper. They keep, covered in plastic wrap at room temperature, overnight. So the caramel doesn't stick to the plastic wrap, set them on a tray with the skewers facing up, and tent plastic wrap over them with the skewers acting as tent poles.

red miso caramel apples

after the hunting trip with pals

When the Spanish came to California, they brought pigs. Today, their feral progeny rampage through parklands, neighborhoods, and farms, wreaking havoc. One responsible solution is hunting. There are lineages of hunting guides on the Central Coast. They take you out on an ATV to a hilltop, and you wait for pigs. If you're lucky, you take a big old boar home.

You can do that here, or you can hunt like my friend and fellow cook Erik and I do, hiking to the top of Big Sur's Silver Peak Wilderness, getting our hides chewed by giant flies. You have to be more aware out there. The wilderness is beautiful but vast, and you're really alone. Your whole rhythm changes. You get up before dawn, then nap during the day, trying to preserve as much energy as you can to go back out there looking for deer in the golden hours. Everything is arduous and it sucks, but you're up there with a purpose: to get food. If you can.

Erik and I have never shot anything, and I've never been more at risk of being bitten by a rattlesnake. But I have also never felt closer to a friend. There's a deep connection that you make with somebody when you go through the

agony and reverie of trying to take down an animal. Guaranteed, if we ever actually bag a deer, we've worked for it. So, we'd better know how to cook it, or any piece of meat for that matter, with respect.

Poison oak, empty water bottles, wildly problematic descents—when you're in the wilderness, you're given all these lessons. Nature raps you a little on the knuckles. "Don't forget," it says, "you have to be really grateful for these things you're given, and you must be careful." After you get schooled, you should go home and feast, deer on your back or not. Cook bold, eat big, tell tall tales, and give enormous love to the people who are with you. That's what this chapter is about.

These are rib-sticking, meat and potatoes recipes: Sage-Grilled Yardbird with Miso-Maple Grits (page 243), Salt-Roasted Purple Potato Salad (page 238). Even broccolini is amped up with loads of pecorino romano and anchovy (page 231). You expelled a bunch of energy to go hunt, and whether you were successful in your mission or not, the hangout afterward is the reward.

Wasabi Dip

½ cup [120 g] crème fraîche, preferably homemade (page 44)

2 Tbsp Fermented Hot Sauce (page 62)

1½ tsp freshly grated or powdered wasabi

1 tsp freshly ground black pepper

½ tsp kosher salt

Zest of 1 lemon, preferably Meyer

Juice of ½ lemon, preferably Meyer

Blooming Shallots

12 medium shallots, peeled

Canola oil, for frying

2 large eggs

1 cup [240 ml] whole milk

2 cups [280 g] all-purpose flour

1 Tbsp Old Bay Seasoning

2 tsp kosher salt

1 tsp freshly ground black pepper

1 tsp cayenne pepper

1 tsp dried oregano

1 tsp smoked paprika

1 tsp freshly ground cumin

Flaky salt, such as Maldon

TIME
1 hour

YIELD
3 or 4 servings

blooming shallots with wasabi dip

We're having a miniature blooming onion party. It's our foray into bar food. This is the snack you want with a drink in your hand. You get sweet, caramelized shallot; crispy, crunchy batter; and lemony, creamy sauce with just enough spice to satisfy your palate's need for heat. It's also a great lesson in organization. You want to set up your dredging station and your landing pad right there next to your hot oil, so you can fry and dry efficiently and serve a hot, full batch of blooming shallots all at once.

The dip gains heat from fresh wasabi, which is plentiful in Half Moon Bay. But it can be hard to find and ridiculously expensive in other places, so the powdered stuff is fine, as long as the jar is freshly opened. It loses its kick pretty quickly hanging out in your pantry.

To make the wasabi dip: In a small bowl, whisk all the ingredients together until they are smooth and fully combined.

To make the blooming shallots: Keeping the root ends intact, cut each shallot lengthwise every ¼ in [6 mm]. Massage the shallots to open them like flowers.

Set a wire rack inside a sheet pan. In a medium Dutch oven or a heavy-walled pot with a candy thermometer attached, heat 3 in [7.5 cm] of oil to 375°F [190°C].

Meanwhile, in a medium bowl, whisk the eggs with the milk.

In a second medium bowl, whisk together the flour, Old Bay, kosher salt, black pepper, cayenne, oregano, smoked paprika, and cumin. Working with three shallots at a time, dredge them in the seasoned flour, followed by the egg mixture, and the seasoned flour again, shaking off excess as you go.

Carefully add the shallots to the hot oil and fry them, moving them around and flipping them, until they are deeply golden and tender, 2 to 3 minutes. Use a spider or slotted spoon to transfer the shallots to the wire rack. Repeat to fry the remaining shallots, bringing the oil back to temperature each time. Sprinkle them with the flaky salt and serve them with the wasabi dip on the side.

Here's a crunchy, hippie salad straight from the heart of California. It's got all the usual suspects: kale, avocado, citrus, grains, nuts. But it's boosted with candied kumquats. I love that you eat kumquats like grapes, tossing them in your mouth, chewing them, seeds and all. I also love how their pucker plays with bittersweet grapefruit. They make this salad pop.

You'd need an awkwardly small amount of syrup to candy just a cup of kumquats, so we're cooking a double batch. Throw the extras into the Goji and Hemp Overnight Oats (page 137) or Homemade Yogurt (page 43), onto a cheese board, or on a ham sandwich. Stir the syrup into a cocktail or sparkling water.

As for the buckwheat, here's wisdom that my pal and co-author Betsy got from her Grandma Syl: Beat an egg into the groats. It helps them toast evenly and plump into nice, separate grains. Grandma Syl used one egg to one cup of groats, so with half as many groats, we're using just the egg white, which works great.

To make the candied kumquats: Put the kumquats in a medium saucepan, then add enough water to cover them by ½ in [13 mm]. Bring them to a boil, then drain them in a fine-mesh strainer. Repeat two more times.

In a medium saucepan over high heat, bring the sugar and 1 cup [240 ml] of water to a boil. Knock the heat down to a simmer and cook it until it thickens slightly, about 8 minutes. Add the blanched kumquats, and simmer them until they are translucent, 10 to 12 minutes. Leave them in the syrup to cool to room temperature.

continued

kumquat and kale

Candied Kumquats

1 pt [365 g] kumquats, cut crosswise into thirds

1½ cups [300 g] sugar

continued

TIME
1 hour

YIELD
6 to 8 servings

Buckwheat

½ cup [90 g] buckwheat groats

1 egg white

1 Tbsp ghee, preferably homemade (page 42)

½ tsp kosher salt

Kale Salad

2 grapefruits

12 oz [340 g] baby kale

¼ cup [60 ml] Hippie Vinaigrette (page 53)

2 avocados, thinly sliced

½ cup [70 g] chopped toasted almonds

To make the buckwheat: In a small bowl, combine the buckwheat groats and the egg white and stir to evenly coat the groats.

In a medium sauté pan over medium heat, toast the groats, breaking apart any clumps with a wooden spoon, until they're golden brown, 3 to 4 minutes.

In a small saucepan, bring the ghee, salt, and 1 cup [240 ml] of water to a boil, then add the buckwheat groats, and give them a stir. Knock the heat down to a simmer, cover it with the lid cracked to let out the steam, and cook it until it's tender and the water is gone, about 15 minutes. Rest it with the lid on tight for 10 minutes, then fluff it and let it cool to room temperature.

To make the kale salad: Use a sharp paring knife to supreme the grapefruits, cutting off the tops and bottoms of the fruit, then running your knife down the sides of the fruit, following its contour to remove the skin, pith, and outer membrane. Free the segments by slicing on either side of the membrane that separates them.

In a large serving bowl, toss the grapefruit segments with half the kumquats, the buckwheat, kale, and vinaigrette. Top the salad with the avocados and almonds.

When I moved to San Francisco, a pal took me to a place called Kingdom of Dumpling, where we ate a sliced pig ear salad that woke me up. I was working at Benu where everything was so precious and uniform. I had come to California to cook that way. But Kingdom of Dumpling threw peanuts whole, chopped, and pulverized in with that pig ear. For me, that was relaxing.

I like crushable dishes that are a bit wabi-sabi. The char on the veg, the chop on the nuts—they don't need to be consistent to be delicious. If you find broccolini that's starting to flower, all the better. It's messed up, it's beautiful, and it's going to be delicious, because you're hitting it with layers of fat, abetted by grains of paradise, a genius African spice that looks like black pepper but tastes like black pepper with cake spices thrown in.

Serve this immediately, while the pecorino romano is still melty. You likely won't use all the anchovy-garlic oil, but the rest will keep, in the fridge in an airtight container, for up to 1 week. Use it to fry Brussels Sprout Latkes (page 140), cook eggs, top steak, or brush on shrimp. It's liquid gold.

charred broccolini with melted anchovy and garlic

Pan spray, if needed

1½ cups [180 g] hazelnuts

7 Tbsp [105 ml] extra-virgin olive oil

8 anchovy fillets

6 garlic cloves, cut into paper-thin slices

2 tsp red pepper flakes, plus more if needed

10 cranks grains of paradise, plus more as needed

2 Tbsp avocado oil

2 lb [910 g] broccolini, flowering if possible, woody ends trimmed and stalks left whole

Kosher salt

1 lemon, preferably Meyer

4 oz [115 g] pecorino romano cheese

Preheat the oven to 350°F [180°C]. Line a sheet pan with a silicone mat or parchment paper; if using parchment, lightly coat it with pan spray.

Spread the hazelnuts on the prepared sheet pan and roast them until glistening, about 12 minutes. Let them cool, then coarsely chop them.

continued

TIME
40 minutes

YIELD
4 servings

In a small pan over medium-low heat, heat 5 tablespoons [75 ml] of the olive oil for 3 to 4 minutes. Add the anchovies and cook them, stirring and breaking them up with a wooden spoon, until they're fragrant, 1 to 2 minutes. Add the garlic and cook it until it's tender but not browned, 4 to 5 minutes. Kill the heat, then add the red pepper flakes and grains of paradise.

Get a cast-iron pan ripping hot over high heat. Add 1 table-spoon of the avocado oil, 1 tablespoon of the olive oil, and then half of the broccolini. Cook, turning it occasionally, until charred on all sides, 3 to 4 minutes. Season it with a pinch of salt, then put it in a serving bowl and repeat with the remaining avocado oil, olive oil, and broccolini.

Add the hazelnuts to the broccolini, then dress it immediately, starting with half of the anchovy-garlic oil and tasting as you go until you hit the amount for you. Zest the lemon onto the broccolini, then cut the lemon in half and squeeze one-half over the broccolini. Toss and season it with more red pepper flakes, if you like, and more grains of paradise. Grate the pecorino romano over the top, smothering the broccolini in cheese, and serve it right away.

1¼ lb [570 g] turnips, preferably small Tokyo turnips with their greens attached

2 Tbsp Umami Oil (page 46)

8 oz [230 g] slab bacon, preferably The Best Bacon (page 65), cut into ½ in [13 mm] pieces

4 oz [115 g] spring onions or very fat green onions, cut lengthwise down the middle

Kosher salt

2 tsp fresh lemon juice, preferably Meyer

1 tsp apple cider vinegar

1 tsp poppy seeds

10 cranks black pepper

I hated turnips. Hated 'em! To me, they were like a radish's miserable cousin. But at Restaurant Eve, we served Virginia ham, and we always had a leftover fat cap. We were getting turnips from Amish families, and a chef there started braising them in that fat with black pepper, cheese, and thyme. That's all I needed to change my mind about this veg. Turnips taste like freshly dug yard. They're sharp. But they sing when you bring in fat. Coated in poppy seeds and roasted spring onion, my riff is like the everything bagel of turnips. It's a luscious little side dish.

In California, we're lucky enough to get Tokyo turnips at farmers' markets. They're small, tender, and sweeter than others, and they come with their greens attached. But if you can't get those or another variety of small turnips on their greens, use the turnips you can find. If the only thing your store has are honking big purple-and-white guys, just cut them into eighths before you roast them.

bacon fat – roasted turnips

Preheat the oven to 425°F [220°C].

If you're using small turnips, split them and their greens down the middle. For larger ones, cut them into eighths.

In a large cast-iron or other oven-safe pan over high heat, heat the umami oil until it's almost smoking, then add the bacon and fry it good and hard until the fat starts to render. Knock the heat down to medium and continue cooking the bacon, stirring every so often, until the fat is fully rendered, about 10 minutes. Use a slotted spoon to scoop out the bacon and save it for a snack or salad topper. Add the turnips and spring onions to the bacon fat in the pan—if their greens poke out of the pan, that's OK. Add a pinch of salt, then put the pan in the oven and roast the turnips until they're golden and tender and their greens are charred, 25 to 30 minutes. Hit the turnips with the lemon juice and vinegar, give them a stir, and season them all over with the poppy seeds, pepper, and ¼ teaspoon of salt. Serve the turnips in the pan, so your people can swipe up some of the pan juices as they fork them.

TIME
45 minutes

YIELD
4 servings

Potatoes

2 Tbsp peppercorns

1 Tbsp whole fennel seeds

1 Tbsp whole celery seeds

1½ tsp whole caraway seeds

1 bay leaf

3 cups [480 g] kosher salt

1½ lb [680 g] golf ball–size purple potatoes or another small, waxy variety

When it comes to potato salad, the way you cook your spuds is key. Salt-baking seasons them, makes them fluffy, and keeps their skins intact. If you can't find purple potatoes, get fingerlings, little reds, whatever small, waxy potato is on deck. Then relax. Cut the spuds any which way, don't worry about getting every grain of salt off them after baking, and if some vinegar from the Pickled Onions (page 48) gets in the dressing, no problem. Potatoes have a way of stealing things. They steal salt, acid, and umami, so you have to go big-time with the other flavors. The dressing has bite and is sweet and anchovy-ish from the Worcestershire. If you marinate the potatoes in it overnight, they'll really be singing. With caraway, red onion, and a pickles-and-mayo sauce, this is a deli-forward spud salad, just right alongside a sandwich. You'll have leftover dressing. Add chopped capers, cornichons, and boiled egg to it, and you've got a sauce gribiche. Drizzle it on gem lettuce or drape it over asparagus or cold roast ham and enjoy.

salt-roasted purple potato salad

To make the potatoes: Preheat the oven to 400°F [200°C].

In a coffee grinder, grind the peppercorns, fennel seeds, celery seeds, caraway seeds, and bay leaf. Put the spice mixture in a medium bowl, then add the kosher salt and mix until they're fully combined. Spread one-third of the seasoned salt in the bottom of a 9 in [23 cm] cast-iron pan. Arrange the potatoes in a single layer in the salt. Add the remaining seasoned salt on top, covering the potatoes but leaving one potato slightly exposed so you can test it.

Bake the potatoes until a cake tester, turkey truss, or fork slides into your test potato with just a bit of resistance, about 35 minutes. If you slice the potatoes while hot, they'll burst. Let them cool in the salt for 1 hour.

TIME
45 minutes active;
1 hour 45 minutes total

YIELD
4 or 5 servings

To make the dressing: In a medium bowl, whisk the mayonnaise, pepper, pickled mustard seeds, honey, and Worcestershire until well combined. Stir in the pickled onions, lemon zest, and lemon juice.

To make the salad: Wipe the salt off the potatoes and cut them into a bowl any way you want. Mix in the apple, celery, celery leaves, and red onion. Stir in 1 cup [240 ml] of the dressing to start, adding more as needed. You want an even coating without it being droopy.

Serve the salad immediately or chill it overnight and reserve ¼ cup [60 ml] of dressing to give it a refreshing sauce bath the next day. Sprinkle on flaky salt just before serving.

Dressing

1½ cups [330 g] The Best Mayonnaise (page 45) or Kewpie

20 cranks black pepper

1 Tbsp Pickled Mustard Seeds (page 50)

1 Tbsp honey

2 tsp Worcestershire sauce

½ cup [110 g] Pickled Onions (page 48)

Zest of 2 lemons, preferably Meyer

Juice of 1 lemon, preferably Meyer

Salad

1 Granny Smith apple, cored and diced

4 celery stalks, cut into ¼ in [6 mm] thick slices, plus ½ cup [20 g] tender celery leaves

½ red onion, diced

Flaky salt, such as Maldon

Every year, the Half Moon Bay Pumpkin Festival holds a competition for the world's biggest pumpkin. The winner in 2023 was a horrifying 2,749 pounds. We are a pumpkin-loving town. By September, squashes of all kinds are in full force at the markets, and some are so meaty that I like to season and sear them like steak. Then, to boost the pumpkin party, I rev up my juicer (you need one for this recipe) and dress the squash steaks in a sauce made with their own juices. Japanese kuri squash have the most beautiful, orangey hue. If you can't find kuris, butternut squash is a great substitute. Bring a rollie cart to the market to haul them; to make both the roasted squash and the sauce, you need 8 pounds total.

Squash are so hard that your knife can slip. The safest, easiest way to break them down is with a serrated bread knife. When you want to plow through anything big and you don't need a finesse cut, use a bread knife. Using the Thai basil is your choice, but I say go for it; it adds a beautiful, herbaceous note to the dish.

To roast the squash: Preheat the oven to 400°F [200°C]. Line two sheet pans with a silicone mat or parchment paper; if using parchment, lightly coat it with pan spray.

Cut the squash lengthwise into quarters and seed it. In a large bowl, coat the squash evenly in ¼ cup [50 g] of the ghee, the curry powder, and the smoked paprika. Spread it evenly on the prepared sheet pan and season it liberally with kosher salt. Bake it until you can push a spoon through the flesh, about 40 minutes. Cool it to room temperature.

continued

seared and sauced kuri squash

Roasted and Seared Squash

Pan spray, if needed

1 large or 2 medium kuri or butternut squash, about 4 lb [1.8 kg] total

¼ cup plus 1 tsp [54 g] ghee, preferably homemade (page 42)

1 Tbsp Madras curry powder

2 tsp smoked paprika

Kosher salt

1 tsp extra-virgin olive oil

continued

TIME
1½ hours

YIELD
4 to 6 servings

SPECIAL GEAR
Juicer

Toasted Pumpkin Seeds

1½ cups [210 g] pumpkin seeds

2 Tbsp ghee, preferably homemade (page 42)

1 tsp Madras curry powder

1 tsp kosher salt

Squash Sauce

1 large or 2 medium kuri or butternut squash, about 4 lb [1.8 kg] total

2 Tbsp honey

½ tsp kosher salt

1 Tbsp white soy sauce

1 tsp white balsamic vinegar

1 tsp Madras curry powder

½ tsp fresh lemon juice, preferably Meyer

1 cup [240 g] crème fraîche, preferably homemade (page 44)

Flaky salt, such as Maldon

Fresh Thai basil leaves, for garnish, if you want

To make the pumpkin seeds: In a medium bowl, coat the seeds evenly in the ghee, curry powder, and kosher salt. Spread them on the other prepared sheet pan and roast them alongside the squash for about 5 minutes. Stir the pumpkin seeds, then continue roasting them until they are crunchy and golden brown, 5 to 8 minutes more.

To make the squash sauce: Peel the squash, then quarter it lengthwise, seed it, and cut it into chunks. Use a juicer to juice the squash. You should have 3 to 4 cups [710 to 945 ml] of juice. Put the juice in a medium saucepan over high heat, then add the honey and kosher salt and bring it to a boil, stirring constantly. Knock the heat down to a simmer and cook it until it is slightly thickened and reduced to 1 cup [240 ml], about 30 minutes.

Transfer the juice mixture to a blender, then add the white soy sauce, vinegar, curry powder, and lemon juice, and blend it until fully combined. Add the crème fraîche and blend it on low to fully incorporate it. The sauce should coat the back of a spoon. Leave it in the blender as you sear the squash so you can give it a final whirl to bring it back together before serving.

To sear the squash: Using a knife as needed, carefully remove the skin from the roasted squash, then cut the squash into 10 to 12 even pieces.

In a 9 in [23 cm] cast-iron pan over medium-high heat, heat the remaining 1 teaspoon of ghee and the olive oil until they are just about smoking. Working in batches, sear the squash, flipping it, until it's caramelized and crunchy, 3 to 4 minutes per side. To serve it, place the squash on a platter, spoon the sauce over the top, and garnish it with the toasted pumpkin seeds, flaky salt, and torn Thai basil leaves, if you want.

sage-grilled yardbird with miso-maple grits

Mountain sage grows everywhere here, a sappy, dewy, aromatic harbinger of spring. I forage it when I'm hiking, bundle it with kitchen twine to make an herb brush, and use it to baste this grilled bird, where its flavor stands out, big, bold, and present.

I grew up with a grandma who always made a pot of grits for breakfast. This is my Californian homage to her. You can't beat stone-ground grits for texture or flavor, but they take longer to cook than others, so plan ahead. Soak your grits overnight to hydrate them. Spatchcock your bird (I teach you how below) and air-dry it overnight, too, so its skin gets taut and crisps on the grill if your fire is right. You want coals that have gone from their red-hot peak to glowing embers in the middle of white ash. Too much heat will burn your bird. Slather any leftover miso-maple butter on waffles, fry eggs in it, brush it on pie crust, or eat it the way Frost did on our recent camping trip: spread on crackers.

To make the miso-maple butter: In a food processor or a medium bowl with an eggbeater or spatula, cream together the butter, maple syrup, red miso, red pepper flakes, and smoked paprika until smooth and uniform. Any leftover miso-maple butter keeps, in an airtight container in the fridge, for 1 month.

To make the grits: In a medium pot, combine the grits and 4½ cups [1 L] of water, then stow the grits in the fridge to soak overnight.

Skim off any schmutz from the pot of grits, then bring the grits and their soaking water to a boil, stirring occasionally. Continue boiling until the grits thicken, 5 to 6 minutes, then remove them from the heat. Stir the grits, then cover them and rest them for 10 minutes to help the cornstarch release and cook evenly. Add the bay leaf, white soy sauce, black pepper, and salt, then put the pot over medium heat and bring it to a simmer. Continue simmering, stirring occasionally, until the grits coat the back of a spoon, 45 minutes to 1 hour. Stir in the miso-maple butter and the hot sauce, then kill the heat, and cover the grits to keep them warm.

continued

Miso-Maple Butter

½ cup [113 g] unsalted butter, diced, at room temperature

1½ tsp maple syrup

1½ tsp red miso

¼ tsp red pepper flakes

¼ tsp smoked paprika

BUTTER TOO COLD? FILL A JAR WITH BOILING WATER, DUMP THE WATER, THEN INVERT THE JAR OVER THE BUTTER. IT'LL BE ROOM TEMPERATURE IN 10 MINUTES.

Grits

1 cup [170 g] stone-ground grits

1 bay leaf

1 Tbsp white soy sauce

1 tsp freshly ground black pepper

½ tsp kosher salt

¼ cup [60 g] Miso-Maple Butter, plus more for serving

1½ tsp hot sauce, preferably Fermented Hot Sauce (page 62)

continued

TIME
2 hours active; overnight total

YIELD
4 to 6 servings

Bird

1 whole chicken, about 3 lb [1.4 kg], giblets removed and neck cut into ¼ in [6 mm] chunks

Kosher salt

1 bunch fresh sage

½ bunch fresh thyme, plus 3 or 4 more sprigs

¼ cup [60 ml] Umami Oil (page 46)

2 shallots, thinly sliced

4 garlic cloves, thinly sliced

Hickory chunks, for grilling

1 bunch wild arugula or 5 oz [140 g] baby arugula

Miso-Maple Butter, for serving

To make the bird: Start by patting it dry inside and out. Then spatchcock it. Set a wire rack inside a sheet pan and keep it nearby. Place the bird, breast-side down, on a cutting board and use kitchen shears to cut it down the back on either side of the backbone. Remove and reserve the backbone, tail, any excess skin, and the neck. Make an incision on the inside to expose the breastbone, then turn the bird over and press down on either side of the breast so it lies flat. Lightly salt the bird all over, then arrange it on the wire rack and stow it, in the fridge uncovered, to dry-brine overnight.

Using kitchen twine, bind the sage and the ½ bunch of thyme together at their stem ends to make a brush.

Hack the reserved backbone into ¼ in [6 mm] chunks. In a medium saucepan over medium heat, heat the umami oil. Add the backbone, along with the reserved tail, neck, and skin, and cook them until the skin is caramel-brown, 8 to 10 minutes. Remove the backbone, tail, and neck, but leave the skin in the pan. Add the shallots, garlic, and the remaining thyme sprigs and cook until the veg are soft and bronzed, 3 to 4 minutes. Dunk your sage brush into this schmaltz marinade and baste both sides of your bird with it.

Build a medium fire in your grill, throw on 2 or 3 hickory chunks, and cook your bird, flipping and basting it every 5 minutes, for about 25 minutes, or until an instant-read thermometer inserted into its thigh reads 165°F [74°C]. Rest the bird for 15 minutes.

COALS HAVE HOT SPOTS. DON'T BE AFRAID TO MOVE YOUR BIRD AROUND TO EVENLY GRILL IT.

Throw the wild arugula right on the grill, or if it's stemmed baby arugula, put it in a 9 in [23 cm] cast-iron pan on the grill. Season it with salt and grill it until charred, 1 to 2 minutes.

To serve, place the charred arugula on a platter, then arrange the bird on top. Drop a knob of the maple-miso butter on the bird and add an extra knob of it on top of the grits. Serve the grits alongside the bird and let your people feast.

Deep and meaty but also super bright with veg, Vietnamese bánh mì are perfectly balanced. They just do all the things you want in a sandwich. I make a loose, ground pork sausage for my riff. It gives me a sausage roll vibe, and sausage rolls are near and dear to my East Coast heart. Generally, the carrots are vinegar-pickled on bánh mì, but an overnight lime bath really punches them up. Serrano chile and a gingery mustard give it a kick, while fish sauce brings the funk. Then you load up your sandos with herbs and vegetables. It's a full-on drippy, multi-napkin meal. And that's what we want. That's the answer.

peppery sausage bánh mì

To make the pickled carrots: In a medium bowl, mix the carrots and serrano, then add enough lime juice to cover them. Put the veg in the fridge to marinate overnight. They'll keep, in the fridge in an airtight container, for up to 1 week.

continued

Pickled Carrots

2 carrots, peeled and cut into thin matchsticks

½ serrano chile, cut into thin rings

Fresh lime juice to cover (from 3 or 4 limes)

continued

TIME
30 minutes active; overnight total

YIELD
3 monster or 4 reasonably sized sandwiches

SPECIAL GEAR
Meat grinder, if using

Sausage

4 oz [115 g] slab bacon, preferably The Best Bacon (page 65)

1 lb [455 g] ground pork

1½ Tbsp fish sauce

1 Tbsp fresh lime juice

1 Tbsp grated fresh ginger

2 tsp grated garlic

2 tsp freshly ground white pepper

1½ tsp toasted sesame oil

Ginger Mustard

½ cup [125 g] Pickled Mustard Seeds (page 50)

½ tsp grated fresh ginger

Sandwiches

1 baguette, split lengthwise

12 crisp, just-washed romaine leaves

Half a cucumber, cut into thin matchsticks

1 bunch fresh cilantro, tough stems removed

To make the sausage: Using a medium die on your meat grinder, or pulsing in a food processor, grind the bacon. Put the bacon in a medium bowl, add the pork, fish sauce, lime juice, ginger, garlic, and pepper, and use your hands to mix everything together until it's well combined. Cover it and stow it in the fridge to marinate for at least 1 hour and up to overnight.

In a 9 in [23 cm] cast-iron pan over high heat, heat the sesame oil until it's smoking. Add the sausage mixture, knock the heat down to medium-high, and fry it, stirring and breaking it up with a wooden spoon, until all the liquid has released and it's well-seared and crumbly, 10 to 12 minutes. Use a slotted spoon to transfer the sausage to a medium bowl.

To make the ginger mustard: In a blender or a food processor, combine the pickled mustard seeds and ginger and blitz them together for 30 seconds.

To make the sandwiches: Generously smear the ginger mustard on the cut sides of the baguette. Pile the sausage on the bottom half of the baguette, then top it with the romaine leaves, cucumber matchsticks, a generous amount of pickled carrots, and a heaping pile of cilantro. Cut into three or four pieces and serve.

BROOKE AND CLAY AVILA, FRONTERA HUNTING

I was nervous the day I met the Avilas. I drove the 101 Freeway, passing ranchland on either side for hours, following Brooke's directions. I got off at a nondescript exit, headed uphill, and the vista exploded into open country. I could see the Pacific to my one side and all the land east of the highway on my other, the oil fields and pastures and trees. Brooke and her husband, Clay, run guided hunts on seven hundred acres of San Luis Obispo County that's been in Clay's family for generations. I was there to nail a pig. We were supposed to start the next day before first light. "Do you want to just go and see if we can find some wild boars right now, so we'll know where they are for the morning?" Brooke asked. We had half an hour before sundown. We jumped in the ATV, set up in a gulch with binoculars, and Brooke spotted one immediately. "There's a big

hog at the top of that hill," she said. Its distance was two hundred yards and some change, but I knew it was a male; I could see the tufts on its head. "Do you feel comfortable taking that shot?" she asked. I wasn't sure. It had been a minute since I last tried to shoot something. But I sat down, took some deep breaths, squeezed one off, and stoned that pig, dead as doornail. Picture perfect. It was two hundred pounds, a good eating size. Clay and their ten-month-old baby, Reese, came and met us. Brooke pulled out her pocket knife, rolled up her sleeves, and gutted that thing, elbows-deep in blood. Its belly was full of green grass and wine grapes. We skinned it, took off its head, stowed it in the cooler to hang for the evening, and that was that. "I just want you to know it never happens that quick," said Brooke. "Never." She is one badass guide.

Cooking meat comes down to this: Season it with intention, let it come to room temperature, and sear the living daylights out of it. Beyond that are the nuances that yield great tenderloin. Whole tenderloin comes with a sinewy side muscle called a chain and connective tissue called silverskin. Make sure your butcher removes these for you because you're looking for butter-tender meat. For even searing, you want uniform thickness, so get yourself some kitchen twine and tie the tenderloin up into a tube shape like a Pringles can. Don't overdo the salt and pepper. You're not curing the tenderloin; you're seasoning it and salt-drying the exterior, which is important because excess moisture in a hot pan is a steam bath waiting to happen. After roasting, don't leave tenderloin soaking in its juice. Set it on a wire rack, and don't touch it. Don't even look at it. It needs rest.

The remainder of this recipe is all about finding that perfect bite: savory-sweet cornbread, seasoned meat, and a dash of hot sauce that's alive. The healthy thing in the cornbread is the chanterelles. When you chop them, stay loose. You want that wabi-sabi thing, where you might get a big chunk in a hunk of cornbread. It's a treasure.

roasted beef tenderloin with chanterelle cornbread

To make the cornbread: Clean the chanterelles without rinsing them by gently scraping down the stem with a paring knife, removing dirt and duff. Heat a dry, 9 in [23 cm] cast-iron pan over medium-high heat. Add the chanterelles and cook them, pushing them around continuously with a wooden spoon, until they're charred, 5 to 10 minutes. Coarsely chop them and set them aside.

Preheat the oven to 375°F [190°C]. Lightly coat a 9 in [23 cm] springform pan with pan spray and set it on a sheet pan.

continued

Chanterelle Cornbread

3 cups [340 g] chanterelles

Pan spray

3 scant cups [400 g] all-purpose flour

¾ cup [100 g] polenta or coarse grits

1 scant cup [175 g] dark brown sugar

5 tsp baking powder

1 Tbsp kosher salt

4 large eggs

1½ cups [360 ml] whole milk

¼ cup [68 g] red miso

½ cup [120 ml] canola oil

⅓ cup [80 ml] extra-virgin olive oil

continued

TIME
1 hour 15 minutes active; 3½ hours total

YIELD
Enough for 6 humans or 4 hungry bears

Beef Tenderloin

1 whole beef tenderloin,
3½ to 5 lb [1.6 to 2.3 kg],
halved crosswise

Kosher salt

Freshly ground black pepper

1½ tsp extra-virgin olive oil

1½ tsp ghee, preferably
homemade (page 42)

Fermented Hot Sauce
(page 62), for serving

In a stand mixer fitted with a paddle attachment or a large bowl with a wooden spoon, mix the flour, polenta, brown sugar, baking powder, and salt. With the stand mixer on medium or while beating with the wooden spoon after each addition, alternate adding each egg with a waterfall of milk and a dollop of miso, until everything is well combined. Fold in the chanterelles.

With the mixer on medium-low or while beating continuously with the wooden spoon, slowly stream the canola oil and olive oil into the batter. Continue beating until the oils are fully incorporated. Pour the batter into the prepared springform pan and bake it for 30 minutes, then rotate the sheet pan and continue baking the cornbread for about 30 minutes more, or until it's golden brown and a cake tester or skewer inserted in the center comes out clean. Cool it for 15 minutes before removing it from the pan. You can slice and serve it warm, stow it in a ziplock or resealable silicone bag with the air squeezed out of it and refrigerate it for up to 1 week, or freeze it for up to 1 month.

To make the tenderloin: Preheat the oven to 425°F [220°C]. Set a wire rack inside a sheet pan and keep it near the oven.

Tie a piece of twine around the meat every two fingers' width down the length of each piece of tenderloin. Season the meat evenly and moderately all over with salt and pepper. Rest it at room temperature for 2 hours.

Get a 9 in [23 cm] cast-iron pan ripping hot over high heat, add the olive oil and ghee, and sear the meat for 4 minutes on one side to form a crust. Roll the tenderloin away from you, stopping where the crust ends, and sear it for another 4 minutes. Repeat until the tenderloin is crusted all around. Flip the tenderloin over, then put it in the oven and roast it for 22 minutes, or until an instant-read thermometer registers 135°F [58°C] for medium-rare. Rest the meat on the wire rack for 15 minutes, then cut it at each piece of twine, removing the twine and pushing the slices over to fan them on your cutting board. Tuck the final slice behind the first slice, so that a pink-red, interior slice is on top. Serve it on the cutting board with the cornbread and fermented hot sauce on the side.

lunch in the vineyard

Now we're taking time out for special occasions. Courtesy of the Central Coast's family-owned wineries, we're making memories over a bottle or two. Folks are sipping a Chamomile–Pink Peppercorn Spritz (page 261), pinkies up, and having a blast. We're pulling out the engagement ring and proposing on the spot. We're impressing all our friends with big-project, crowd-worthy cooking that, with a little planning, we've made look like a snap. It might take us a few days to prep some of this, but it's going to be one helluva picnic.

The Central Coast is a sleeper wine region, but it's a beautiful place to grow grapes, particularly as more-famous areas like Napa warm up under climate change. The vineyards here are close to the sea, and the Pacific fog rolls in, refreshing the fruit and giving it that lip-smacking balance of depth and acid that leads to great wine.

I love the renegade winemakers on this coast, scraping it together with a couple of acres of vines here and there in the Santa Cruz Mountains, the Santa Rita Hills, and the Edna and Arroyo Grande Valleys. A lot of them are farming organically and biodynamically, taking care of the ecosystem, and vinifying whatever varieties they want. Yeah, sure, they make Pinot Noir and Chardonnay, but also Sangiovese, Riesling, Chenin Blanc—grapes you don't find a lot of in California. They remind us that, once upon a time, even stalwart Napa and Sonoma were planted by hippie iconoclasts. Lady of the Sunshine, Scar of the Sea, Camins2Dreams, my friends at Dunites Wine Company (see page 276)—It's just a magical community of people here on the Central Coast doing their best, with all the challenges and the expense of making wine, to produce something chug-able that speaks to the seaside terroir where it was grown.

For them and the wildly biodiverse plots they tend, the kinds of places that give you a little head rush when you're sipping under the sun and walking the rows, here's a chapter of recipes that are a little bit softer and more ethereal. Tuck your Chicken Liver Mousse with Persimmon Pudding (page 270), your Meyer Lemon Curd with Blueberry Sauce (page 283), and the Hippie Vinaigrette (page 53) for your Seasonal Herb Salad (page 278) in mason jars; cure your salmon and roe (page 267), braise and press your Head Cheese (page 271), and carve your Shio Koji–Roasted Goat Leg (page 282) ahead of time. Then pack it all up and tote it in a wicker basket to spread on a picnic table with a view of the vines. Pass plates around, day drink a little, and enjoy the afternoon sun for a few hours with your homies. Take it easy. Take it light.

An Aperol spritz is a fine afternoon sipper, but with Anthony's help, this version is more complex. If you can find Bodegas Hidalgo La Gitana, have a nice taste before you infuse it. It's not as oxidative as other Manzanillas. It's dry and clean with brioche-y, salty notes. Chamomile grows as groundcover all over the Central Coast, and pink peppercorn bushes line the highways, so we forage fresh ingredients for this one, and they speak to the terroir expressed in the wine. At home, you can use dried chamomile flowers and peppercorns. Mix leftover pink peppercorn syrup with sparkling water, use it to dress a fruit salad, or swap it in for the simple syrup to candy the fruit for the Kumquat and Kale (page 229).

When you're pouring cocktails out in a vineyard, field, or park, it's nice to garnish them with what's around you. Walking the vineyard with Tyler and Rachel of Dunites (see page 276), I grabbed lavender, Meyer leaves, and peppercorn branches off plants and trees bordering the rows. But garnish this with a dandelion if that's what's available. Just make it pretty, because this is a fancy picnic drink.

chamomile—pink peppercorn spritz

Chamomile Sherry

One 500 ml bottle Manzanilla sherry, preferably Bodegas Hidalgo La Gitana

2 oz [55 g] dried chamomile flowers

Pink Peppercorn Syrup

1 cup [200 g] sugar

¼ cup [16 g] freshly ground pink peppercorns

Spritz

1½ oz [45 ml] Aperol, chilled

1 oz [30 ml] Chamomile Sherry, chilled

1 barspoon (about 1 tsp) Pink Peppercorn Syrup, chilled

Big splash of dry California sparkling wine, chilled

To make the chamomile sherry: Pour the sherry into a mason jar and stir in the chamomile flowers, pressing down to submerge them. Stow the jar in the fridge to infuse overnight.

Strain the infusion through a chinois into an airtight container, pressing on the flowers to extract the liquid. Discard the flowers. You should have about 1½ cups [360 ml] of chamomile sherry, which is enough for ten drinks. It keeps, in the fridge in an airtight container, for up to 2 weeks.

To make the pink peppercorn syrup: In a small saucepan over medium-high heat, dissolve the sugar in 1½ cups [360 ml] of water. Knock the heat down to low, simmer it for 5 minutes, then kill the heat. Stir in the peppercorns and steep them for 30 minutes. Strain the syrup through a fine-mesh strainer into an airtight container and put it in the fridge to chill. You should have about 1 cup [240 ml] of pink peppercorn syrup. It keeps, in the fridge in an airtight container, for up to 1 month.

To make the spritz: Pour the Aperol, chamomile sherry, and pink peppercorn syrup into a chilled wineglass. Top with sparkling wine until the glass is three-quarters full.

TIME
15 minutes active; overnight total

YIELD
1 drink

Country Toast

2 loaves sourdough bread, cut into 1 in [2.5 cm] thick slices

¼ cup [60 ml] extra-virgin olive oil

country toast bar

I make this spread, which includes the next five recipes, when I have some free days to get it done in advance. Then I can spend more time at the picnic hanging out with friends rather than tending to the food. There's a lot of technique (you'll need a piping bag and star tip) and some heavy prep, but on party day, the only thing left to do is buy a loaf of crusty bread and make toast out of it. When you tell your crowd that you made everything else from scratch, that's just damned impressive.

Really, you want to do this step last on the day of the picnic when all the good stuff that you'll pile on top of the bread is already prepped. But it's the heart and soul of the Country Toast Bar. To make the toast, place the bread slices on a sheet pan and drizzle them with the olive oil. Heat a 9 in [23 cm] grill pan or cast-iron pan over medium-high heat. Working in batches, toast one side of the bread slices until they're golden and crusty, 3 to 4 minutes. Remove the toasts to a sheet pan and cut them in half, if you want, to serve.

TIME
3 days total

YIELD
4 to 6 servings

smoked mackerel
with lemon-dill relish

Smoked Mackerel

¼ cup [40 g] kosher salt

2 Tbsp mustard powder

Two 8 oz [230 g] skin-on
mackerel fillets

Hickory chunks, for smoking

continued

Fatty, flavorful mackerel is revered in Korea. But in the States, a lot of fishermen just use it for bait. Catching macks with a sabiki rig, a sort of whirligig made lethal with tiny hooks, I'd sometimes pull up one or two that were eight to twelve inches long. That's too big for bait, so I'd throw them back. By chance, I brought a few home, and a Korean pal of mine said, "Woah, you caught mackerel? We can eat this." That's this recipe's origin story. I went from thinking of mackerel almost as bycatch to prepping it into something delicious. The idea is that every catch is important in its own right. A mackerel can lure a huge lingcod, but if all you catch is mackerel, well, then, you've got yourself dinner—or, in this case, a beautiful foundation for a smoky, tangy party dish.

To make the smoked mackerel: In a small bowl, combine the salt and mustard powder, and mix well. Heavily season both sides of the mackerel with the salt mixture, then set it on a wire rack and rest it at room temperature for 30 minutes. Rinse it, pat it dry, and stow it in the fridge, uncovered, for at least 2 hours. You want it firm and dry, so it doesn't leach moisture and flavor during smoking.

Prep your smoker. This is a nice one for a stovetop smoker. If you're using a charcoal grill, bank your coals to one side and wrap the other side of the grate with aluminum foil. When the coals are glowing and no longer on fire, throw a handful of hickory chunks on them. There's no need to soak the wood chunks. For a gas grill, heat one side on high, place the hickory chunks in a smoker box, and place the smoker box over the flame. Decrease the heat to low once the wood starts smoking. Set a wire rack inside a sheet pan and put it near the smoker or grill.

continued

TIME
1 hour 15 minutes active;
3 hours 45 minutes total

YIELD
4 to 6 servings

SPECIAL GEAR
Grill or smoker
Lump charcoal

Let the first blast of acrid smoke blow off, then place the fish directly on the foil, and close the lid. If you're using a charcoal grill, position the vents over the fish. Checking its temp at 30 minutes and every 15 minutes after that, leave it to smoke until an instant-read thermometer inserted into the meatiest part of the fillet reads 150°F [65°C], about 1 hour. Transfer the fish to the rack, and let it cool to room temperature. It keeps, in the fridge in an airtight container, for up to 6 days.

To make the relish: Using a sharp paring knife, supreme the lemons, cutting off the tops and bottoms of the fruit, then running your knife down the sides of the fruit, following its contour to remove the skin, pith, and outer membrane. Free the segments by slicing on either side of the membrane that separates them. Dice the segments, put them in a small bowl, and fold in the confit garlic, chives, dill, and pepper.

To serve, grab your sharpest knife, and cut the mackerel, on the bias, into ¼ in [6 mm] thick pieces, slicing off the skin at the end of each cut or, if you enjoy eating the skin like I do, cutting right through the skin. Serve a slice of mackerel and some relish on your country toast.

Relish

4 lemons, preferably Meyer

6 cloves Confit Garlic (page 47), mashed into a paste

½ cup [20 g] chopped fresh chives

¼ cup [5 g] fresh dill sprigs, tough stems removed

3 or 4 cranks black pepper

From April to October during salmon season in Central California, I sometimes get lucky and nab a fish full of roe. Then I make this deliciousness, using the same curing process for the fish that I use for the Lox 'n' Tacs (page 148). If you can't get wild salmon fresh, buy it frozen, and thaw it in your fridge before curing it. Remember that curing the salmon takes 24 hours. As for the roe, if you fish the roe yourself or buy it fresh, the brining process tightens up the eggs, removes the membranes around them, and cleans any residue. Then the roe is ready for a flavorful cure. But in all likelihood, you'll buy jarred, brined roe, i.e., salmon caviar or what is called ikura in Japanese, and then you can skip the brining step. Just make sure the roe is not pasteurized because the taste isn't the same.

½ cup [120 g] fresh or brined salmon roe

¾ tsp kosher salt, if brining

¼ cup [60 ml] Junmai or Junmai Daiginjo sake

2 Tbsp mirin

¾ tsp tamari

Cured Salmon (page 149), for serving

Crème fraîche, preferably homemade (page 44), for serving

If you're using brined roe, skip the brining. If you're using fresh roe, place it in a medium bowl. Dissolve the salt in ¼ cup [60 ml] of ice-cold water and pour it over the roe. Chill it for 30 minutes, then gently roll the eggs around with your hands, removing and skimming any loose membranes from the water. Drain the roe in a fine-mesh strainer, rinse it, and remove any remaining membranes.

Put the roe in a medium bowl, add the sake and ¼ cup [60 ml] of ice-cold water, and cure the roe for 5 minutes. Drain the roe in a fine-mesh strainer and rinse it gently, as it's now quite delicate. Put the roe in a mason jar, add the mirin and tamari, and cure it for at least 1 hour. It keeps, in the fridge in an airtight container, for up to 4 days.

To serve, grab your sharpest knife and cut the salmon, on the bias, into ¼ in [6 mm] thick pieces, slicing off the skin at the end of each cut. Serve the salmon on country toast with a schmear of crème fraîche and a mound of roe, scooping it out of the jar with a slotted spoon.

cured salmon with roe and crème fraîche

TIME
30 minutes active; 2 hours total

YIELD
6 to 8 servings

18 quail eggs

6 Tbsp [90 g] The Best Mayonnaise (page 45) or Kewpie

2 tsp Dijon or spicy brown mustard

2 or 3 pinches of kosher salt

I like my deviled eggs small and straightforward. These are one-biters. The key to success here is patience. Peeling quail eggs is a meditation. The shell is soft, so it can shatter on you, and the eggs are fragile, so if you're rough with them, the whites will tear. But once you get a good purchase on the membrane, a big swath of shell will peel away. Most importantly, clean your knife between each slice of egg. A clean knife slices smooth and clear. A dirty one catches on the egg white and rips it.

deviled quail eggs

Fill a large bowl with ice water and line a bowl with paper towels.

In a medium saucepan, cover the eggs with 1 in [2.5 cm] of water and bring them to a boil. Immediately remove the pan from the heat, cover it, and let it stand for 3 minutes. Transfer the eggs to the ice bath and cool them down, 8 to 10 minutes.

With the hilt of a paring knife, tap into the air pocket at the bottom of each egg. Use the knife or your fingers to remove the membrane and shell around the air pocket. The rest of the shell should peel off easily. Place the eggs in the paper towel–lined bowl.

Cut the eggs lengthwise in half, cleaning your knife after each cut. Transfer the yolks to a food processor. Add the mayo, mustard, and salt and pulse until smooth. Place a small star tip inside an uncut piping bag. Add the deviled yolk to the piping bag, and holding the bag closed at its opening, swing it around to force the yolk into the tip end. Twist and tie the bag closed, cut the end of the bag around the star tip, and pipe the yolk into the egg white halves. Arrange them on a platter for serving.

TIME
40 minutes

YIELD
36 deviled eggs

SPECIAL GEAR
Piping bag and star tip

Chicken Liver Mousse

1 lb [455 g] chicken livers, trimmed of fat and veins

1½ tsp plus a pinch of kosher salt

¼ tsp pink curing salt

1 cup [226 g] unsalted butter

½ white onion, thinly sliced

2 garlic cloves, thinly sliced

½ cup [120 ml] heavy cream

Persimmon Pudding

4 ripe Hachiya persimmons

TIME
25 minutes active; overnight total

YIELD
Three 1 pt [475 ml] jars

chicken liver mousse with persimmon pudding

For this blender-method mousse, the machine does double duty, blitzing and poaching the livers at once. Brining the livers beforehand seasons them and prevents oxidation so they stay pink. The persimmon pudding adds a sweet contrast. If the persimmons you buy aren't quite ripe enough, massage them every so often for a few days to break down their cells. They'll soften up. If you're looking for another delicious thing to do with the mousse, hold some back after blitzing. Don't top it with persimmon pudding and use it instead to make Shrimp and Chicken Liver Grits (page 84).

To make the chicken liver mousse: Combine the livers, ¾ teaspoon of kosher salt, and the pink salt with ½ cup [120 ml] of cold water in an airtight container, and brine them overnight in the fridge.

Strain and rinse the chicken livers well, then drain them and pat them dry with a double layer of paper towels, removing all the moisture. Put them in a blender or a food processor.

In a small saucepan over medium-low heat, melt the butter. When it stops bubbling, add the onion, garlic, and a pinch of salt and cook until the onion is translucent, about 5 minutes. Add the heavy cream and bring it to a boil, then pour the hot liquid over the chicken livers, and blitz them until smooth, 1 to 1½ minutes. Strain the mousse through a chinois into three pint-size [475 ml] mason jars. Stow the jars in the fridge, uncovered, to chill it until the mousse is set, 2 to 4 hours. Place plastic wrap on the surface of the mousse before screwing on the lids. It keeps, in the fridge covered in plastic, for up to 5 days.

To make the persimmon pudding: Just before serving, halve the persimmons, squeeze their pulp into a blender, and blitz on high until it comes together into a thick sauce, 30 to 45 seconds. Pour the pudding over the set chicken liver mousse and serve it from jars, with country toast on the side.

My mom is a head cheese fanatic. She once called me while on her way out to California to visit me. "I'm getting a slice of head cheese before I get to the airport, so I can eat it on the plane," she said. I thought, "Do you think the person crammed in next to you wants to deal with you eating a big old hunk of head cheese?" But she likes it so much, she doesn't give a wit what anyone else thinks.

This recipe is for people like her and cooks like you. It's fun to eat and super fun to make. First, you're going to procure a pig's head from a local farm, your butcher, or online. Then you're going to brine it for two days before braising and setting it. Because some places sell it halved, you can work with half a pig's head, too, and only make one terrine. Just keep the brine ingredients and water at the same amount, but halve the ingredients that go into the terrine, as you'll have half as much meat. You need fortitude, a huge container, a giant stockpot, one or two loaf pans, and lots of room in your fridge.

head cheese with charred onion mustard

To make the head cheese: Wrap the peppercorns, allspice, fennel seeds, and bay leaves in cheesecloth. In a large pot, combine the spice sachet, sugar, kosher salt, pink curing salt, and 6 quarts [5.7 L] of water and bring it to a boil. Transfer the brine and spice sachet to a 12 qt [11.3 L] container and fill it with ice up to the 10 qt [9.5 L] mark. Add the pig's head, then stow it in the fridge to brine for 48 hours.

Remove the head from the brine and rinse it; discard the brine. Put the head in a 12 qt [11.3 L] stockpot and add enough water to cover the head by 3 in [7.5 cm]. Bring it to a boil, then knock the heat down to a simmer and cover it with the lid cracked to let the steam out. Braise the head until the meat pulls away from the bone and the skin pierces easily, 4 to 6 hours. Rest the head in the braising liquid until it's cool enough to pull out with kitchen gloves on, about 2 hours.

continued

Head Cheese

¼ cup [50 g] peppercorns

1 Tbsp whole allspice

1 Tbsp whole fennel seeds

3 bay leaves

1⅔ cups [330 g] sugar

3¾ cups [600 g] kosher salt

4½ Tbsp [85 g] pink curing salt

1 whole pig's head, 12 to 15 lb [5.4 to 6.8 kg]

1 cup [320 g] Dijon mustard

½ cup [80 g] chopped shallots

½ cup [20 g] chopped fresh chervil, or ¼ cup [10 g] chopped fresh parsley and ¼ cup [10 g] chopped fresh tarragon

¼ cup [10 g] chopped fresh parsley

¼ cup [10 g] chopped fresh chives

Zest and juice of 2 lemons, preferably Meyer

6 to 8 very coarse cranks black pepper

2 cups [475 ml] chicken stock, preferably The Best Chicken Stock (page 63)

Pan spray

continued

TIME
2 hours active;
3 days total

YIELD
Two 9 by 5 by 3 in [23 by 13 by 7.5 cm] terrines

SPECIAL GEAR
12 qt [11.4 L] container
12 qt [11.4 L] stockpot
Two 9 by 5 by 3 in [23 by 13 by 7.5 cm] loaf pans

Remove the head from the braising liquid; reserve the liquid. Peel away and discard the skin. Pull the meat, fat, and cartilage from all the pockets and dice it. Put it in a large bowl. Thinly slice the ears, remove and discard the skin from the tongue, dice the tongue, and add the ear and tongue meat to the bowl. Add the mustard, shallots, chervil, parsley, chives, lemon zest, lemon juice, and pepper and mix well with your hands.

In a medium saucepan, bring 1 cup [240 ml] of the reserved braising liquid and the chicken stock to a boil. Knock the heat down to a simmer, and cook it, skimming any fat, until it's reduced by about half, 12 to 15 minutes.

Lightly coat two 9 by 5 by 3 in [23 by 13 by 7.5 cm] loaf pans with pan spray, then line them with plastic wrap, leaving some hanging over the sides.

Divide the meat mixture between the prepared loaf pans, pressing it in and squeezing out any air. Pour the braising reduction over the top. That's the glue that holds the meat together. Fold the plastic wrap tightly over the top, then stow the terrines in the fridge to chill for 12 hours.

To make the charred onion mustard: In a 9 in [23 cm] cast-iron pan over medium-high heat, heat the oil until it's ripping hot. Add the onion. It will sizzle and whine. When it quiets down, stir it with a wooden spoon to release the moisture. Cook it, stirring occasionally, until it's caramelized, 8 to 10 minutes. Transfer the onion to a food processor, then add the pickled mustard seeds and pulse the mixture until it has a grainy texture. Cool it to room temperature, then put it in a jar. It keeps, in the fridge in an airtight container, for up to 2 weeks.

To serve, unwrap the plastic wrap from the top of a terrine and pull it, along with the head cheese, out of the loaf pan. Cut the head cheese into ¼ in [6 mm] thick slices and serve it with smears of charred onion mustard on the country toast.

Charred Onion Mustard

1½ tsp canola oil

1 white onion, cut into thin half-moons

1 cup [250 g] Pickled Mustard Seeds (page 50)

TYLER AND RACHEL ECK, DUNITES WINE COMPANY

In the 1920s and 1930s, a group of renegade bohos carved out a utopian community in the dunes at Oceano, where they robbed from the rich, started a magazine, and attracted a bunch of nudists, mystics, and artists like Georgia O'Keefe, John Steinbeck, Ansel Adams, and John Cage. They were rad. And very Californian. They called themselves the Dunites.

I learned about them from winemakers Rachel and Tyler Eck, who named their label, Dunites Wine Company, in tribute. It fits. Both Rachel and Tyler seemingly play by the rules during the day, working for larger producers, but in their off-hours, they're alchemists, farming a wild and windblown little organic vineyard a few miles from the sea, raising a toddler, and making small-batch, terroir-driven, beautiful wines from grapes like Grenache and Albariño that other winemakers don't work with here. Their bosses at the big wineries ask them, "Why are you making these weirdo varietals?" But Rachel and Tyler stay true to their vision, producing natural ferments to sell out of their San Luis Obispo tasting room: sulfur-free Syrah, Blanc de Noirs pét-nat, a briny-fresh white blend they call Moy Mell after the original Dunites' meeting house, along with Pinot Noir as gorgeous as any on this coast. All the while, they're using a portion of their profits to support the Guadalupe-Nipomo Dunes Center that works to protect the coastal ecosystem that inspired their brand. That's the Central Coast for you. It's scrappy and true and close to nature, with some sweet folks making cool shit and giving back.

2 bunches fresh parsley

2 bunches fresh mint

2 medium fennel bulbs, stalks removed and tender fronds reserved

1 bunch mixed radishes with their greens

2 big handfuls pea shoots

2 big handfuls sunflower sprouts

1 bunch fresh chives, ends trimmed and cut into 2 in [5 cm] pieces

¼ cup [60 ml] Hippie Vinaigrette (page 53), plus more as needed

1 handful edible flowers, such as oxalis, mustard blossoms, or arugula blossoms

This salad is a visceral experience, like you ran through the garden with a weed whacker. Made up of pieces of fresh herbs that are just shy of being too big to eat, it's a wild and reckless bowl of green with a sexy crunch. At Dad's, it stands up to the wrath of a greasy diner burger and a yolk-exploding mushroom sandwich. The ingredients list is anarchic; you can decide for yourself what your handfuls are, changing up the herbs and sprouts as others come into season. You can use a salad spinner to wash it all, but I like to get my hands in it, mix it up well, and let it drip dry. Then you'll dress it with Hippie Vinaigrette (page 53), and your folks will chomp on it like they're herbivores.

seasonal herb salad

Set a colander inside a bowl and use kitchen shears to prune the parsley and mint into it, making big pieces and discarding any tough stems.

Trim the root end of the fennel, halve the bulbs, and remove the cores. Slice the remaining fennel into ¼ in [6 mm] thick half-moons.

Trim the radish greens to 1 in [2.5 cm] above the top and, using the green ends as a handle, mandoline the radishes into ⅛ in [3 mm] thick slices.

Add the fennel and fronds, radishes, pea shoots, sunflower sprouts, and chives to the colander.

Fill the bowl with cold water and mix the salad with your hands. Drain and wipe the bowl and rest the colander inside. Mix the salad with your hands again, shaking the colander. When the last bit of water has leaked into the bowl, wipe it dry again and put the salad in it. Dress the salad, starting with ¼ cup [60 ml] of vinaigrette and adding more as needed. Garnish the salad with edible flowers and serve it immediately.

TIME
30 minutes

YIELD
4 to 6 servings

barley and wine grape salad

For this hearty chopped salad, I use something I can find in abundance in Central Coast vineyards: wine grapes. Sweet and tart but tannic, they have just enough abrasiveness that you can't just chomp a handful. But when mixed with whole grains and veg, they balance beautifully. If you can't get wine grapes, use whatever thick-skinned grapes you can find. If you need to, add an extra tablespoon of sherry vinegar to offset their sweetness and make the salad come alive.

A hard toast on the raw barley adds deep magic. Before simmering, you'll throw the grains in the oven until they're fragrant and deeply bronzed. You know a cookie's baked when you can smell it. Same with grains.

The veg also gets extra love to bring out its goodness. Peel just half of the cuke skin off, making alternating stripes of skin and exposed flesh, because a small amount of peel lends a nice bitter note. The salad sits marinating, soaking up the vinaigrette. What puts it over the edge is mixing in a ridiculous amount of basil and parsley just before bringing it to the table. "Elvis Parsley!" Frost calls it. I love that knucklehead.

Preheat the oven to 350°F [180°C].

Spread the barley on a sheet pan and toast it, checking it and stirring it every 5 minutes, until it's deeply bronzed, about 25 minutes. Put the barley in a medium pot, then add the kombu, white soy sauce, and 3 cups [710 ml] of water. Bring it up to a boil, then knock the heat down to a simmer and cook until the barley is plump and tender and there's no water left in the bottom of the pot, 40 to 50 minutes. Cool to room temperature.

In a small jar, combine the olive oil, vinegar, lemon juice, liquid aminos, honey, salt, and pepper and shake to fully combine.

In a large serving bowl, toss the broccoli, grapes, cukes, and snow peas. Add the cooled barley and toss to incorporate it. Pour ½ cup [120 ml] of the dressing onto the salad and mix well with a wooden spoon to coat it evenly. Stow the salad in the fridge to chill for at least 6 hours and up to overnight. Just before serving, toss in the basil, parsley, green onions, and lemon zest. Give the salad a good stir, freshen it up with a bit more dressing, as needed, and bring it to your people.

1 cup [200 g] pearl barley

2 by 2 in [5 by 5 cm] piece kombu

1½ Tbsp white soy sauce

¼ cup [60 ml] California extra-virgin olive oil

3 Tbsp sherry vinegar

Zest of 2 lemons, preferably Meyer, and 2 Tbsp fresh lemon juice, preferably Meyer

2 Tbsp Bragg Liquid Aminos

2 Tbsp honey

Pinch of kosher salt

4 or 5 cranks black pepper

1 cup [50 g] broccoli florets

10½ oz [300 g] wine grapes or other thick-skinned grapes, halved

2 Persian cucumbers, half the peel removed in stripes, halved lengthwise, and cut into chunks

1½ cups [130 g] snow peas, stems and ribs removed, and halved on the bias

1 cup [40 g] fresh basil, chopped or left whole

1 cup [40 g] fresh parsley, chopped or left whole

¼ cup [15 g] thinly sliced green onions

PLEASE DO NOT BUY PACKAGED BROCCOLI FLORETS. GET A WHOLE HEAD AND DEFOREST IT.

TIME
1 hour active;
7 hours total

YIELD
6 to 8 servings

1 cup [240 ml] shio koji, preferably homemade (page 54)

4 garlic cloves, minced

1 Tbsp minced fresh ginger

1 Tbsp honey

One 4 lb [1.8 kg] bone-in goat leg

2 Tbsp canola oil

A whole roasted goat leg is a pretty big statement to throw on the table. It's not for every day. But when I want to show off, I like to cook a honker like this. It's a cool thing to have on deck for a celebration, and once you do it, you'll feel capable of pulling off other big roasts—because it's a lot easier than you might imagine.

You can buy a goat leg fresh or get it frozen and thaw it in your fridge overnight before you marinate it. The shio koji marinade tenderizes and flavors it. Then you leave it to do its thing in the oven. After it's rested, you slap it on a board, and cut hunks out of it with a sharp knife and a cool-ass granny fork like it's medieval times. On a big piece of meat like this, you'll hit different layers of doneness, so you can please pals who like it juicier and redder, as well as pals who need it more well-done. Do the same to cook a whole lamb's leg. It's a carnal, caveman-y treat. The veg in this chapter—the Seasonal Herb Salad (page 278), the Barley and Wine Grape Salad (page 281)— are great to go alongside.

shio koji–roasted goat leg

In a small bowl, mix the shio koji, garlic, ginger, and honey. Slather it all over the goat leg. Put the goat leg inside a couple of clean, doubled-up turkey bags, compress all the air out of them, and stow the leg in the fridge to marinate overnight.

Preheat the oven to 325°F [165°C]. Free the goat leg from the bags and pat it dry, removing the marinade. In a large cast-iron pan over high heat, heat the canola oil. Add the goat leg and sear the meaty parts, turning it to get a good crust on them.

Transfer the goat leg, bone-side down, to a large roasting pan and roast it until a meat thermometer inserted into the thickest section of meat at the ball joint registers 145°F [63°C] for medium-rare, 2 to 3 hours. Let it rest for 30 minutes.

To carve the goat leg, hold it by the hoof end and run a sharp knife down the leg, shaving off thin strips until you reach the bone. You can also make bigger hunks by cutting the thigh meat into ¼ in [6 mm] thick pieces. Serve it piled on a platter.

TIME
30 minutes active; overnight total

YIELD
6 to 8 servings

coastal

meyer lemon curd
with blueberry sauce

It bears repeating: There is no lemon like a Meyer lemon. This dessert celebrates its flowery sweetness. Lemon curd is just sugar, butter, eggs, and citrus, but it amounts to the lightest, brightest, most refreshing thing to eat at the end of a meal. It's a little twee, but it doesn't lean overly sweet, and with blueberry sauce on top, it's visually beautiful. It's also portable if you set it in mason jars. As for the blueberry sauce, you can also just whip that up separately any time you want to drizzle it on waffles, pancakes, ice cream, yogurt, whatever.

To make the curd: Bloom the gelatin in 3 tablespoons of water.

In a medium saucepan, whisk together the sugar, lemon juice, and eggs until smooth. Whisking, bring the mixture to a boil over medium-high heat. Cook it, whisking, for 1 minute more. Transfer the mixture to a blender and with the blender running, add the butter, a few cubes at a time. When all the butter is incorporated, add the bloomed gelatin. You'll have about 4 cups [945 ml] of curd. Pour it into four to six mason jars, leaving room for the blueberry sauce. Without screwing the lids on, put the curd in the fridge to set, about 2 hours. Then screw on the lids. It keeps, in the fridge in airtight containers, for up to 3 days.

To make the blueberry sauce: In a small bowl, stir the cornstarch into ¼ cup [60 ml] of water.

Put half of the blueberries in a medium bowl.

In a stainless steel saucepan over medium-high heat, bring the remaining blueberries, sugar, vanilla, ginger, and ¾ cup [180 ml] of water to a boil. Add the cornstarch slurry and bring the mixture back to a boil. Knock the heat down to a simmer and, stirring and smashing the blueberries, cook it until it thickens slightly, 4 to 5 minutes. Pour the cooked blueberries over the reserved blueberries, then remove the ginger and add the lemon juice. Mix until well combined. Cool for 5 minutes, then fold in the lemon zest. You should have about 4 cups [945 ml] of sauce. It keeps, in the fridge in an airtight container, for up to 1 week.

To serve, pour the blueberry sauce over the set curd in the mason jars, and sprinkle it with pretzel crispies, if you want.

Lemon Curd

3 sheets silver gelatin or ¾ package powdered gelatin (about 2 tsp)

1 cup plus 1 Tbsp [215 g] sugar

1 cup [240 ml] fresh Meyer lemon juice (from about 5 lemons)

4 large eggs

1½ cups [340 g] unsalted butter, cold and cubed

Blueberry Sauce

1 Tbsp cornstarch

4 cups [560 g] blueberries

¼ cup [50 g] sugar

½ tsp vanilla extract

Two ⅛ in [3 mm] thick slices peeled fresh ginger

Zest of 1 Meyer lemon and 2 tsp fresh Meyer lemon juice

Pretzel Crispies (page 340), for topping, if you want

TIME
**1 hour active;
3 hours total**

YIELD
4 to 6 servings

grilling on pismo beach

The border between San Luis Obispo and Santa Barbara Counties is a working class–meets–old money zone, where fun-lovin' Pismo Beach gives way to tony Santa Barbara. If you linger in Pismo, though, you can lose yourself in the sky-scraping sand hills of one of the biggest coastal dune ecosystems on the planet. This is where the Chumash left massive midden piles five millennia ago, feasting on bivalves and chucking their shells. It's where free-love radicals, dreamers, and outlaws took to the dunes in the 1920s to form an alternative society. It was the Clam Capital of the World, until the clam population crashed in the 1990s from overharvesting. The clams are just now creeping back. Pismo Beach is a place unto itself. You can build a fire and ride a dune buggy on the sand here.

Summer's come again, and we're farther down the Central Coast. The air is getting warmer, and the recipes are getting more straightforward. We're ripping Tamarind Mezcal Americanos (page 288) and bringing Korean BBQ Pear Butter Ribs (page 304), Grilled Eggplant Yakitori (page 289), and Ghee-Roasted Oysters with Fire Cider Mignonette (page 301) to life over the flames. This chapter is like an Igloo cooler commercial circa 1990, all splashy and bright with people in swimsuits playing volleyball and lotioning up in the sun. It's a picture-perfect California day. Shirtless time. Bikini time. There are palm trees and a wide stretch of warm sand before the waves. We're throwing a BBQ on the beach. You're learning to grill and ember-roast.

In my mind, there's nothing better than sweating in front of a fire as it crackles and roars, watching logs and coals burn down to pea-size pieces, so you can sear off a hunk of deliciousness. But since food, and yourself, can get burned, let me dispel a common misconception: When you cook over fire, you're not throwing stuff onto live flames. You're making a really nice, glowing coal bed and learning to control its heat. There's this dance that you do, a give-and-take between leaving the Santa Maria Rib Eye (page 307) alone on the grates or moving it around to bring some more char to parts of it or to cool it down. You develop a sense of timing for when the coals are too hot or when you need to build the bed up. It's elevated camp cooking, based on embers, ingenuity, and rhythm. You're burying sweet potatoes (page 292) in that glowing pile and pulling them out perfectly roasted; you're coaxing delicate things like head-on shrimp (page 295) and snap peas (page 291) to just-doneness. You're working with the nuances of the heat, getting better at it as you go.

Tamarind Syrup

6 oz [170 g] tamarind, about 6 pods

1 cup [200 g] turbinado sugar

Americanos

One 750 ml bottle mezcal, preferably Espadín

One 250 ml bottle bitter amaro, preferably Amargo Vallet

6 Tbsp [90 ml] Tamarind Syrup

Peel of 2 lemons, preferably Meyer

California is Mexican in more ways than one, and this drink of Anthony's gives gratitude to the folks and foods hailing from Mexico who have made the cuisine of the Central Coast what it is today. Espadín is the most widely planted agave in Oaxaca, so it speaks of that place. An aggressive, high-proof, extra-bitter amaro, Mexico's Amargo Vallet is a centuries-old infusion of ingredients that grow all the way down the coast to Baja. And the tamarind, well, that's a legume with a singular pucker that originates in Africa but has been naturalized in Mexico. You're going to batch this one out for the BBQ. Leftover tamarind syrup is great for shaking in a margarita or stirring into soda water.

tamarind mezcal americanos

To make the tamarind syrup: Break open the tamarind pods, remove the husk and the ribbing, and put the pulp in a small saucepan. Add the sugar and 1 cup [240 ml] of water and bring it to a simmer. Continue simmering over medium-low heat for 15 minutes. Strain it through a chinois into a blender and blitz it on high for 2 minutes, then transfer it to an airtight container. You should have about 1½ cups [360 ml] of syrup. It keeps, in the fridge in an airtight container, for up to 2 weeks.

To make the Americanos: Fill a pitcher halfway with ice, then add the mezcal, amaro, tamarind syrup, and lemon peels and stir for 30 seconds. Strain the drink into ice-filled glasses.

TIME
25 minutes

YIELD
16 drinks

coastal

grilled eggplant yakitori

This recipe is an homage to Ippuku in Berkeley, where you go for chicken livers, hearts, and gizzards, plus shishito peppers and king trumpets all grilled on a stick. This young man from Virginia had never eaten yakitori before moving to California. Ippuku was where I learned you can basically put anything on a skewer, and I will love it, even eggplant, which I had never loved before. When you poach eggplant in soy sauce and sugar and then grill it, it's like candy. The hole in the parchment cloche's center lets liquid over the top to hold the cloche down, which keeps the eggplants submerged in their delicious bath so that they cook all the way through. Then you throw them on the fire and burn the heck out of them, which brings out their wild florality. Buy sturdy, chubby eggplants, not skinny ones. Keep the skewers on them so people can pick them up and walk off with them at the cookout.

Cut a square piece of parchment paper a bit bigger than your braising pot. Fold it into quarters, then fold it in half to create a triangle with the gathered corner at the tip. Fold it in half two more times to make a narrower triangle. Lay the triangle with its tip centered inside a medium Dutch oven. Crimp the other end of the parchment where it meets the inside edge of the pot. Cut along the crimp. Cut off the tip of the triangle. Open it up. You should have a round cloche with a center hole.

Prick the eggplants all over with a fork. Add them to the braising pot with the soy sauce, brown sugar, granulated sugar, vinegar, and 2½ cups [600 ml] of water. Lay the cloche on top of the braise and bring it to a boil. Knock the heat down to a simmer, cover it with the lid cracked to let out some steam, and cook the eggplants until they're custardy soft and a skewer goes through them easily, 30 to 40 minutes. Kill the heat and cool the eggplants in the braising liquid until you can handle them, about 20 minutes.

Meanwhile, build a fire in your charcoal grill and let the coals get white-hot, light your gas grill to high, or heat a grill pan over high heat on your stove.

Remove the eggplants from their braising liquid; discard the liquid. Push two skewers, evenly spaced, crosswise through each eggplant. Grill the eggplants until their skin is charred and crackly, 1 to 2 minutes per side. Serve them on the skewers.

1½ lb [680 g] fist-size eggplants (6 to 8 eggplants)

2½ cups [600 ml] soy sauce

1 cup [200 g] packed dark brown sugar

1 cup [200 g] granulated sugar

½ cup [120 ml] rice vinegar

12 to 16 skewers, soaked for 30 minutes in water if wooden

TIME
1 hour 15 minutes

YIELD
4 to 6 servings

Here's a dish that Frost and I call our Inner Smile Salad. It's everything you want for a cookout. It's super easy, so you can make it ahead and bring it in a Tupperware. Or you can prop a cast-iron pan on the beach flames and make it right there and then. After a hot fire, lots of sun, and piles of grilled meat, it's a hydrating, cooling, creamy, green gift that's fun to eat, with a mix of savory elements tucked amid the sweetness that Frost loves. We hammer bowls of it.

The dressing is my knockoff of a Japanese probiotic milk drink called Yakult. It's fermented with a different strain of bacteria than yogurt, and that's where it gets its citrusy tang. But we can zhush our Homemade Yogurt (page 43) to achieve the same effect.

To make the Yakult-style dressing: In a small bowl, mix all the ingredients until fully combined. It keeps, in the fridge in an airtight container, for up to 1 week.

To make the roasted snap pea salad: In a 9 in [23 cm] cast-iron pan over high heat, get the sesame oil ripping hot and smoking. Drop in the peas and cook them without moving them until one side gets good and charred, 3 to 5 minutes. When they're hissing at you and barely wanting to stay inside the pan, give the peas a push. Some will turn over. Add the salt and continue cooking the peas for 3 to 4 minutes more. You want them unevenly charred. Put the peas on a sheet pan and stow them in the fridge or pop them in a cooler to get nice and cold, about 15 minutes.

Remove the tops and bottoms of your cukes. Holding your knife at a 45-degree angle, cut a chunk of cuke. Roll the cuke 180 degrees and cut again to get weird, triangular pieces. Repeat with all the cukes, then smash all the pieces with the side of your blade. They'll hold together because their shape gives them maximum skin. Add the cukes and chilled snap peas to a serving bowl.

Add enough dressing to the serving bowl to heavily coat the veg and mix well. Toss in the chives and all the sesame seeds and serve.

Yakult-Style Dressing

½ cup [120 g] yogurt, preferably homemade (page 43)

1 Tbsp honey

2 tsp fresh lime juice

1 tsp fresh lemon juice, preferably Meyer

Roasted Snap Pea Salad

1 Tbsp toasted sesame oil

12 oz [340 g] sugar snap peas, stems and fibrous ribs removed

¾ tsp kosher salt

3 Persian cucumbers

½ bunch fresh chives, cut crosswise into thirds

1 tsp toasted white sesame seeds

1 tsp black sesame seeds

roasted snap pea salad with yakult-style dressing

TIME
30 minutes

YIELD
2 or 3 servings

Farmer's Cheese

3 cups [710 ml] whole milk

1 cup [240 ml] heavy cream

1 tsp fine salt, such as Maldon

2 Tbsp fresh lemon juice

continued

I went to New Brighton State Beach for a weekend of camping and surfing with my pals Nate and Josh. We were three dudes in a tent, hanging out, having a trippy time in the Santa Cruz woods. We took a bunch of mushrooms and heaved a bunch of vegetables into the embers, and the foil-wrapped sweet potatoes were the only thing that survived to the next morning. So, we ate sweet potatoes for breakfast and paddled around the ocean like silly kids.

When you cook with fire, you don't want raging flames. You want well-controlled embers. For these sweet potatoes, use a shovel to break the embers into small pieces to create a uniform bed of mellower heat to bury them in. Leather fireplace gloves help for moving stuff around.

I like to use this simple method for making farmer's cheese when I'm cooking with Frost. It's a cool way to show a kid how things work in the kitchen. The leftover whey is full of probiotics. You can dissolve sugar into it for simple syrup, cook it down for caramel, stir it into seltzer for probiotic soda, and even cure vegetables in it.

ember-roasted sweet potatoes

To make the farmer's cheese: In a medium saucepan over medium-high heat, bring the milk, heavy cream, and salt to a boil, stirring continuously. Add the lemon juice and stir once to incorporate it, then knock the heat down to a simmer and don't touch it for 2 minutes. If you whisk it, you get fine curds. We are looking for big, full pieces. Kill the heat, cover the pan, and let the cheese hydrate in its whey until it cools to room temperature, about 1 hour.

Pour the cheese into a cheesecloth-lined fine-mesh strainer set over a bowl, then stow the strainer and bowl in the fridge and let it sit for at least 1 hour or overnight to drain. The cheese keeps, in the fridge in an airtight container, for up to 3 days.

continued

TIME
**30 minutes active;
3½ hours total**

YIELD
4 servings

coastal

Sweet Potatoes

4 medium sweet potatoes

4 Tbsp ghee [50 g], preferably homemade (page 42)

4 tsp kosher salt

Honey, for serving

Red pepper flakes, for serving

Flaky salt, such as Maldon

Hot sauce, preferably Fermented Hot Sauce (page 62), for serving

To make the sweet potatoes: Wrap each potato in aluminum foil with 1 tablespoon of ghee and 1 teaspoon of salt.

Build a large fire in your firepit or grill, and let it burn down to glowing embers. Break up the embers into smaller pieces with a fireplace shovel, then bury the potatoes in the embers, making sure there are embers above and below them. Cook time will vary, depending on how hot your embers are. Start testing the spuds at 30 minutes. Untwist a metal coat hanger to poke them with. If it slides right in, they're ready, 45 minutes to 1½ hours.

Pull the potatoes out of the fire and carefully unwrap them. Split them in half, dollop on the farmer's cheese, drizzle on honey, sprinkle on red pepper flakes and flaky salt, and serve with fermented hot sauce on the side.

YOU CAN USE THE EMBERS LEFT OVER FROM GRILLING THE OTHER DISHES IN THIS CHAPTER.

There's magic in Pacific spot prawns. They're meatier than other shrimp but also sweeter, more ethereal. At Saison, they lived in the fish tank. There's nothing like dunking your hand into ice-cold salt water and pulling out a live shrimp to cook it à la minute (or popping one in your mouth when no one is watching).

A few years ago, for my birthday, I got a fishhook tattoo on my palm. Then I went out on a boat with a friend who had some spot prawn traps. "Every buoy is ours," he said. "Start pulling." The pots were full of prawns. We were eating them raw like candy. But he didn't get off his ass. I damn near rubbed the new tattoo off my palm hand-lining thousands of feet of rope, while my friend kicked back and smoked pot. Somehow, that's a fond memory for me.

grilled spot prawn cocktail

To make the Coastal Cocktail Sauce: In a medium bowl, whisk together all the ingredients until they're well combined but still have a chunky texture. Stow the sauce in the fridge for 2 hours to marry the flavors. You'll have about 1¼ cups [300 ml] of sauce. It keeps, in the fridge in an airtight container, for up to 2 weeks, so you can also use it for Fries with Eyes (page 213).

To make the grilled spot prawns: Holding a paring knife perpendicular to its belly, slice the legs off each prawn from the bottom of the head to the tail, then use your knife to get under the shell and peel it off the bodies. Keep the heads on. Make slits down the back of the prawns and remove the veins. Pat the prawns dry.

Fire up your grill and let the coals turn white-hot, or heat a grill pan on the stove over high heat until it's smoking. Brush the spot prawns with the sesame oil, and if you are cooking them on the grill, place them in a wire rack or wire grill basket. Add a pinch of salt and sear them on one side until the color has crept halfway up their bodies, 1 to 2 minutes. Flip them and sear them until cooked through, 1 to 2 minutes more.

To serve, arrange the prawns around the perimeter of a serving platter, and put a small serving bowl of the cocktail sauce in the center.

Coastal Cocktail Sauce

½ cup [120 ml] ketchup

¼ cup [65 g] Oven-Dried Tomatoes (page 67), chopped

1 Tbsp plus 2 tsp white soy sauce

1 Tbsp gochujang

1 Tbsp Worcestershire sauce

1 Tbsp furikake, preferably homemade (page 70)

Zest of 1 lemon, preferably Meyer

Juice of ½ lemon, preferably Meyer

2 tsp rice vinegar

1 tsp Confit Garlic (page 47)

1 tsp horseradish

¼ tsp freshly ground black pepper

Grilled Spot Prawns

1 lb [455 g] head-on spot prawns or shrimp

1 Tbsp toasted sesame oil

Pinch of kosher salt

I HATE TO USE KETCHUP, BUT YA GOTTA HERE. GET A GOOD ORGANIC ONE.

TIME
15 minutes active;
2 hours 15 minutes total

YIELD
4 servings

NEAL MALONEY, MORRO BAY OYSTER COMPANY

A remnant of an ancient volcano, Morro Rock sticks up like a 581-foot thumb from the Pacific. A landmark for sailors, a sacred place to the Chumash and Salinan, it marks the border between a gnarly break and Morro Bay, one of the country's most biodiverse estuaries, fed by Chorro and Los Osos Creeks. Millions of birds from more than two hundred species winter in the salt marsh of the Morro Bay National Estuary Preserve. Harbor seas loll on the banks, otters float with their fur babies on their chests, stingrays and shovelnose guitarfish thrash in the water, and eagles, ospreys, and pelicans dive for fish. It's here, just on the calm side of the Sandspit, that Neal Maloney keeps his oyster barge.

Neal is a salty young pirate with a crew out there growing oysters in bags in a manner that's harmonious with this protected zone. Pacific Golds, the oysters he's developed, are super fat and creamy, with a bowl-like shell. Like all mollusks, they're filtering the water as they grow, giving back to the bay. Neal brings the oysters to his shop and eatery on the Embarcadero, selling them out of tanks and shucking them right there, so you can slurp them facing the Rock. I love that dichotomy. The shepherd of the water cruises, tranquil and attuned, through the clean, cold estuary in his aluminum boat, while on the other side of that seawall, the ocean is pure chaos.

coastal

It took a seaweed-pulling slog through the tidal pools at Estero Bluffs, a visit to the oyster barge in the Morro Bay estuary, a breakdown-lane harvest of pink peppercorns on the 101 Freeway, and a lungful of air that revived a pile of overnight embers we found on Pismo Beach to get to this recipe. I was flying by the seat of my pants, and the payoff was an early-morning oyster roast.

At Morro Bay Oyster Company (see page 296), the Pacific Golds have super deep cups. If you find similar oysters, cradled in their shells like babies, you'll have nice little bowls for all the goodness you're ladling on them. Luscious, spicy, and full of umami, these oysters explode with flavor. Use any seaweed for the garnish, except kombu, which gets goopy. Give the shallot time to cure in the fire cider, and you're good to go.

1 shallot, minced

¼ cup [60 ml] fire cider, preferably Pre-Surf Fire Cider (page 136)

¼ cup [60 ml] white soy sauce

2 Tbsp ghee, preferably homemade (page 42)

2 dozen oysters

Fresh or dried and rehydrated seaweed, chopped, for garnish

Lemon zest, preferably Meyer, for garnish

Freshly ground pink peppercorns, for garnish

In a small bowl, mix the shallot in the fire cider and let it marinate for 2 hours, then stir in the white soy sauce.

Meanwhile, build a medium fire, or heat a gas grill to medium.

In a small saucepan, melt the ghee over the fire; keep it warm.

Grill the oysters, cup-side up, until just open, about 5 minutes. Using tongs, remove them from the heat, and pry off the top shells, retaining the liquor. Spoon ½ teaspoon of ghee onto each oyster, return them to the grill, and cook them for 2 minutes more. Remove them from the heat, top each with 1 teaspoon of the fire cider mignonette, and garnish each with seaweed, lemon zest, and peppercorns. Serve immediately, everyone slurping the oysters out of their shells.

ghee-roasted oysters with fire cider mignonette

TIME
45 minutes active;
2 hours 45 minutes total

YIELD
2 dozen oysters

1 cup [240 ml] Pear Butter
(page 51)

½ cup [120 ml] yuzu soda

½ cup [120 ml] rice wine
vinegar

⅓ cup [80 ml] white soy sauce

1 Tbsp toasted sesame oil

1 tsp freshly ground black
pepper

½ tsp gochujang

1 white onion, coarsely
chopped

10 garlic cloves, peeled

One 2 in [5 cm] knob fresh
ginger, peeled

3 lb [1.4 kg] flanken cut beef
short ribs

2 tsp toasted white
sesame seeds

2 heads romaine lettuce

Steamed short-grain rice,
for serving

Fresh cilantro sprigs,
for serving

Sliced green onions,
for serving

Kimchi, preferably Whole
Napa Cabbage Kimchi
(page 58), for serving

Chile Jam (page 60),
for serving

TIME
**1 hour active;
at least 7 hours total**

YIELD
4 servings

In high school, I got a job as a furniture mover. We'd all work our tails off, then go to this place called Honey Pig and destroy a big pile of Korean BBQ. In my mind, Korean BBQ is still about being hungry and getting sated with your friends around you.

Make sure to buy flanken cut ribs, which are sliced thin across the bone. You can find them in Asian and kosher markets. The Pear Butter (page 51) brings sweetness to the marinade. Vinegar and soy sauce break down the meat. So does the citrus soda. It's like putting a dirty penny in a cup of Coca-Cola and it comes out clean; soda is a tenderizer. When you cook this meat, some bits get dark, some stay light, and it's nice, when you're folding it in lettuce, to have different textures and flavors going on. As Frost says, "It makes my stomach happy."

korean bbq pear butter ribs

In a blender or a food processor, combine the pear butter, soda, vinegar, white soy sauce, sesame oil, pepper, gochujang, onion, garlic, and ginger and blitz it until the marinade is smooth.

Put the short ribs in a bowl and pour the marinade over the top. Sprinkle on the sesame seeds. Cover the bowl and stow it in the fridge to marinate for at least 6 hours or preferably overnight.

Bring the ribs to room temperature, about 30 minutes.

Meanwhile, separate the lettuce into individual leaves, dunk them in ice-cold water, and pat them dry.

Pull the ribs from the marinade and wipe off most of the excess. Don't bother to pat them dry; you want some marinade on the meat but not so much that it scorches.

Fire up your grill and let the coals turn white-hot, or heat a grill pan on the stove over high heat until it's smoking. Working in batches, grill the ribs until they're charred in places and cooked through, 2 minutes on each side. Serve them on a platter with the lettuce leaves, rice, cilantro, green onions, kimchi, and chile jam.

2 Tbsp unsalted butter

8 oz [230 g] slab bacon, preferably The Best Bacon (page 65), cut into ¼ in [6 mm] lardons

4 shallots, cut into ¼ in [6 mm] thick rings

2 cups [475 ml] bone-dry hard cider

½ cup [120 ml] Calvados

2 Tbsp white soy sauce

2 by 3 in [5 by 7.5 cm] piece kombu

1 tsp red pepper flakes

2 lb [910 g] littleneck clams, purged, washed, and scrubbed

1¼ cups [15 g] fresh chervil or ¾ cup [9 g] fresh parsley and ½ cup [6 g] fresh tarragon

6 green onions, thinly sliced

Lemon slices, preferably Meyer, for serving

Crusty bread, for serving

This dish is an homage to the annual Pismo Beach Clam Festival and all the other clam-themed things that make Pismo so unique. Would that we could braise a pot of huge, shiny Pismo clams, but they're still making their comeback and need time to recuperate. Littlenecks are great, though.

For me, apples and clams—sweet and salty—mix really well. Add bacon, and a clam jus with all those flavors is a sauce you want to dunk crusty bread into. The Calvados amps up the richness and depth. Kombu brings the body.

Frost asked me why I don't chop the herbs for this one. I told her that when you use the herb leaves whole, they're toothsome and become part of the dish, rather than a thing that kind of melts into it. "Does that make sense?" I asked her. She just shouted at me, "Yeah!" She's gonna be a helluva cook.

hard cider clam bake

In a medium Dutch oven over medium heat, melt the butter. Add the bacon and cook it until the fat starts to render and it gets a little color, 5 to 6 minutes. Add the shallots and sauté them, 2 to 3 minutes. Add the cider, Calvados, white soy sauce, kombu, and red pepper flakes. Bring it up to a good, rumbling boil, then add the clams, give them a stir, slam the lid on tight, and steam them until they open, 5 to 8 minutes. Garnish the clams with the chervil and green onions. Serve them in the pot with the lemon slices, and bread on the side, if you want.

TIME
30 minutes

YIELD
2 or 3 servings

coastal

The Central Coast is vaquero country. Those Mexican cowboys gave us Santa Maria BBQ, a style that doesn't rely on rubs or sauces. It's just burning heartwood, meat, and salt. There's a purity to it that I admire.

I have three rules for grilling proteins: Air-dry them, season them correctly, and care for them assiduously. Letting a bare steak hang out in the fridge tightens the exterior, ensuring a nice sear. Full coverage with salt and pepper brings out flavor. And whether it's grass- or grain-fed, bone-in or -out, cooked on a yard kettle or stovetop grill pan, you want to use white-hot heat and baby the meat. You have to strike a balance between leaving it be and moving it around. When it's done, you rest it as long as a California shower, by which I mean ten minutes because this is a drought state, and we don't waste water here.

There's no shame in eating your meat. But eat your veggies too. I throw the salad right on top, so the steak gets seasoned with bittersweet, oniony, potato-y goodness.

To make the steak: Set a wire rack inside a sheet pan. Pat the steak dry, put it on the wire rack, and stow it, uncovered, in your fridge. Let it hang there overnight, turning it once.

Pull out the steak and very, very generously season it with kosher salt and pepper. Flabbergast yourself with how much seasoning you use and press it into the meat so it doesn't fall off during grilling. Set a wire rack inside a sheet pan and put it near the grill.

continued

Steak

1 lb [455 g] rib eye, preferably grass-fed

Plenty of kosher salt

Plenty of cranks of black pepper

Flaky salt, such as Maldon

continued

santa maria rib eye and mustard greens

TIME
40 minutes active; overnight total

YIELD
2 or 3 servings

Salad

2 Tbsp plus a pinch of kosher salt

8 oz [230 g] small red potatoes

2 Tbsp Umami Oil (page 46)

2 Tbsp rice vinegar

1 Tbsp chopped shallots

1 Tbsp sweet white miso

1 Tbsp honey

1 Tbsp white soy sauce

1 tsp Pickled Mustard Seeds (page 50)

½ tsp Oriental hot mustard powder

A couple cranks black pepper

4 oz [115 g] tender mustard greens, flowering if you can get 'em, tough stems removed and leaves halved lengthwise

DON'T BE SCARED TO MOVE FOOD AROUND WHILE COOKING. IT'S ALL ABOUT GETTING IT THE WAY YOU WANT IT.

Fire up your grill and let the coals turn white-hot, or heat a grill pan on the stove over high heat until it's smoking. Grill the rib eye until it's deeply crusted, striped from the grates, and sexy, 3 to 4 minutes per side for medium-rare.

Place it on the rack and let it rest for 10 minutes.

Slice and finish it with flaky salt.

To make the salad: Fill a large pot with 4 qt [3.8 L] of cold water and the 2 tablespoons of kosher salt. Add the potatoes and bring it to a boil, then knock the heat down to a simmer and cook until the potatoes are fork-tender, 12 to 15 minutes. Drain and run them under cold water until they're cool.

In a medium bowl, whisk together the umami oil, vinegar, shallots, miso, honey, white soy sauce, pickled mustard seeds, mustard powder, pepper, and a pinch of kosher salt until fully combined. Fold the potatoes and mustard greens into the dressing. You can serve the salad in a bowl on the side, but I like piling it on and hiding the steak under a bunch of spicy green stuff.

grilled and chilled melon

Sometimes you learn lessons when you're least expecting them. This recipe came from being hammered and hungry at the end of a shift at Benu. There was this Canary melon in the kitchen. We grilled it, scooped ice cream on top of it, and that was a go. Grilling makes melons' texture creamier, and it transforms melons' flavor, bringing out savory squash notes.

In their wild array of varieties, California melons are otherworldly. You can use any dense melon for this recipe. The uglier the exterior, the sweeter the inside. Heinously marred with a big yellow stain? That's the melon that's been lying in a field getting ripe. Grab it. If it's gushy, eat it out of hand. Get sloppy. But, for this recipe, you want a melon that's ripe but not too juicy, or it won't char correctly. Squeeze and smell before you buy. You want it to be heavy, fragrant, and firm.

To get a good grill on a melon, you start the day prior. Cut off both ends, then cut the melon lengthwise into quarters, scoop out the seeds, and cut each quarter crosswise into quarters. Put the melon pieces, skin-side down, on a sheet pan, then stow them in the fridge to dry out the flesh overnight. The leathery surface is better for grilling.

Clean the grate of your grill, so there's no old meat schmutz on it. Fire up your grill and let the coals turn white-hot, or heat a grill pan on the stove over high heat until it's smoking. If grilling, rub the grates with canola oil.

In a medium bowl, mix the sugar and Tajín-style spice. Dip the melon pieces in the mixture, liberally coating the flesh to ensure caramelization. Arrange the melon pieces, flesh-side down, on the grill and grill them until they caramelize, 5 to 10 minutes.

Transfer the melon pieces back to the sheet pan and stow them in the fridge until they're nice and cold, about 15 minutes. Sprinkle the melon with more Tajín-style spice, squeeze the lime over the top, and let your people at them.

1 large melon, such as Piel de Sapo, Canary, honeydew, or cantaloupe

Canola oil, for the grill

1 cup [200 g] sugar

2 Tbsp Tajín-Style Spice (page 68), plus more for garnish

1 lime, halved, for squeezing

TIME
30 minutes active; overnight total

YIELD
6 to 8 servings

Every coastal taqueria has a bouncy horchata made of ground rice, sweet milks, and cinnamon. When we get tacos, it's a treat for the kiddo. This is a fun way to bring that happiness home. Since I'm feeding a child, I lean toward easy, breezy, but intensely flavored desserts. Frost and I make these and keep them in the freezer instead of buying pints of ice cream.

I use short-grain rice, but you can use whatever white rice you have. It's not going to change the world if it's jasmine or basmati or short-grained. Just don't forgo the cheesecloth because that extra filter helps you nail a silky texture. And if you're a no-lactose household, sweetened and condensed coconut milk and evaporated coconut milk make an awesome paleta, too. Then buy yourself a cheap set of silicone popsicle molds. You'll use them again and again.

1 cup [200 g] white rice

½ tsp vanilla extract

¼ tsp ground cinnamon

¼ tsp ground ginger

1 cup [240 ml] sweetened condensed milk

¾ cup [180 ml] evaporated milk

horchata paletas

Soak the rice in 4 cups [945 ml] of water in a covered bowl on your countertop overnight.

Put the rice and its water in a blender with the vanilla, cinnamon, and ginger. Rip it on high for 4 minutes to smash up all the bits and pieces. You can't over-blend it, so just go for it.

Strain the mixture through a fine-mesh strainer lined with a double layer of cheesecloth into a pitcher. Pour in the sweetened condensed milk and evaporated milk and give it a good stir to blend everything well. Fill your popsicle molds, leaving some room at the top for expansion, and freeze the paletas at least overnight. Pop one out when a craving hits.

TIME
20 minutes active; 2 days total

YIELD
About 15 paletas

SPECIAL GEAR
Popsicle molds

sailing to the channel islands

Opulent green waves, emerald lagoons, big blue sky, and the Technicolor that's right below the surface—the Pacific Ocean is ravishing. Out in the Channel Islands on *Beyond Reason*, my pal's thirty-eight-foot sloop, we immerse ourselves in the pelicans' world. We coax the most out of the least ingredients in a tiny galley using a single pot. We pull fresh food from the sea. We're breaking open urchins for Sea Urchin Cacio e Pepe (page 325) and reeling in mackerel to confit them for Homemade "Tinned" Fish (page 321). It's a pirate's life for us.

I had never seen the Milky Way until I sailed the Channels. A group of eight rocks teeming with life twenty miles offshore, the Channel Islands are sacred and abundant. Seven millennia ago, the northern Channels, which are now part of Santa Barbara County, supported Chumash towns of thousands of people. Everywhere you look is something delicious you can survive on.

But we don't mess with land species here, because the northern Channels are protected. Three-quarters of Santa Cruz Island, where we mainly sail, is the property of the Nature Conservancy. The National Park Service handles the remainder. You can catch a ferry out to camp overnight with hopes of glimpsing the elusive island fox, one of sixty species of living things found exclusively on this rock.

On *Beyond Reason*, however, our focus is the sea. It starts with Captain Dan Baron, a Napa winemaker and friend of mine, loading bottles of his Complant Wine on board, playing tunes on his mandolin, and going over the safety measures with our crew of five. It's like the restaurant kitchen brigade system, the captain calling the shots so the trip goes smoothly, everyone falling into their roles, all of it meaningful. You plan for a trip like this. You make the cookies and the pastry cream ahead of time, so all you have to do to finish your Onboard Oreos (page 341) is stuff them.

You sail out past piles of fleshy harbor seals sunning on a buoy. Waves break over the bow, the boat goes squirrely, you heave up the sails. The ride out through the shipping channel can be stomach-churning. But four hours later, you're throwing anchors at Cueva Valdez, an inlet surrounded by sea caves, where sea lions bellow like monsters. It takes you aback, how Jurassic and alive the island feels. Dan and Betsy pull on scuba tanks and plunge in to pry scallops from crags so I can slice them raw and we can dip them in citronette (page 318). I'm pulling up buckets of seawater for Sea-Blanched Broccoli (page 322) and kayaking around with my rod, looking for where the rockfish lurk so I can char one on the propane grill that's clamped to the pulpit and sauce it in an aromatic green curry (page 328). The birds sound clearer. The stars are way brighter. The camaraderie is fierce.

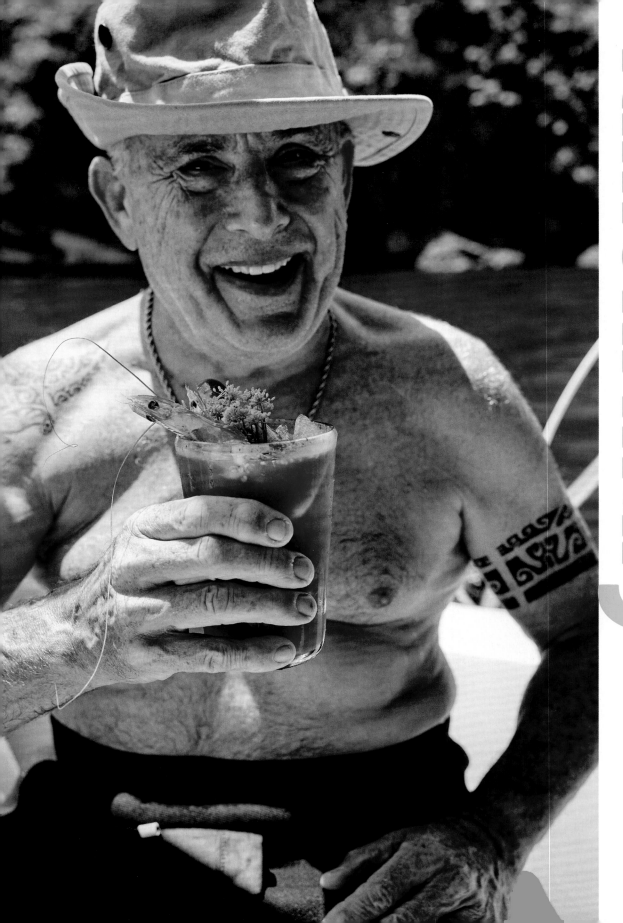

kimchi mary

I enjoy the reverence people have for Bloody Marys. There's a sport to the random garnishes people put in them, like waffles and sliders on skewers. It's hilarious, and that inspires me to make them, especially on a boat, because the Bloody Mary is a sailor's drink. In fact, the science of Bloody Mary love is real. In the cabin with the engine on, or on deck in the wind when we're sailing, the noise can affect your ability to taste. In those circumstances, biologically speaking, the flavor that makes the strongest impression is umami. Bloody Marys are full-on umami. They're also spicy and tangy. This one is all that and more. It's smoky from mezcal, funky with kimchi, and briny-sweet from head-on shrimp, which is a garnish to end them all.

To make the infused mezcal: In a lidded container, combine the mezcal and chili flakes, give it a shake, and infuse it overnight on your countertop.

To make the tomato base: In a lidded container, combine the tomato juice, dill pickle brine, kimchi brine, dill pickles, kimchi, white soy sauce, and gochujang and shake it well.

To make the shrimp: Peel and devein the shrimp but keep the heads on (see page 295).

Fill a large bowl with ice.

In a medium pot, combine 4 cups [945 ml] of water with the onion, celery, peppercorns, and bay leaf and bring it to a boil. Knock the heat down to a simmer, then add the shrimp and cook them until they're gently poached through, about 1½ minutes. Plunge the shrimp in the ice bath.

To make the Bloody Marys: Fill four 12 oz [360 ml] glasses with ice, then pour 4 oz [120 ml] of the tomato base over the ice in each glass. Top each with 2 oz [60 ml] of the infused mezcal. Garnish the drinks with the pickle spears, fennel, and shrimp. Start sipping.

Infused Mezcal

8 oz [240 ml] mezcal

3 Tbsp coarse Korean chili flakes

Tomato Base

12 oz [360 ml] tomato juice

3 oz [90 ml] dill pickle brine

2 oz [60 ml] kimchi brine, preferably from Whole Napa Cabbage Kimchi (page 58)

3 Tbsp minced dill pickles

3 Tbsp minced kimchi, preferably Whole Napa Cabbage Kimchi (page 58)

4 tsp white soy sauce

1 Tbsp gochujang

Shrimp

4 head-on shrimp

½ white onion

2 celery stalks

1 Tbsp peppercorns

1 bay leaf

Bloody Marys

4 pickle spears

4 fennel stalks with fronds, flowering, if possible

TIME
30 minutes active; overnight total

YIELD
4 drinks

1 lb [455 g] fresh, cold scallops

2 Tbsp kosher salt

¼ cup [60 ml] fresh lemon juice, preferably Meyer, or fresh lime or grapefruit juice

¼ cup [60 ml] white soy sauce

4 kumquats, seeded, very thinly sliced

1 lemon, preferably Meyer

One 2 in [5 cm] knob fresh ginger, peeled

Captain Dan likes to spend his dives hunting. The water temperature out in the Channel Islands is around 60°F [16°C] in August. Seven millimeters thick, his wetsuit makes him look like the Michelin Man, but he grabs his dive knife and goes for it. In the caves beneath these islands, huge scallops cling to crannies in the walls, cemented in by sticky filaments. With a permit, you can take thirty-five of them a day, and Dan comes up with a full net. Fresh, cold, and raw, they taste like sweet ocean.

Store-bought scallops are also tasty if they're bristling fresh. Ask a trusted fishmonger if you can eat theirs raw, and if they say yes, do. Keep them iced in your fridge until you slice them and prepare them fast. Scallops aren't going to wait overnight for you. Get them, make them, and eat them right away. Citronette honors these delicious, stubborn mollusks, and it will change the way you eat other raw foods. Toss it with thinly sliced squash, mushrooms, and other raw veg, and pour it over rice. It's a good thing to have in your tool kit.

raw scallops with citronette

Chill a plate in your fridge. Set a wire rack inside a sheet pan.

Clean your scallops by dunking them in a large bowl filled with 4 qt [3.8 L] of ice water and the kosher salt and agitating them gently. Let them firm up in the salted ice water for 3 to 5 minutes, then pull them out, pat them dry, and rest them on the wire rack in the fridge.

In a small bowl, whisk together the lemon juice and white soy sauce. Add the kumquats and let them marinate for 15 minutes.

Using a very sharp knife, at a 45-degree angle, cut the scallops into ¼ in [6 mm] thick slices. Arrange the scallops, slices overlapping like fallen dominoes, on the chilled plate. Zest the lemon and grate the ginger over the top, then serve the scallops right away, with the citronette on the side for dipping.

TIME
25 minutes

YIELD
4 servings

coastal

On our last voyage, not many rockfish were biting, but the mackerel sure were, their silver skin flashing in the night amid phosphorescent squid. You can passively fish and get dinner, just plucking them out of the ocean when they swarm the bait. Those little oily guys bring a ton of flavor and nutrition to the table; it feels good when you can give them the culinary respect they deserve. This dish came together organically. I saw what I caught, took stock of what we had onboard, and made something work. Out at sea, less is more. Just a few ingredients knocked it out of the park. If you catch these guys, I assume you know how to butterfly them. On land, luckily, you don't have to butterfly your own. Ask your fishmonger to do it for you, and the rest is a snap.

Season the fish inside and out with the salt and let them hang out that way for 15 minutes, so the salt penetrates. Put the fish in a pot wide enough to lay them flat, then add the garlic and fennel fronds, and pour the oil over the top to cover them. Bring the pot up to a simmer over medium heat, then immediately kill the heat. Let the fish sit in the oil for 1 hour. Serve them with crusty bread on the side.

4 small mackerels or sardines, about 4 oz [115 g] each, butterflied

2 tsp kosher salt

8 garlic cloves, peeled

4 cups [128 g] fennel fronds

2 cups [475 ml] olive oil

Crusty bread, for serving

homemade "tinned" fish

TIME
15 minutes active;
1½ hours total

YIELD
2 servings

2 big heads broccoli

8 qt [7.5 L] clean seawater or
8 qt [7.5 L] tap water and
4 Tbsp [40 g] kosher salt

1 Tbsp toasted white sesame
seeds

2 tsp toasted sesame oil

sea-blanched broccoli

On a boat, fresh veg is a nice reprieve from the packaged snack foods you're always grabbing from the galley. It's also just fun to dunk a clean bucket into the ocean and pull it up sloshing with seawater. If you're not out at sea, the concept is the same: Salt the blanching water like it's the ocean, which is basically how you would salt it for pasta water. Keep the salt coming, even in the ice bath. Color is the key to successful blanching; you're watching for the broccoli to pop to a bright green. The sesame is a riff on the type of flavor you get with Korean banchan or at a Japanese omakase. It adds elegance to an easy side dish.

Slice the crowns off the broccoli and pull them apart to make uniform-size florets. Reserve the stems for another use, like cutting them into matchsticks to swipe in Herby Buttermilk Ranch Dip (page 116).

Fill a bowl with plenty of ice and 4 qt [3.8 L] of clean, clear seawater or 4 qt [3.8 L] of tap water and 2 tablespoons of the salt.

In a large stockpot, bring 4 qt [3.8 L] of seawater or 4 qt [3.8 L] of tap water and the remaining 2 tablespoons of salt to a boil. Add the broccoli, give it a stir to submerge it, and watch it until it turns an eye-popping green, about 3 minutes. Drain it in a colander, then plunge it immediately into the salted ice bath. When the broccoli is cool, about 1 minute, drain it into a colander, and let it drip dry.

Put the broccoli in a serving bowl, add the sesame seeds and sesame oil, and zhush it until it's well coated.

TIME
15 minutes

YIELD
4 to 6 servings

coastal

I'm a firm believer that fresh seafood and cheese don't go together—except in this recipe. The urchin butter brings that caramelly Maillard effect. The key to making it is pliable butter, so make sure it's at room temperature and soft before you work with it. Other than that, the recipe is easy, and it makes one sexy dish. You're eating the reproductive glands of a weird sea creature, the sharp cheese melding with the silky, saline urchin tongues barely warmed from the hot pasta. Out in the Channel Islands, with the proper permits, we scuba or free dive the rock walls, pulling urchins from the sea, and cracking into them, trying to avoid embedding spines in our skin. You have to respect a creature covered in sharps, and the work of hunting and foraging for them makes the dish all the more satisfying.

sea urchin cacio e pepe

Sea Urchin Butter

5 Tbsp [75 g] unsalted butter, at room temperature

8 sea urchin tongues

Pinch of sea salt

Pasta

2 Tbsp kosher salt

12 oz [340 g] fresh or dried spaghetti

2 tsp freshly cracked black pepper

1 Tbsp white soy sauce

¾ cup [25 g] freshly grated Parmesan cheese

½ cup [30 g] freshly grated pecorino romano cheese

10 sea urchin tongues

To make the sea urchin butter: In a small bowl, whisk together the butter, sea urchin tongues, and salt, breaking up the tongues until they're fully incorporated. Form the urchin butter into a log, wrap it in plastic wrap or wax paper, and stow it in the fridge.

To make the pasta: In a large pot, combine 4 qt [3.8 L] of water with the salt and bring it to a boil. Add the pasta and cook it until al dente. Reserve 1 cup [240 ml] of the pasta water, then drain the pasta and return it to the pot.

In a small saucepan over medium heat, melt 3 tablespoons of the sea urchin butter. Add the pepper and let the butter caramelize, about 5 minutes. Pour this over the pasta, then add the white soy sauce and stir it with a wooden spoon until the pasta is coated and the sauce thickens. If the pasta is clumping, add the reserved pasta water, a couple tablespoons at a time. Add the remaining 2 tablespoons of sea urchin butter, the Parmesan, and the pecorino romano and stir until it's creamy, adding pasta water again if it needs loosening up. Put the pasta in a big bowl or portion it, arrange the remaining urchin tongues over the top, and serve it immediately.

TIME
30 minutes

YIELD
4 servings

rockfish curry

2 Tbsp coconut oil

6 oz [170 g] chopped shallots

6 oz [170 g] chopped fresh ginger

6 garlic cloves, chopped

4 lemongrass stalks, chopped

3 or 4 serrano chiles, chopped

2 Tbsp toasted white sesame seeds

2 Tbsp whole coriander seeds

2 Tbsp whole cumin seeds

2 star anise pods

½ cinnamon stick

Two 14 oz [415 ml] cans coconut milk

6 makrut lime leaves

Peel of 2 limes, pith removed

¼ cup [60 ml] white soy sauce, plus more as needed

1 whole, cleaned rockfish or snapper, 1½ to 2 lb [680 to 910 g]

2 Tbsp canola oil

2 tsp kosher salt

6 baby bok choys

Steamed short-grain white rice, for serving

TIME
1 hour 15 minutes

YIELD
4 servings

On the boat, the heady scent of this Thai-style green curry fills the cabin and makes everyone go nuts. Firm and flaky yet subtle, Pacific rockfish absorbs all that flavor beautifully, and I love to catch them. They just hang out on a reef and wait for something to make them mad enough to strike, so you can drop some squid on a hook and easily pull up a monster. You never know which you'll get because there are dozens of types. Bocaccio, Canary, Chilipepper rockfish; Vermilion rockfish, tinted red from eating urchins and shrimp—the diversity is part of the adventure. On the East Coast, black bass or red snapper are good substitutes. Out sailing, we clean the fish ourselves, but to save yourself the trouble, ask your fishmonger to do it for you.

In a medium saucepan over medium-high heat, melt the coconut oil. Add the shallots, ginger, garlic, lemongrass, and serrano chiles and sauté them until you can really smell them, about 5 minutes. Add the sesame seeds, coriander seeds, cumin seeds, star anise, and cinnamon stick and toast them, stirring, for 5 minutes. Add the coconut milk and bring it to a boil. Knock the heat down to a simmer and cook for 30 minutes. Hand-crush the lime leaves, then add them, along with the lime peels, to the broth and cook them until they turn drab, 3 minutes. Immediately strain the broth through a chinois into a clean pot, then stir in the white soy sauce, cover the pot, and keep it warm while you grill the fish.

Pat the fish dry inside and out. With your knife at a 45-degree angle, make three deep scores all the way down to the rib, on each side of the fish, from the top fin to the belly. This will ensure it cooks all the way through on the grill. Brush the exterior with the canola oil and season it all over, inside and out, with the salt.

Build a medium-hot fire in your grill or heat a grill pan on the stovetop to medium-high. Add the fish and grill it, using a fish spatula to flip it and cook it on all sides, including the top and bottom of the head, until the skin is crispy and the meat is white all the way through, 10 to 15 minutes total.

Cut the baby bok choy in half and rinse out the sand. Add the bok choy to the strained curry, then bring the curry back to a simmer over medium heat and cook the bok choy until it's just wilted, about 5 minutes. Place the fish in a shallow serving bowl, ladle the curry and bok choy all over it, and serve it with rice on the side.

WALLY KLUHGERS, QUEEN OF HEARTS SPORTFISHING

A classic boat captain, Wally likes to be efficient, catch fish, smoke cigarettes, and talk trash. He guides sportfishing and crabbing expeditions out of Half Moon Bay's Pillar Point Harbor aboard the *Queen of Hearts*, a fifty-foot, wooden-hulled vessel with its name painted on its blue-and-white sides. Wally knows how to get it done. An East Coaster like me, he spent eight seasons out on the *Queen of Hearts* before buying it from its previous owner, and he's full of salty knowledge. He'll tell you himself he's a great fisherman. He'll steal your rod and pull up a lingcod half the size of his body with total nonchalance. But, like the best of his class of operators, his real talent is helping other people get their catch: rockfish, salmon, Dungeness crab—whatever you want to grab and eat. With twenty people onboard, imagine how dynamic Wally has to be in order to make sure everyone stays safe and gets their catch. Maybe three of those people know how to fish. The rest are completely awash with a rod, and it's Wally's job to get their lines off the rocks, figure out who's tangled with whom, and get people some fish in the short time they have out there. The crabbing trips are especially intense. One year, I went out with just him and his crew on New Year's Eve, the last day of the season. The seas were rocking, the *Queen of Hearts* was slamming down between breaks, and my stress level was off the charts—until I looked at Wally. He was just ripping smokes and chilling, like it was nothing. That calmed me right down. Afterwards, he told me, "That's the worst I've ever seen it, and we shouldn't have been out there." At least he waited until we got back to the dock to say it.

On my first outing with my fellow cooks at Benu, we went to Tadich Grill, the state's oldest restaurant, and ate cioppino. A cornucopia of whatever Gold Rush–era Genoese immigrants fished from the Pacific, that stew gave me insight into the cooking of Old California. The stupid bibs we wore just made it better.

My riff gets fire and funk from kimchi. Not long after the Genoese, Korean communities started coming to California in numbers. This recipe is my way of taking influences from these Californian cooks who have come before me to make a dish from what's living around us.

On the northern Central Coast, Dungeness crab season runs from November to July. Farther south, spiny lobsters come in from October to March. But use the seafood available near you. Blue crabs, American lobster, even precooked snow crab legs—it's all good.

When you're cooking in a giant pot, taste as you go. You start with a fumet, then infuse your homemade fish stock with layers of other seafood, bringing all these delicious flavors to the party. With that kimchi spark, this cioppino is even more fun to eat, bib or not.

kimchioppino

To make the fumet: Set a ladle and a bowl of clean water next to the stove.

Rinse the bones well, then cut them into 2 in [5 cm] chunks and put them in a medium Dutch oven with 10 cups [2.4 L] of water, the clam juice, fennel, onion, garlic, and salt. Bring the stock to a boil, then knock the heat down to a simmer, and cook it, skimming off any foam with the ladle and rinsing the ladle in the water bowl, for 15 minutes. Add the coriander seeds, white peppercorns, fennel seeds, black pepper, and bay leaves. Simmer the stock for 1 hour, or until it's reduced to about 6 cups [1.4 L]. Do not let it boil, or it will cloud up. You want it rich and deep but not murky. Add the parsley and tarragon, stir for 30 seconds, and immediately kill the heat. Strain the stock through a chinois into a bowl.

continued

ASK YOUR FISHMONGER FOR SKELETONS LEFT OVER FROM FILLETING. USE HEADS, TAILS, AND ALL. THE COLLAGEN ADDS BODY TO THE STEW.

Fumet

2 lb [910 g] bones from white-fleshed fish, like halibut or rockfish

1 cup [240 ml] bottled clam juice

1 large fennel bulb, quartered

1 large white onion, quartered

6 garlic cloves, peeled

Pinch of kosher salt

1 tsp whole coriander seeds

1 tsp white peppercorns

½ tsp whole fennel seeds

½ tsp freshly ground black pepper

2 bay leaves

4 fresh parsley sprigs

4 fresh tarragon sprigs

continued

TIME
3½ hours

YIELD
8 servings

SPECIAL GEAR
Mondo-size stockpot

Kimchioppino

1 Dungeness crab or 2 spiny lobsters, one 1 lb [455 g] American lobster, 3 or 4 blue crabs, or 1 lb [455 g] precooked snow crab legs (see note opposite)

¼ cup [60 ml] extra-virgin olive oil

1 Tbsp unsalted butter

1 white onion, halved and cut lengthwise into ⅛ in [3 mm] thick slices

1 fennel bulb, halved and cut lengthwise into ⅛ in [3 mm] thick slices, fronds reserved

6 garlic cloves, very thinly sliced

4 oz [115 g] tomato paste

1½ tsp red pepper flakes, plus more as needed

1½ cups [350 g] chopped kimchi, preferably Whole Napa Cabbage Kimchi (page 58)

1 cup [240 ml] kimchi brine, preferably from Whole Napa Cabbage Kimchi (page 58)

1 cup [250 g] Oven-Dried Tomatoes (page 67)

1 cup [240 ml] dry white wine

6 cups [1.4 L] Fumet (page 337), warm

Fat pinch of kosher salt

1 lb [455 g] littleneck clams (about 1 dozen clams)

1 lb [455 g] mussels, rinsed and debearded (see note)

1 lb [455 g] white-fleshed, bone-in fish, like halibut or rockfish, cut into 1 in [2.5 cm] chunks

1 lb [455 g] shrimp, preferably head-on, peeled and deveined (see page 295)

Country Toast (page 262), for serving

To make the kimchioppino: Ask your fishmonger to dispatch the Dungeness crab, or to do it yourself the most humane way, put it in the freezer for 15 to 20 minutes to knock it unconscious. Flip the crab onto its back with the pincers facing you and shove the tip of your sharpest knife into its body at the tip of the triangular piece that forms its abdomen. Force your knife blade downward through the head and between the eyes. Turn the crab around, pull up the triangular abdomen, stick your knife under the base of the triangle between the top shell and the body, and yank the crab free of its top shell. Cut it in half, pull the gills off, and clean the guts out.

In the biggest pot you've got over medium heat, heat the olive oil and butter until the butter stops frothing. Add the onion and fennel and sauté them until they're translucent, about 5 minutes. Add the garlic and cook it for 2 minutes. Add the tomato paste and red pepper flakes and cook them, stirring, until the tomato paste caramelizes, turning from Marlboro red to deep maroon, 7 to 10 minutes. Stir in the kimchi, kimchi brine, and oven-dried tomatoes. Add the wine, then crank up the heat and bring it to a boil, scraping to deglaze the pot. Add the fumet and salt, then bring it back to a boil. Knock the heat down to a simmer, cover it with the lid cracked to let out the steam, and cook for 35 to 40 minutes, just letting it love on itself. Add the crab, crank the heat to medium-high, and cook for 10 minutes. Add the clams and cook them for 2 minutes. Add the mussels and cook until they start to open, 3 to 4 minutes. Add the fish and cook for 4 minutes. Lay the shrimp on top and bring it to a boil, then immediately kill the heat and cover the pot so the shrimp steams, 5 to 10 minutes. Dress the broth with the reserved fennel fronds. Serve it with country toast. Now you're living.

THE BEARD IS A THREAD BETWEEN THE SHELLS THAT CLINGS TO ROCKS. REMOVE IT. SQUEEZE ANY OPEN MUSSELS. IF THEY DON'T SHUT, THEY'RE DEAD. CHUCK 'EM.

To swap in spiny or American lobster: Ask your fishmonger to dispatch the lobster, or to do it yourself the most humane way, put the lobster in the freezer for 15 to 20 minutes to knock it unconscious. Then, starting with the lobster's eyes facing you, blast the tip of a sharp knife straight down into the shell about a centimeter behind the eyes, and force the blade downward all the way through the front of the head between the eyes. Grip the head and tail with a kitchen towel and twist the tail to pull it off. Dunk the tail in ice-cold water and agitate it to clean it. Lay it on a cutting board upside down and, using kitchen shears, cut down its length on either side where the undercarriage meets the shell. Tear away the undercarriage to expose the meat. With a spoon, scrape along the length of the shell under the meat. Holding the tail flap, pull the meat from shell. This will also devein it. If you're working with American lobster, crack the raw claws and pull out the meat. Clean the meat in ice-cold water, then pat it dry and cut it into ½ in [13 mm] thick slices. Add it at the end to steam along with the shrimp.

To swap in precooked snow crab legs: If they're frozen, thaw them in the fridge, then add them when you add your shrimp.

To swap in blue crabs: Add them in whole before you add the other seafood and let them die in that beautiful broth. When I'm ready to go, that's how I want to do it. Just leave me to perish in a perfect fumet.

Pan spray, if needed

1 lb [455 g] thin salted pretzels

1 cup [226 g] unsalted butter

12 oz [340 g] marshmallows

Pinch of kosher salt

Hide these from yourself, your significant other, your children, your neighbors, and the general world, because they're horrifying. We were having a riff in the restaurant, and we decided to come up with the most mega-stoner snack imaginable. How do you make a one-stop shop of sweet, salty, crunchy, sticky, and chewy? That's Rice Krispies, but then you also need savory. I thought: What can you break down to the size of Rice Krispies and cook similarly? Pretzels won out. Eat the whole tray in your underwear watching Netflix, or lying on the deck of a boat as it rolls on its anchors, watching stars shoot across the nighttime sky. There's no culinary genius behind it. It's just got-stoned-and-gotta-eat food. Pretzels, butter, and marshmallows, baby. That's it.

pretzel crispies

Line a sheet pan with a silicone mat or parchment paper; if using parchment, lightly coat it with pan spray.

Working in batches as needed, in a food processor, pulse the pretzels ten to twenty times until they're crumbs with a few larger chunks, wabi-sabi style.

In a medium Dutch oven over medium-high heat, melt the butter. When it stops frothing, knock the heat down to medium, add the marshmallows, and stir with a rubber spatula until they're melted, 2 to 3 minutes. Add the pretzels and stir until they're well coated. Spread the mixture on the prepared sheet pan. Lay another silicone mat or another piece of parchment coated with pan spray upside down on top of the crispies and use a rolling pin to roll it out to about ⅛ in [3 mm] thick. Peel the parchment off the top, finish it with a pinch of salt, and let it cool before slicing and eating it, or just scarf it up warm from the pan.

NO FOOD PROCESSOR? STAB A COUPLE HOLES IN THE PRETZEL BAG TO DEFLATE IT AND POUND THE HECK OUT OF IT WITH YOUR FISTS.

NO ROLLING PIN? USE THE PAN SPRAY CAN AS A ROLLING PIN, OR JUST PUSH IT TOWARD THE EDGES WITH YOUR FINGERS.

TIME
20 minutes

YIELD
Feeds a dozen crewmates or 1 mega-stoned stowaway

Oreos are such a delicious snack, but they're not big enough. If you make them yourself, they can be twice as large. Baking, creaming, and piping are fun, hands-on techniques, and you get to create something nostalgic, but also give it more beauty and class. Plus, I like recipes that take the mystique out of packaged goods. You'd think you could never make them yourself, and then it turns out to be incredibly straightforward. If you're boarding a boat, bake the cookies ahead of time and tuck them into a snug airtight container where they won't jostle and break. Bring the two pastry creams along in piping bags. Dessert is ready onboard as fast as you can cut the bags' tips and fill your cookies.

To make the cookies: In a stand mixer fitted with the paddle attachment, a food processor, or a large bowl with a whisk, mix the flour, granulated sugar, cocoa powder, baking soda, baking powder, and salt together until they're well combined. Add the butter and egg and mix the dough until it just comes together, about 5 minutes. Place a big piece of plastic wrap on a work surface, drop the dough onto it, and form it into a log about 2 in [5 cm] in diameter. Wrap the log, twisting the ends of the plastic to tighten it, and chill the dough for at least 1 hour.

Preheat the oven to 375°F [190°C]. Line a sheet pan with a silicone mat or parchment paper; if using parchment, lightly coat it with pan spray.

Slice the log into ⅛ in [3 mm] thick cookies and arrange them on the prepared sheet pan 1½ in [4 cm] apart. Bake them for 8 minutes, then check them by pressing a few with your finger. If the cookies resist denting, they're done. Repeat with the remaining dough. Cool to room temperature.

continued

onboard oreos

Cookies

1⅓ cups [185 g] all-purpose flour

¾ cup [150 g] granulated sugar

½ cup [40 g] cocoa powder

1 tsp baking soda

¼ tsp baking powder

¼ tsp kosher salt

10 Tbsp [150 g] unsalted butter, cut into small pieces, at cool room temperature

1 large egg, at room temperature

Pan spray, if needed

continued

TIME
45 minutes active;
1 hour 45 minutes total

YIELD
12 to 16 cookies

SPECIAL GEAR
2 piping bags and tips

Pastry Cream

1 cup [226 g] unsalted butter, at room temperature

2½ tsp vanilla extract

2 cups [240 g] powdered sugar

⅛ tsp kosher salt

2 Tbsp black sesame powder

GET BLACK SESAME POWDER AT A KOREAN GROCERY STORE OR ONLINE.

To make the pastry cream: In a stand mixer fitted with the paddle attachment, a food processor, or a large bowl with eggbeaters, beat the butter, vanilla, powdered sugar, and salt until light and fluffy, 3 to 5 minutes. Do not overmix it. You will see the pastry cream change from glossy to pale, and it will stand up in soft peaks. Stop right then.

Place tips inside two uncut piping bags. Transfer half the pastry cream to a piping bag. Transfer the other half to a medium bowl, and with a rubber spatula, fold in the black sesame powder until it's well incorporated. Transfer the sesame pastry cream to the other piping bag. Holding one piping bag closed at its opening, swing it around to force the pastry cream into the tip end. Twist and tie the bag closed, cut the end of the bag around the tip, and pipe the pastry cream double-stuffed style, about ¼ in [6 mm] thick, onto a quarter of the cookies. Top the cream with another quarter of the cookies. Then repeat with the other piping bag and the remaining cookies.

back home with the kid

After our whirlwind of movement and motion, we're back in that cozy place. We come home after traveling with that feeling of, "Wow, we just did something." We drop our bags, hit the couch, and return to the sweet adventure of daily life. A road trip is so magnificent, but we're living this home life every day, and it's the cherry on top. The most beautiful thing we do is sit down and have a meal with people we love. With wholesome, nourishing, and good-time recipes, this chapter is about that connection. It's also about how you get a six-year-old to eat her vegetables.

There are a couple of things in my journey as a parent that have hit me hard. Here's one: Time is fleeting, and patience is tested. We get tired and rocked from the world and the day's events, but we also want to be great parents. There are pitfalls where you can mess up and judge yourself. But, in all of that, the best thing you can do for your child is to remember what it was like to be a kid yourself. For me, the emotions that come from that are strong. When I can take a moment through all the madness, there are memories that stick with me of being at home cooking in the kitchen with my mom or dad, eating pumpkin bread covered in butter and salt (page 350). Moments like that are core. Gooey queso fundido for swiping beefy taquitos (page 364); a sheet-pan pizza loaded up with kid-friendly stuff (page 361)—these recipes bring love to the table. But if something

happens in the middle of cooking, it's OK to stop what you're doing and just be with someone who needs you. It's a lesson I am teaching myself after years of giving it all away in Michelin kitchens: Be here now. Ram Dass your life a little bit.

The other day, I worked, went for a big run, then picked up Frost from school, and I was taking a moment for myself, catching up on emails and reading a book. She came in and asked, "Will you come play soccer?" I said, "No, I'm in the middle of things." But what was I really doing? Emailing? I stopped myself, went out there, and gave the kids a run for their money at soccer. That's my kind of experience now. Everything else can wait.

This chapter echoes that story. It's nourishing because those formative moments add up. At the end of the Central Coast journey, these recipes are scrumptious and full: a Fish Stick Hand Roll Bar (page 358), Matcha Mochi Waffles with raspberry coulis and whipped mascarpone (page 367), and a Watermelon Agua Fresca (page 349) to wash it all down. I hope you get to cook them, and I hope there's zero stress in doing it and that you have a fun time. But if it doesn't happen, and you can't cook right now, that's OK, too, because nothing is as important as dropping everything when you need to and being with your people, whoever your people may be.

Taquerias all have these big jars full of wild colors and flavors: hibiscus, tamarind, pineapple. I love going for tacos made from face parts and getting a sweet liquid treat as well. Watermelon agua fresca is so simple, hydrating, and tasty. Buy a big, ripe melon, and you'll need half of it, or score a sweet, little baby, and you'll use it all up. (Pickle the rind, if you want, using the method for Pickled Onions, page 48.) Be careful to remove the seeds, though if some end up blitzed in the blender, no worries; you're straining it afterwards anyway. For kids, just pour a glass over ice. For grown-ups, you can do a Tajín-Style Spice (page 68) rim and a lime wedge, throw a sliced serrano chile in the blender for some heat, or garnish a glass with a Genovese basil sprig—whatever you think is delicious.

1 lime, plus 1 lime wedge, for garnish, if you want

6 cups [915 g] watermelon chunks

¼ cup [50 g] sugar

Tajín-Style Spice (page 68), for garnish, if you want

Using a sharp paring knife, cut the top and bottom off the lime, then cut down between the peel and the pulp all the way around the fruit to remove all the peel. (Save the peel for the lime powder for Tajín-Style Spice, page 68.) Cut the lime pulp into chunks. Throw it in the blender with the watermelon and sugar and blitz it until it's smooth. Strain the agua fresca through a fine-mesh strainer into a mason jar and stow it in the fridge. Watermelon agua fresca tends to separate, so when you're ready to serve it, give it a good shake. If you're doing the Tajín-style spice rim, place some of the spice on a small plate. Wipe the rim of a glass with the lime wedge, and roll the rim in the spice so it sticks. Fill the glass with ice and pour the agua fresca over the top. Garnish the glass with the lime wedge. The agua fresca keeps, in the fridge in a jar or bottle, for up to 3 days.

watermelon agua fresca

TIME
10 minutes

YIELD
4 to 5 cups [945 ml to 1.2 L]

Pan spray

1 small sugar or pie pumpkin, 1½ to 2 lb [680 g to 910 g]

½ cup [113 g] unsalted butter, plus more for serving

2 large eggs

½ cup [100 g] packed dark brown sugar

½ cup [100 g] granulated sugar

2 tsp molasses

1½ cups [210 g] all-purpose flour

1 tsp baking soda

1 tsp ground ginger

½ tsp ground cinnamon

½ tsp freshly ground cardamom

½ tsp kosher salt

½ cup [60 g] chopped pecans

½ cup [45 g] chopped crystallized ginger

Flaky salt, such as Maldon

TIME
30 minutes active; 2 hours 15 minutes total

YIELD
1 loaf

I fell into a love affair with pumpkin bread when I happened to buy a hunk from a stand at the Santa Cruz Community Farmers' Market (see page 355). It was so pumpkin-y and molasses-y. I'm always looking for a reason to blast some butter into my face, and pumpkin bread is a justification. So, I got inspired and made my own, hard-roasting fresh sugar pumpkin and swapping the ubiquitous pumpkin-spice flavor for a hot-spicy vibe. Crystallized ginger and pecans bring texture and booming flavor. Cut a slice fresh off the caramelly, hot loaf, or grill it in a pan later. Either way, throw on a melty knob of butter, and finish it with crunchy, flaky sea salt. This is not just "sit there" bread. It's popping.

pumpkin bread with salty butter

Preheat the oven to 350°F [180°C]. Lightly coat a 9 by 5 in [23 by 13 cm] loaf pan with pan spray.

Halve the pumpkin and scoop out the seeds. Salt and roast the seeds for a snack, if you want. Place the pumpkin, flesh-side down, on a sheet pan. Use a fork to poke a bunch of holes in the pumpkin and bake it until it's soft and caramelly, 45 minutes to 1 hour. Cool it to room temperature, then scrape all the caramelized bits and velvety flesh into a measuring cup. You need 1 cup [225 g] of purée. You can reserve the rest to top oatmeal, but if you're like me, you'll just spoon it up and eat it there and then. Leave the oven on.

In a small saucepan over medium-high heat, heat the butter until it stops foaming. Continue cooking it, stirring, for 2 to 3 minutes more, or until it's dark brown and fragrant. Cool it to room temperature.

In a medium bowl, whisk together 1 cup [225 g] of the pumpkin purée, the browned and cooled butter, the eggs, brown sugar, granulated sugar, molasses, and ¼ cup [60 ml] of water until smooth.

In another medium bowl, whisk together the flour, baking soda, ground ginger, cinnamon, cardamom, and kosher salt. With a rubber spatula, gently fold this mixture into the pumpkin mixture until everything is well incorporated. Fold in the pecans and crystalized ginger. Transfer the batter to the prepared loaf pan. Slam the pan on the counter once or twice to knock out the air and even the top. Bake the bread for 30 minutes, then rotate the pan and continue baking for about 30 minutes more, or until a cake tester or fork inserted in the center comes out clean. Cool it for 5 minutes before popping it out of the pan.

Cut a nice, 2 in [5 cm] slice, slather on butter, and finish it with flaky salt.

If you want to heat it the next day, slather on butter, then grill it, butter-side down, in a cast-iron pan over medium-high heat until it's golden, 2 to 3 minutes, and finish it with flaky salt. It keeps, tightly wrapped in plastic wrap on the countertop, for up to 4 days, in the fridge for up to 1 week, or in the freezer for up to 1 month.

2 Tbsp Umami Oil (page 46)

1 lb [455 g] green beans, ends trimmed

8 oz [230 g] shishito peppers

½ cup [150 g] ground pork

1 tsp sesame oil

3 garlic cloves, thinly sliced

3 dried chiles de árbol, seeds removed and torn into small pieces

4 oz [115 g] shiitake mushrooms, halved and hard stem bulbs removed

2 Tbsp Chile Jam (page 60)

1 Tbsp dark soy sauce

Green beans hold a special place in my heart. At my grandmother's farm, I could always find her sitting on the porch, wielding an ancient, bowed-out paring knife and splitting green beans. She would just blast them all day long. God bless her soul, then she'd boil the life out of them. But when I'm processing peak-season California green beans, I still always think of her.

The technique here is thanks to the chefs at California's Szechuan restaurants. Dry frying is a way of maximizing flavor. You grab a wok and fry stuff in super hot oil without any batter, so the outside burns in places and the inside heats up, concentrating the taste. You want all your mise en place organized before you start because the beans cook fast, and the rest is simple, if you're ready to go. Then you sit back, tolerate a little char, and let the flavors marry on their own.

dry-fried green beans

Heat a wok or a 9 in [23 cm] cast-iron pan over high heat. Add the umami oil, and when it's smoking, add the green beans and shishito peppers. Leave them alone to char on one side, about 5 minutes, before flipping them and charring the other side, 5 minutes more. Transfer them to a bowl. Add the ground pork and sesame oil to the wok and cook it, using a wok spatula or wooden spoon, to break up the meat, for 2 minutes. Add the garlic and chiles de árbol, and cook them until the garlic is toasted, 1 minute. Add the mushrooms and cook for 2 minutes. Return the green beans and shishito peppers to the wok, then add the chile jam and dark soy sauce. Mix well to coat everything, pull it from the heat, and serve it right away.

TIME
20 minutes

YIELD
4 servings

SPECIAL GEAR
Wok

DOWNTOWN SANTA CRUZ
COMMUNITY
FARMERS' MARKET

Frost going bananas eating a cone from The Penny Ice Creamery, ice cream melting down her arm. Frost chomping on an Asian pear from Kashiwase Farms. Frost snacking on a Dos Hermanos pupusa and dancing to the tunes strummed by some busking guitarist. It's so rad to take your kid to a farmers' market here. You can't beat them for their diversity of products, and Santa Cruz's are just about the best. The town is located at an agricultural crossroads, between Driscoll and the other big-ag operations of Watsonville and the family-owned micro-plots that stake out their place in all the little zones and corners.

The mission of the Santa Cruz Community Farmers' Markets is to showcase the artisan producers, and it's cool to give my kid a couple of bucks to hand to a vendor and show her how those dollars can go to the right place: Four Sisters Farm's purslane, miner's lettuce, and other soft herbs; persimmons from fifth-generation Mora Family Farms; Vasquez Farm's strawberries and blueberries from second-generation growers whose parents came up from Jalisco and San Luis Potosi. Frost has been coming to this market since she was strapped to my chest in an Ergobaby. When we're in the truck cruising the coast, we always stop at any and all markets on the way, because in California, that's where so much of local life goes on. From the north's hardier rutabagas and sweet potatoes to the guavas and other tropical fruits of southern growers, each market beats its own drum. We meet the people growing the creamiest avocados or the most sought-after citrus, but we also find flower farmers, food vendors, musicians, and small-batch craftspeople, who've fired mugs and made soaps in their own backyards. We get to sink a bit into each coastal community.

Kimchi Mayo

1 cup [220 g] The Best Mayonnaise (page 45) or Kewpie

¼ cup [60 g] hand-squeezed, chopped kimchi, preferably Whole Napa Cabbage Kimchi (page 58)

Marinated Cucumber

½ cup [120 ml] seasoned rice vinegar

¼ cup [60 ml] white soy sauce

2 Tbsp sugar

1 tsp toasted sesame oil

1 tsp freshly ground black pepper

2 English cucumbers

continued

fish stick hand roll bar

On a lake-flat day, I paddled a good mile and a half out to the halibut grounds. I was the only idiot in a kayak, fishing amid huge boats. Fishermen are notoriously competitive, but I could talk to folks, because you can only do so much damage in a kayak. When a fellow fisherman saw I wasn't catching anything, he yelled, "Do you have live squid?" He heaved a bag of seawater and squid at me, and with that, I started knocking 'em dead. There's nothing like pulling up a twenty-eight-inch halibut and knocking it out with a baseball bat while it's thrashing in your lap on a kayak.

When I got back to shore, I dreamed up this DIY party platter for me and the kid and some friends. The key is to have your nori and all your garnishes prepped before you fry, so the fish is hot when folks build their bites. You can also throw pickled ginger, malt vinegar, Fermented Hot Sauce (page 62), even ketchup on the table. Whatever floats your boat.

To make the kimchi mayo: In a small bowl, mix the mayonnaise and kimchi. It keeps, in the fridge in an airtight container, for up to 3 days.

To make the marinated cucumber: In a medium bowl, whisk together the vinegar, white soy sauce, sugar, sesame oil, and pepper until the sugar is dissolved. Peel half the skin from the cukes in stripes, then use a mandoline to cut them into paper-thin slices right into the bowl. Stir to coat them in the marinade, then stow them in the fridge to marinate for 45 minutes.

continued

TIME
1 hour 15 minutes

YIELD
6 servings

Fish Sticks

1½ lb [680 g] boneless, skinless halibut, cod, or haddock fillets

Kosher salt

Freshly ground black pepper

1 cup [120 g] Wondra flour

4 large eggs, beaten

2 cups [160 g] panko

Canola oil, for frying

Hand Rolls

12 seasoned, roasted nori sheets

3 cups [540 g] cooked short-grain rice

2 bunches green onions, thinly sliced, for garnish

Everything Seasoning (page 71), for garnish

To make the fish sticks: Set a wire rack inside a sheet pan. Cut the fillets crosswise into 1 in [2.5 cm] wide fish sticks. Season them generously with salt and pepper, then lay them on the wire rack and put them in the fridge to chill for 30 minutes.

Place the Wondra flour in one bowl, the eggs in a second bowl, and half the panko in a third bowl. Working with two fish sticks at time, dredge all the fish sticks in the flour, shaking them off and placing them back on the wire rack. Working with two fish sticks at a time, dredge half the fish sticks in the egg, letting the excess egg drip off, then dredge them in the panko, and return them to the wire rack. Add the remaining panko to its bowl, and dredge the remainder of the fish in the egg and panko.

Set another wire rack in a sheet pan, and put it beside the stove. In a medium Dutch oven or a heavy-walled pot with a candy thermometer attached, heat 3 in [7.5 cm] of canola oil to 375°F [190°C]. Using a spider or slotted spoon, carefully lower three or four fish sticks into the oil and fry them, moving them around and flipping them at least once, until they're golden brown and opaque all the way through, about 2 minutes. Put them on the clean rack and repeat with the remaining fish sticks.

Show your people how to make a roll: Rip a sheet of nori in half along a perforation, then spread rice crosswise over one-quarter of it. Spread the kimchi mayo on the rice, lay a fish stick on top of the mayo, and garnish it with some cukes pulled right out of their marinade. Sprinkle on green onions and everything seasoning and wrap the nori on the bias like an ice cream cone to eat the roll out of hand. Let your guests build the rest of the hand rolls themselves with the remaining nori and filling.

date, sopressata, arugula, and smoked gouda pizza

It was pizza night, and at the grocery store, Frost headed straight for Humboldt Fog cheese and prosciutto. Then she said, "I think our pizza would be good with pickles." Her finale? Chick-fil-A sauce. She wanted a stinky goat cheese, pickle, and pig pizza that she could dip. "You're a monster," I told her. "I love you." Like Frost, I ask myself, what can I do to make a pizza sing?

I always have extra sauce and dough in the freezer, so the components that take the longest are already on deck. To ramp up the dough's flavor, I swap the water for a cold-infused ancho chile stock. But you can infuse it with any fruit or veg that contains sugars to feed the yeast. Forget the pizza peel. It's easier to use a sheet pan set right on top of the pizza stone. With toppings, I make sure every bite incorporates sweet, spicy, meaty, and fresh things. The honey is optional; use it if you want.

To make the dough: In a cast-iron pan over medium heat, heat the chiles for 30 seconds, then put them in a medium bowl. Pour 4 cups [945 ml] of cold water over them, cover the bowl tightly, and steep the chiles overnight.

Strain the stock through a fine-mesh strainer into a bowl. In a medium bowl, whisk 1½ cups [360 ml] of the chile stock with the granulated sugar and yeast and let it sit for 10 minutes. Reserve the chiles and the rest of the stock for other uses, like making Fermented Hot Sauce (page 62).

Add the flour to the chile stock mixture, ½ cup [70 g] at a time, and mix with a wooden spoon or your hands until it's fully incorporated. Add the olive oil and mix with your hands for 5 minutes until it's fully incorporated (or put the dough in a stand mixer fitted with a dough hook and knead it on medium).

Put the dough on a floured surface and knead it by hand until it's smooth, about 10 minutes. Add the flaky salt and knead it for 3 to 4 minutes more. The dough should be soft and a bit springy. Form it into a ball and rub oil all over it, then put it in a medium bowl, cover it tightly, and let it ferment in the fridge for 24 hours.

continued

Dough

- 4½ oz [130 g] dried ancho chiles
- 3 Tbsp granulated sugar
- ½ tsp instant yeast
- 3½ cups [490 g] bread flour
- 2 Tbsp extra-virgin olive oil, plus more as needed
- 1 Tbsp flaky salt, such as Maldon

continued

TIME
2½ hours active; 2 days total

YIELD
1 pizza

SPECIAL GEAR
Pizza stone

Put the dough on a floured surface, cover it with a damp kitchen towel, and let it rise until doubled in size, 2 to 4 hours. Using a dough scraper, split the dough in half. Cover one piece with a damp kitchen towel, or if you're not making a second pizza right away, stow it in the fridge in an oiled bag for up to 5 days or in the freezer for up to 3 months. (Thaw it in the fridge, and then let it come to room temperature before using it.) Gently flatten the remaining dough ball. Fold it like a taco, then fold it again four or five times, as the dough tightens. Form a taut ball, place it in a bowl, cover it tightly, and leave it at room temperature until it's doubled in size again, smells beery, and keeps an indent when poked, about 2 hours.

To make the pizza sauce: In a food processor, a blender, or in a medium bowl with an immersion blender, blitz the tomatoes for a few seconds, leaving them a bit chunky.

In a medium Dutch oven or stainless steel saucepan, melt the butter over medium-high heat. Once it stops foaming, add the oil and heat it until just before smoking, about 1 minute. Add the onion and garlic and cook, stirring, until they're just caramelized, about 15 minutes. Stir in the tomatoes, brown sugar, kosher salt, red pepper flakes, and basil. Bring the sauce to a boil, then knock the heat down to a simmer and cook it for 1 hour. Cool the sauce to room temperature, then discard the basil. You'll have about 4 cups [945 ml] of sauce. It keeps, in the fridge in an airtight container, for up to 1 week or in the freezer for up to 1 month. Thaw it in the fridge before using it.

To make the pizza: Place a pizza stone on the top rack in your oven, and preheat the oven to 450°F [230°C].

Spread olive oil all over a half sheet pan, babying the corners and edges. Ease the dough onto the pan. With your fingertips, press outward, working the dough into the corners of the sheet and up its edges. Be firm but gentle; any tear is a start-over scenario.

With a silicone spatula or brush, paint a thin layer of sauce all the way to the dough's edges. Evenly top it with the sopressata and dates. Grate the Gouda over the top like it's a snowstorm, blanketing the pizza. Place the pan on top of the pizza stone and bake the pizza for 15 to 20 minutes, until the crust is golden and the cheese and dates start to caramelize. Let it cool for 5 minutes, then drizzle on the honey, if you're into it. Slice the pie, scatter on the arugula and the lemon zest, if you want, and grind black pepper on top. Serve it right away.

Pizza Sauce

One 28 oz [840 g] can whole, peeled tomatoes, preferably San Marzanos

2 Tbsp unsalted butter

2 Tbsp extra-virgin olive oil

½ medium white onion, very thinly sliced

4 garlic cloves, very thinly sliced

2 tsp packed dark brown sugar

Monster pinch of kosher salt

Monster pinch of red pepper flakes

½ bunch fresh basil, both stems and leaves

Pizza

Olive oil, as needed

1 ball Dough (page 361)

½ to ¾ cup [120 to 180 ml] Pizza Sauce, depending on your love of sauce

12 thin slices sopressata, about 4 oz [115 g]

8 dates, pitted and halved crosswise

3 oz [85 g] aged smoked Gouda

1 Tbsp honey, if you want

2 cups [40 g] baby arugula

Lemon zest, preferably Meyer, for garnish, if you want

As many cranks black pepper as you want

Pulled Chuck Roast

1 Tbsp mustard powder

1 Tbsp packed dark brown sugar

1 Tbsp kosher salt

1 Tbsp freshly ground black pepper

2½ to 3 lb [1.1 to 1.4 kg] beef chuck roast

Mesquite wood chunks, for smoking

Mop

1 cup [240 ml] chicken stock, preferably The Best Chicken Stock (page 63)

2 Tbsp apple cider vinegar

2 tsp chili powder

TIME
6 hours active; overnight total

YIELD
6 servings

SPECIAL GEAR
Lump charcoal

taquito party

There were always El Monterey Taquitos in the freezer at my mom's house. We'd microwave and eat those things by the dozens while we waited for her to come home from work. I gravitate toward recipes that are thoughtful, homemade versions of packaged foods like that. It's fun to figure out how to make them for my own kid and our pals. This party is West-meets-West. Sweet, savory, and fatty, the chuck roast is Texas BBQ style, with a flavorful mop to drench the smoked meat. It's a good one to pregame. You can smoke the meat a day ahead and keep it in the fridge unshredded. You can also fry the taquitos in advance and freeze them until party time. The tortillas and all the fixings are thanks to every taqueria I've ever stopped in along the Central Coast. You have options for serving the taquitos: You can pile them up in a tower and garnish them; bake queso fundido to dip them in; or get wild and do both simultaneously.

To make the pulled chuck roast: Set a wire rack inside a sheet pan.

Slather the mustard powder, brown sugar, salt, and pepper all over the chuck roast. Set it on the wire rack and stow it in the fridge to rest overnight.

To make the mop: In a small bowl, whisk together all the ingredients until fully combined.

Prep your smoker. If you're using a charcoal grill, bank your coals to one side. When the coals are glowing and no longer on fire, throw a handful of wood chunks on them. There's no need to soak the wood chunks. For a gas grill, heat one side on high, place the wood chunks in a smoker box, and place the smoker box over the flame. Decrease the heat to low once the wood starts smoking.

Let the first blast of acrid smoke blow off, then lay the chuck roast on the cool side of the grill and close the lid. If you're using a charcoal grill, position the vents over the chuck roast, and leave it to smoke. After the first 30 minutes, start basting the chuck roast with the mop. Continue smoking the chuck roast, basting it every 30 minutes and adding more coals and wood chunks as needed, until a meat thermometer inserted into the thickest part reads at least 165°F [74°C], about 3 hours.

Pull the chuck roast off the grill and place it on a double layer of aluminum foil with the edges turned up. Drench it in the remaining mop and wrap it up in the foil. Put the wrapped chuck roast back on the grill and smoke it, adding more coals and wood chunks as needed, until it shreds easily with a fork, 3 to 4 hours more. Rest the chuck roast for at least 30 minutes, then shred it with your hands or two forks.

To make the taquitos: Put 3 tablespoons or so of meat across the center of a homemade tortilla, roll it like a cigar, and fasten it with two toothpicks. Repeat for the rest of the meat and tortillas. In a 9 in [23 cm] cast-iron pan over high heat, heat the oil to 350°F [180°C]. Working in batches of four, fry the taquitos until they are golden brown, 30 to 45 seconds on each side. The taquitos keep, in an airtight container in the fridge, overnight or in the freezer for 1 month; reheat them in a 350°F [180°C] oven for 10 minutes.

To make the queso fundido: Preheat the oven to 400°F [200°C]. Line a plate with paper towels.

Crumble the chorizo into a cast-iron pan and sauté it over medium-high heat until it's nicely rendered and starting to crisp, 3 to 5 minutes. Transfer it to the paper towel–lined plate.

Remove and discard all but 1 tablespoon of fat from the pan, then add the onion and garlic, and sauté them over medium-high heat until they're just caramelized, 15 minutes. Transfer them to a medium bowl.

Over a gas burner on high or in a cast-iron pan over high heat, char the chiles, turning them until blackened all over, 5 to 10 minutes. Seal them in a paper bag to steam for 10 minutes. Peel, stem, and dice them. Add them to the garlic and onions.

Mix the cheeses together in a medium bowl.

In a small baking dish, layer one-third of the cheeses, half the sautéed vegetables, and half the chorizo, then repeat with one-third of the cheeses, half the veg, and half the chorizo, and top with the final layer of cheese. Bake the queso fundido until the cheese is oozing and bubbly, 12 to 15 minutes.

In a medium bowl, mix the fresh and oven-dried tomatoes, lime juice, and salt. Sprinkle the cilantro over the queso fundido, and using a slotted spoon, pile the tomato mixture in its center. Serve immediately with the taquitos for dipping.

To make the taquito tower: Arrange the taquitos in a pyramid on a platter and mound the crema, Cotija, pickled onions, tomato, and cilantro on top, with hot sauce on the side.

Taquitos
Double batch Homemade Tortillas (page 72)

2 cups [475 ml] canola oil

Queso Fundido
8 oz [230 g] fresh chorizo, casings removed

1 medium white onion, diced

3 garlic cloves, thinly sliced

2 Hatch or poblano chiles

12 oz [340 g] Monterey Jack cheese, grated

4 oz [115 g] Manchego cheese, grated

2 Early Girl or other medium tomatoes, diced

¼ cup [65 g] Oven-Dried Tomatoes (page 67)

Juice of 1 lime

Pinch of kosher salt

½ cup [20 g] chopped cilantro

Taquito Tower
1 cup [240 g] crema or sour cream

1 cup [225 g] Cotija polvo granulado cheese

Pickled Onions (page 48), for garnish

1 big beefsteak tomato, diced, for garnish

1 bunch fresh cilantro, tough stems removed, roughly chopped, for garnish

Hot sauce, preferably Fermented Hot Sauce (page 62), for serving

Whipped Mascarpone

8 oz [230 g] mascarpone

4 oz [115 g] chèvre

4 oz [115 g] crème fraîche,
preferably homemade
(page 44)

¼ cup [85 g] honey

¼ cup [60 ml] whole milk

Raspberry Sauce

2 Tbsp pink peppercorns

1 pt [240 g] raspberries

3 Tbsp honey

1 Tbsp fresh lemon juice,
preferably Meyer

4 cranks black pepper

continued

Like any good parent, I trick my kid into doing what I want by giving her sweets. That said, Frost's palate is oddly refined for a six-year-old, so with waffles, we get weird. Rice flour, or mochi, brings a super chewy texture. Then there's the color: a green waffle? That's so cool, and we get there not with food coloring, but with matcha. The matcha contrasts the waffles' sweetness with tannic flavor, and the briny chèvre in the mascarpone that's served on top helps too. Adding raspberry sauce is a chef-y thing: When you're introducing hard-to-fathom flavors, hide them under a raspberry coulis. Works every time, especially with Central Coast berries, which are the best.

To make the whipped mascarpone: In a stand mixer fitted with the paddle attachment, a food processor, or a large bowl with an immersion blender, whip the mascarpone, chèvre, crème fraîche, honey, and milk on medium-high until it has soft peaks, 1½ to 2 minutes. Keep it chilled until serving. It keeps, in the fridge in an airtight container, for up to 1 week.

To make the raspberry sauce: In a small skillet over medium heat, toast the pink peppercorns until fragrant, 30 to 45 seconds. Grind them in a coffee grinder or mortar and pestle into a powder, then put half of the powder in a medium bowl, reserving the rest for garnish. Add the raspberries, honey, lemon juice, and black pepper to the bowl and, wearing gloves, squeeze the ingredients together to macerate the sauce, making it as smooth or pulpy as you want. Keep it chilled until serving. It keeps, in the fridge in an airtight container, for up to 1 week.

continued

TIME
1 hour

YIELD
6 waffles

SPECIAL GEAR
Waffle iron

matcha mochi waffles

Waffles

2½ cups [350 g] sweet rice flour, preferably Koda Farms Mochiko

½ cup [100 g] sugar

2 Tbsp matcha powder

2½ tsp baking powder

1½ cups [360 ml] whole milk

2 large eggs

Pan spray

Lemon zest, preferably Meyer, for garnish

To make the waffles: In a medium bowl, mix the rice flour, sugar, matcha powder, and baking powder.

In a second medium bowl, whisk together the milk and eggs. Pour this mixture into the flour mixture and stir to form a loose, tacky dough.

Lightly coat the top and bottom of your waffle iron with pan spray, then make the waffles as per the machine's instructions. If you haven't used one before, I'll tell you: Basically, you plug the thing in, and a light goes on when it's hot. Mochi batter is thicker than your regular waffle batter, so spoon it in rather than pouring it, filling the bottom of the waffle iron without overflowing it. Close the lid and presto! When the light goes off, the waffle is done. It's 3 to 5 minutes to crusty. Use oven mitts to handle the machine and a fork to coax out the waffle.

Serve the waffles warm, with a big spoonful each of the whipped mascarpone and raspberry sauce dolloped on top, a sprinkling of lemon zest and reserved ground pink peppercorns to finish. Then let the kids go wild on them. Leftover waffles keep, in the freezer in a ziplock or resealable silicone bag, for up to 1 week. Cool them to room temperature before wrapping and freezing, so they don't get soggy. Reheat them in a 300°F [150°C] oven for about 10 minutes. But this is all probably unnecessary because, for real, when are there ever leftover waffles?

miso, walnut, and chocolate chip cookies

Let's make it easy on ourselves when we get home. This recipe uses the same base as the White Chocolate, Pistachio, and Rose Cookies (page 128) we were munching on the road. These cookies echo the journey, but they're simpler, more grounded, deeper, richer. I got the idea from the Nescafé that Mimi (see page 97) drinks at Dad's, slammed with milk and sugar. The coffee adds this whisper of goodness. Just don't let the kiddies devour too many cookies, or they'll be bonkers. In fact, the dough is meant to be sliced as you go. Keep it frozen and slice off ¾ in [2 cm] chunks when you need to satisfy cookie urges.

In the bowl of a stand mixer fitted with a paddle attachment or a large bowl with a fork, mix the brown sugar, granulated sugar, instant coffee, salt, and baking soda until uniform. Adding the butter a few chunks at a time, cream the butter into the sugar mixture until it's fully incorporated.

In a medium bowl, mix the eggs, miso, and vanilla. Add this to the sugar mixture and mix it in, scraping down the bowl as you go, until it's the consistency of wet sand, about 1 minute. Fold in the walnuts and chocolate chips. With the stand mixer on the lowest setting or mixing by hand with a spatula, add the flour, ½ cup [70 g] at a time, until the dough is uniform.

Place a large piece of plastic wrap on a work surface and drop one-third of the dough onto it, then form it into a log about 2 in [5 cm] in diameter and wrap the log, twisting the ends of the plastic to tighten it. Repeat with the remaining dough. Refrigerate the dough for at least 2 hours and up to 2 days or freeze it for up to 1 month.

Preheat the oven to 350°F [180°C]. Line a sheet pan with a silicone mat or parchment paper; if using parchment, lightly coat it with pan spray.

Slice the cold or frozen dough ¾ in [2 cm] thick (or 85 g by weight). Working in batches, place the dough slices on the prepared sheet pan—you can fit six cookies on a half sheet. Bake them on the oven's center rack for 9 minutes, then rotate the pan, and bake for about 9 more minutes, or until crunchy on the outside but still soft on the inside. Let them cool to room temperature. The cookies will keep in an airtight countainer on the countertop for 2 days.

2 cups [400 g] packed dark brown sugar

1½ cups [300 g] granulated sugar

⅓ cup [20 g] instant coffee grounds

1 Tbsp kosher salt

2 tsp baking soda

1 lb [455 g] unsalted butter, cut into small pieces, at room temperature

DON'T LET YOUR BUTTER GET TOO WARM; YOU WANT IT SORT OF SOFT, NOT VERY SOFT.

4 large eggs

6 Tbsp [100 g] sweet white miso

2½ Tbsp vanilla extract

1⅔ cups [200 g] roughly chopped walnuts

1 cup [180 g] chocolate chips, preferably 60% cacao

5 cups [700 g] all-purpose flour

Pan spray, if needed

TIME
45 minutes active;
2 hours 45 minutes total

YIELD
30 cookies

This is it. The last recipe in the book. A nighttime potion. A finale. A wrap. After all our adventures, we've landed back home, where I have this trifecta waiting on my bar for drinking guests who drop by. There's no out-of-state substitute for the bittersweet richness of Greenbar's amaro infused with California poppies or for the mellow botanicals in the gin from St. George Spirits, a pioneer of post-Prohibition distilling in our state. There's nothing you need to cook here, nothing you need to do but go and buy the same bottles, stir 'em up together for a good, long time, and sip. The kid's in bed, the truck's in the driveway, and the moon is rising over the churning Pacific. It's another day done on the Central Coast, or wherever you are. Cheers and goodnight, my friend.

In a mixing glass half filled with ice, combine the gin, amaro, and Barolo Chinato and stir for a good 90 seconds. Strain the drink into a chilled rocks glass, without ice, and garnish it with the orange twist.

1¾ oz [50 ml] St. George Spirits Botanivore Gin

½ oz [15 ml] Greenbar Poppy Amaro

½ oz [15 ml] Barolo Chinato, preferably Cocchi

1 orange twist

dad's sleepy time nightcap

TIME
3 minutes

YIELD
1 drink

acknowledgments

To my mom and dad ● Mom, thank you for always believing in me and encouraging me to follow my dreams no matter how absurd and erratic they are. You are strong, smart, and full of love. I'm lucky to have you in my corner and proud to be your son. Dad, thank you for never giving up on me, even when it seemed like the only logical thing to do. I'll always be indebted to you for literally dragging me out of bed, getting me outside no matter the weather, and making me fish. Sorry for stealing and almost sinking your bass boat that one time.

To the family at Dad's, past and present ● Anthony Keels, Erik Andreassen, Joe Levitt, Wen Yu, Noemi "Mimi" Peña, Alexis Liu, Luca Balbi. Without your tireless work, impeccable attitude, and devotion, none of this would be possible. I appreciate you more than I could ever put into words. It's an absolute joy and honor of mine to come to work and see your faces.

To the community of Half Moon Bay ● Thank you for accepting this wild man into your world and giving me the ability to thrive in town.

To the farmers, fishers, hunters, and gatherers who showed me your world and shared with me your passion and expertise ● I am forever grateful. This is your story, and I hope I honored you all in it.

To the team at Chronicle ● Sarah, Alex, and everyone (Jessica, Steve, Tera, Keely, Elora), you took a chance and gave us the ability to put our hearts on paper.

Victoria ● Thank you for your patience and for taking the time to show me how to slow down and savor this life, to breathe and be at peace.

Betsy Andrews ● It's been a fucking long one getting this to print. Your wit, grit, and steadfast drive is an inspiration. You are one of the most badass people I've ever met. There is not a moment that goes by where I don't recognize how much you've poured into these pages. It shows, and it's beautiful.

Cheyenne Ellis ● Your impeccable eye and outrageous ability to capture precious moments is second to none. Your presence brings me and everyone around you calm and joy. Behind every image is a gorgeous person with an incredible story. You're just so cool, man.

And, finally, **Frost Quartz Liu Clark** ● My bear, my bean, my sweet, wonderful girl, I adore you, darling. Your daddy loves you. My life gained a meaning when you came into it that changed me forever. I cannot believe I get to be your dad every single day till the end of time. You are a gift, a force, and a presence. Please never change, honey.

— SCOTT CLARK

To my Grandma Kay ● Thank you for instilling the love of cooking in me young.

To my husband Ryan ● for being my forever guinea pig when I cook. I love you and that appetite forever.

Beth Protass ● We couldn't have done this book without your genius and patience.

For the gorgeous and thoughtful design, thank you, **Lizzie Vaughan** ● for bringing our vision to life on these pages. **Sarah Billingsley**, thank you for believing in us and giving us the greatest team to collaborate with at Chronicle.

To my agent **Alyssa Pizer** ● Your unwavering support and devotion to my career over the years has allowed me to do what I love for a living.

To Scott ● for teaching me so much more than I ever knew possible in the kitchen. And to Betsy for bringing me full circle on this journey and trusting me with your creative projects near and far. To you both, for the adventure of a lifetime.

You have all allowed me to create in the food world with my camera, and for that I am incredibly grateful.

And to **every purveyor, fisher, forager, hunter, and resident of the Central Coast** ● who allowed us to learn so much more about where we live and what it provides us, thank you!

—— CHEYENNE ELLIS

To Scott ● for your story, your poetry, your one-of-a-kind vision, and your damned delicious cooking, and to Cheyenne, for the beauty of your eye, your transporting photography, and your soul, which is one with California: This writer thanks you, team!

Heartfelt appreciation goes out to ● my lady **Jeanne Baron**, and to **Eva Mantell**, **Joel Beck**, and **Felix Zimmerman-Beck**, for always tasting with love. Thanks to **Laiko Bahr** for introducing me to Scott; **Carolyn Malcoun**, who assigned the *Eating Well* story that sparked this book; **Bill Mazza** and **Lisa Michurski** for helping with the look of the proposal; **Lindsey Bowen** for a sharp eye with contracts; our agent, **Stacey Glick**, for enthusiastically shepherding us; and **Sarah Billingsley** and her team at Chronicle for supporting and believing in this project.

Big gratitude to our fearless (and opinionated!) cross-testers ● Allison Amend, Nancy Andrews, Helen Baldus, Gwenyth Baron, Katie Baron and Ian Stewart, Penny Baron, Stella Bellow, Sarah Blackwood and Ames and Owen McKenna-Blackwood, Ted Boerner and Oren Postrel, Liz Bonsal, Dana Carlson, Claire Conway, Joshua David, Carol Diuguid, Katy Fertel, Georgia Freedman, Lisa Futterman, Ellie Herman, Sam Jarden, Kenny Kirschner, Ellen and Evelyn Kochansky, Diane Lent, Harlan Mandel, Linda Matalon, Carolyn Monastra, Linda Monastra, Peggy Monastra, Jennie Altman Nemroff, Jane Roomberg, Farideh Sadeghin, Sarah Schenck and John Donohue, Robin Sheldon, and Kit Soleil.

We acknowledge and thank the ancestral and continuing stewards of the unceded Central Coast ● the **Chumash**, **Esselen**, **Salanin**, and **Ohlone People**.

—— BETSY ANDREWS

index

After-Surf Sundae 157–59
Agua Fresca, Watermelon 349
Albacore Pea Shoot Bowl 198–99
almonds
    Kumquat and Kale 229–30
amaro
    Dad's Sleepy Time Nightcap 371
    Tamarind Mezcal Americanos 288
anchovies
    Charred Broccolini with
    Melted Anchovy and Garlic 231–33
Andreassen, Erik 96, 97, 225
Aperol
    Chamomile–Pink Peppercorn Spritz 261
apples
    Coastal Kraut 56–57
    Goji and Hemp Overnight Oats 137–38
    Red Miso Caramel Apple 222
    Salt-Roasted Purple Potato Salad 238–39
Artichokes, Fried, with Artichoke Dip . . 164–65
arugula
    about 34
    Date, Sopressata, Arugula, and
    Smoked Gouda Pizza 361–63
    Porcini with Guanciale Ravigote 200–201
    Sage-Grilled Yardbird with
    Miso-Maple Grits 243–44
Asparagus Grain Bowl Benedict 146–47
Avila, Brooke and Clay 249

bacon
    Bacon Fat–Roasted Turnips 234
    Bacon-Gouda Dutch Baby 156
    The Best Bacon 65
    California PBLT 183–85
    Fried Artichokes with Artichoke Dip . . . 164–65
    Hard Cider Clam Bake 306
    Peppery Sausage Bánh Mì 245–46
    Red-Eye Gravy 203
    Rye Berry Salad 146
bagels
    Smoked Tongue Reuben 94–95
Balbi, Luca 96, 97
Bánh Mì, Peppery Sausage 245–46

Barley and Wine Grape Salad 281
Barolo Chinato
    Dad's Sleepy Time Nightcap 371
Baron, Dan 313, 318
bay leaves 34
beans
    Dry-Fried Green Beans 352
    Falafel Party 181–82
    Miso-Braised Gigante Beans 179–80
Béarnaise 147
beef
    Hen of the Woods or Hamburger Sandwich . 91–93
    Korean BBQ Pear Butter Ribs 304
    Roasted Beef Tenderloin with
    Chanterelle Cornbread 253–54
    Santa Maria Rib Eye and Mustard Greens . . 307–8
    Shio Koji–Cured Jerky 115
    Smoked Tongue Reuben 94–95
    Taquito Party 364–65
beer
    IPA Caramel 159
Benu 20, 151, 231, 309, 337
Blueberry Sauce 283
bonito flakes
    about 34
    California Kimbap 122–24
    Cherry Blossom Vinaigrette 167
    Sweet Soy Glaze 55
    Umami Oil 46
bread. *See also* sandwiches
    Chanterelle Cornbread 253–54
    Country Toast Bar 262–73
    Jimmy Nardello Panzanella 168
    Pumpkin Bread with Salty Butter 350–51
Brisa Ranch 161, 173
broccoli and broccolini
    Barley and Wine Grape Salad 281
    Charred Broccolini with Melted
    Anchovy and Garlic 231–33
    Sea-Blanched Broccoli 322
Brownies, Rhubarb 105
Brussels Sprout Latkes 140
buckwheat
    Kumquat and Kale 229–30
butter
    Ghee 42
    Sea Urchin Butter 325
Buttermilk Ranch Dip, Herby 116

C

cabbage
Coastal Kraut 56–57
Whole Napa Cabbage Kimchi 58–59
California Kimbap **122–24**
California PBLT **183–85**
CA Muddy Buddies **131**
caramel
IPA Caramel 159
Red Miso Caramel Apple 222
carrots
Carrot Salad 181
Curried Carrot Soup 80
Pickled Carrots 245
chamomile
Chamomile–Pink Peppercorn Spritz 261
Chamomile Sherry 261
Channel Islands **313, 318, 325**
cheese
aged smoked Gouda 34
Bacon-Gouda Dutch Baby 156
Charred Broccolini with Melted Anchovy
and Garlic 231–33
Date, Sopressata, Arugula, and
Smoked Gouda Pizza 361–63
Duck Egg Brie Bake 154
Farmer's Cheese 292
Feta Dip 140
Fig, Feta, and Radicchio Hand Salad 169
Hen of the Woods or Hamburger Sandwich . 91–93
Mac 'n' Cheese with Puffed Rice Topping . . 82–83
making 143
Maple Mascarpone 103
Queso Fundido 365
Roasted Corn and Smoked Blue Cheese Salad . 170
Sea Urchin Cacio e Pepe 325
Smoked Tongue Reuben 94–95
Taquito Party 364–65
Whipped Mascarpone 366
Cherry Blossom Vinaigrette **167**
chervil **34**
Chex cereal
CA Muddy Buddies 131
chicken
The Best Chicken Stock 63–64
Chicken Liver Mousse with
Persimmon Pudding 270
Sage-Grilled Yardbird with
Miso-Maple Grits 243–44
Shrimp and Chicken Liver Grits 84–85
Smoked Chicken with Smoked Chimichurri . 87–88
chiles
Chile Jam 60
Fermented Hot Sauce 62

Pre-Surf Fire Cider 136
Smoked Chimichurri 88
Tajin-Style Spice 68
Chimichurri, Smoked **88**
chives
chopping 116
Herby Buttermilk Ranch Dip 116
chocolate
Miso, Walnut, and Chocolate Chip Cookies . 369
Onboard Oreos 341–42
Rhubarb Brownies 105
cider
Hard Cider Clam Bake 306
Pre-Surf Fire Cider 136
cioppino
Kimchioppino 337–39
clams
Hard Cider Clam Bake 306
Kimchioppino 337–39
Coastal Cocktail Sauce **295**
Coastal Kraut **56–57**
Cocktail Sauce, Coastal **295**
coconut milk
Curried Carrot Soup 80
Goji and Hemp Overnight Oats 137–38
Rockfish Curry 328
cod
Fish Stick Hand Roll Bar 358–60
coffee
Miso, Walnut, and Chocolate Chip Cookies . 369
Red-Eye Gravy 203
cookies
Miso, Walnut, and Chocolate Chip Cookies . 369
Onboard Oreos 341–42
White Chocolate, Pistachio, and
Rose Cookies 128–29
corn. *See also* grits
Chanterelle Cornbread 253–54
Furikake Popcorn 112–13
Roasted Corn and Smoked Blue Cheese
Salad 170
Country Toast Bar **262–73**
crab
Dungeness Crab Rice 218–21
Kimchioppino 337–39
Crème Fraîche **44**
Cruz Hernández, Cristóbal **173**
cucumbers
Barley and Wine Grape Salad 281
Fish Stick Hand Roll Bar 358–60
Jimmy Nardello Panzanella 168
Roasted Corn and Smoked Blue Cheese
Salad 170
Roasted Snap Pea Salad with
Yakult-Style Dressing 291
Curry, Rockfish **328**
Custard, Smoked Mussel **151**

d

Dad Sauce 91
Dad's Luncheonette   17, 21, 24, 25, 75, 79, 80, 82, 91, 97, 100, 105, 128, 133, 173, 202, 278, 369, 371
Dad's Potato Chips 79
Dad's Sleepy Time Nightcap 371
dandelion greens
    Roasted Corn and Smoked Blue Cheese Salad 170
Date, Sopressata, Arugula, and Smoked Gouda Pizza, 361–63
desserts
    After-Surf Sundae 157–59
    Earl Grey Icebox Pie 100
    Grilled and Chilled Melon 309
    Horchata Paletas 311
    Meyer Lemon Curd with Blueberry Sauce 283
    Miso, Walnut, and Chocolate Chip Cookies 369
    Onboard Oreos 341–42
    Pretzel Crispies 340
    Rhubarb Brownies 105
    White Chocolate, Pistachio, and Rose Cookies 128–29
Deviled Quail Eggs 268
dips
    Artichoke Dip 164–65
    Feta Dip 140
    Herby Buttermilk Ranch Dip 116
    Maple Mascarpone 103
    Queso Fundido 365
    Wasabi Dip 228
Donuts, Yeasty Drop 103–4
drinks
    Chamomile–Pink Peppercorn Spritz 261
    Dad's Sleepy Time Nightcap 371
    Kimchi Mary 316–17
    Perfect Meyer Lemonade 111
    Pre-Surf Fire Cider 136
    Smoked Huckleberry Old Fashioned 190
    Tamarind Mezcal Americanos 288
    Watermelon Agua Fresca 349
dry frying 352
Duarte's Tavern 213
Duck Egg Brie Bake 154
Dunites Wine Company 257, 276
Dutch Baby, Bacon-Gouda 156

e

Earl Grey Icebox Pie, 100
Eck, Tyler and Rachel, 261, 276
Eggplant Yakitori, Grilled, 289

eggs

Asparagus Grain Bowl Benedict, 146–47
Bacon-Gouda Dutch Baby, 156
Deviled Quail Eggs 268
Duck Egg Brie Bake 154
Lox 'n' Tacs 148–50
Smoked Mussel Custard 151
Everything Seasoning 71
Everything Tortillas 150

f

Falafel Party 181–82
Farmer's Cheese 292
Fig, Feta, and Radicchio Hand Salad 169
fish
    Albacore Pea Shoot Bowl 198–99
    Charred Broccolini with Melted Anchovy and Garlic 231–33
    Confit Tuna Salad with Sea Salt Lavash 126–27
    Cured Salmon with Roe and Crème Fraîche 267
    Fish Stick Hand Roll Bar 358–60
    Fries with Eyes 213–15
    Homemade "Tinned" Fish 321
    Kimchioppino 337–39
    Lingcod Ceviche 210–12
    Rockfish Curry 328
    Smoked Mackerel with Lemon-Dill Relish 263–64
fishing 187, 328, 333
Fish Sauce Mayo 213
foraging 187, 202, 206
Four Sisters Farm 355
Fries with Eyes 213–15
Frontera Hunting 249
Furikake 70
    Furikake Popcorn 112–13

g

garbanzo beans
    Falafel Party 181–82
garlic
    about 34
    Charred Broccolini with Melted Anchovy and Garlic 231–33
    Confit Garlic 47
    peeling 47
    Pre-Surf Fire Cider 136
    Umami Oil 46
gear 30–33
Gerbino, Anthony 201, 206
Ghee 42

gin
    Dad's Sleepy Time Nightcap 371
ginger
    Ginger Mustard 246
    Pre-Surf Fire Cider 136
    Pumpkin Bread with Salty Butter 350–51
Goat Leg, Shio Koji–Roasted **282**
Goji and Hemp Overnight Oats **137–38**
gooseberries
    Lingcod Ceviche 210–12
graham crackers
    Earl Grey Icebox Pie 100
grapefruit
    Fig, Feta, and Radicchio Hand Salad 169
    Kumquat and Kale 229–30
grapes
    Barley and Wine Grape Salad 281
Gravy, Red-Eye **203**
green onions **34**
grilling **285, 307**
grits
    Chanterelle Cornbread 253–54
    Miso-Maple Grits 243
    Shrimp and Chicken Liver Grits 84–85
Guanciale Ravigote, Porcini with **200–201**

haddock
    Fish Stick Hand Roll Bar 358–60
halibut
    Fish Stick Hand Roll Bar 358–60
    Kimchioppino 337–39
Harley, Dee **140, 143**
Harley Goat Farm **143**
hazelnuts
    Charred Broccolini with Melted Anchovy
    and Garlic 231–33
Head Cheese with Charred Onion Mustard . . . **271–73**
Hemp Overnight Oats, Goji and **137–38**
Hen of the Woods or Hamburger Sandwich . . . **91–93**
herbs
    Herby Buttermilk Ranch Dip 116
    Seasonal Herb Salad 278
Hippie Vinaigrette **53**
Hodad's **183**
Hoffman, Jeremy **20**
honey **34**
Honey Pig **304**
Horchata Paletas **311**
Hot Sauce, Fermented **62**
huckleberries
    Smoked Berry Syrup 190
    Smoked Huckleberry Old Fashioned 190
hunting **225, 249**

ice cream
    After-Surf Sundae 157–59
    Vanilla Ice Cream 157
IPA Caramel **159**
Ippuku **288**

jams
    Chile Jam 60
    Rhubarb Jam 105
Jerky, Shio Koji–Cured **115**

kale
    Kumquat and Kale 229–30
    Miso-Braised Gigante Beans 179–80
Kashiwase Farms **355**
Keels, Anthony **96, 97, 190**
Keller, Thomas **20**
Kimbap, California **122–24**
kimchi
    Kimchi Mary 316–17
    Kimchi Mayo 358
    Kimchioppino 337–39
    Whole Napa Cabbage Kimchi 58–59
Kingdom of Dumpling **231**
Kluhgers, Wally **333**
kombu **34–35**
Korean BBQ Pear Butter Ribs **304**
kumquats
    Candied Kumquats 229
    Kumquat and Kale 229–30
    Raw Scallops with Citronette 318

Latkes, Brussels Sprout **140**
Lavash, Sea Salt **127**
Lee, Corey **20**
lemons
    Meyer 35
    Meyer Lemon Curd with Blueberry Sauce 283
    Perfect Meyer Lemonade 111
    Raw Scallops with Citronette 318
    Smoked Mackerel with Lemon-Dill Relish 263–64
limes
    Lingcod Ceviche, 210–12
    Tajin-Style Spice, 68

Lingcod Ceviche 210–12
Linn's 190
Liu, Alexis 21, 96, 97
liver
    Chicken Liver Mousse with Persimmon
    Pudding, ... 270
    Shrimp and Chicken Liver Grits 84–85
lobster
    Kimchioppino 337–39
Lox 'n' Tacs 148–50

m

mackerel
    Homemade "Tinned" Fish 321
    Smoked Mackerel with Lemon-Dill Relish . . 263–64
Mac 'n' Cheese with Puffed Rice Topping . . 82–83
Maggiano's Little Italy 18
Maloney, Neal 216, 296
maple syrup
    Maple Mascarpone 103
    Miso-Maple Grits 243
Marley, Spencer 191, 195
Marley Family Seaweeds 195
marshmallows
    Pretzel Crispies 340
masa harina
    Homemade Tortillas 72
Matcha Mochi Waffles 366–68
mayonnaise
    The Best Mayonnaise 45
    Fish Sauce Mayo 213
    Kimchi Mayo 358
    Oven-Dried Tomato Mayo 183
    Smoked Padrón Mayo 216–17
Mazariegos-Anastassiou, Verónica and Cole . . . 173
Melon, Grilled and Chilled 309
Meyer, Frank 111
mezcal
    Kimchi Mary 316–17
    Tamarind Mezcal Americanos 288
miso
    about 35
    Miso-Braised Gigante Beans 179–80
    Miso-Maple Grits 243
    Miso, Walnut, and Chocolate Chip Cookies . . 369
    Red Miso Caramel Apple 222
    Seaweed-Shiitake Miso Soup 191
    White Chocolate, Pistachio, and
    Rose Cookies 128–29
Mora Family Farms 355
Morro Bay Oyster Company 296, 301
Muddy Buddies, CA 131
mushrooms
    California Kimbap 122–24

Chanterelle Cornbread 253–54
Chicken-Fried Morels with Red-Eye Gravy . . 202–3
Dry-Fried Green Beans 352
Duck Egg Brie Bake 154
foraging for 187, 202, 206
Hen of the Woods or Hamburger
Sandwich 91–93
Porcini with Guanciale Ravigote 200–201
Seaweed-Shiitake Miso Soup 191
Umami Oil 46
mussels
    Kimchioppino 337–39
    Smoked Mussel Custard 151
mustard
    Charred Onion Mustard 273
    Ginger Mustard 246
    Pickled Mustard Seeds 50
    Santa Maria Rib Eye and Mustard Greens . . 307–8

n

nori
    California Kimbap 122–24
    Fish Stick Hand Roll Bar 358–60
    Furikake 70

o

Oats, Goji and Hemp Overnight 137–38
Oil, Umami 46
Old Bay Seasoning 35
Old Fashioned, Smoked Huckleberry 190
Old Jerusalem 181
Onboard Oreos 341–42
onions
    Charred Onion Mustard 273
    green 34
    Pickled Onions 48
    white 37
Oreos, Onboard 341–42
oysters
    about 296
    Ghee-Roasted Oysters with Fire Cider
    Mignonette 301
    Oyster Po'boys with Smoked Padrón Mayo . . 216–17

p

Paletas, Horchata 311
Panzanella, Jimmy Nardello 168

parsley
- Seasoned Vinegar 52
- Smoked Chimichurri 88
- Umami Oil 46

pasta
- Mac 'n' Cheese with Puffed Rice Topping . . . 82–83
- Sea Urchin Cacio e Pepe 325

pears
- Korean BBQ Pear Butter Ribs 304
- Pear Butter 51

peas
- Barley and Wine Grape Salad 281
- Roasted Snap Pea Salad with Yakult-Style Dressing 291

pea shoots
- Albacore Pea Shoot Bowl 198–99
- Seasonal Herb Salad 278

pecans
- After-Surf Sundae 157–59
- Candied Pecans 159
- Pumpkin Bread with Salty Butter 350–51

Peña, Mimi 96, 97, 369

The Penny Ice Creamery 355

Peppercorn Syrup, Pink 261

pepper flakes, red 35

peppers. *See also* **chiles**
- Chile Jam 60
- Dry-Fried Green Beans 352
- Jimmy Nardello Panzanella 168
- Smoked Padrón Mayo 216–17

Per Se 20

Persimmon Pudding, Chicken Liver Mousse with . 270

Pie, Earl Grey Icebox 100

Pie Ranch 173

pineapple
- California PBLT 183–85

Pink Peppercorn Syrup 261

Pismo Beach 285, 306

pistachios
- White Chocolate, Pistachio, and Rose Cookies 128–29

pizza
- Date, Sopressata, Arugula, and Smoked Gouda Pizza 361–63
- Pizza Sauce 363

plums
- Fig, Feta, and Radicchio Hand Salad 169
- Summer Squash and Plum Salad 167

Po'boys, Oyster, with Smoked Padrón Mayo . 216–17

Popcorn, Furikake 112–13

poppy seeds
- Everything Seasoning 71

pork. *See also* **bacon**
- Dry-Fried Green Beans 352
- Head Cheese with Charred Onion Mustard . 271–73
- Peppery Sausage Bánh Mì 245–46
- Porcini with Guanciale Ravigote 200–201

potatoes
- Dad's Potato Chips 79
- Salt-Roasted Purple Potato Salad 238–39
- Santa Maria Rib Eye and Mustard Greens . 307–8
- Shredded Potato Salad 118–19

Pre-Surf Fire Cider 136

Pretzel Crispies 340

Pumpkin Bread with Salty Butter 350–51

pumpkin seeds
- Seared and Sauced Kuri Squash 241–42
- toasting 242

Quail Eggs, Deviled 268

Queen of Hearts 333

Queso Fundido 365

Radicchio Hand Salad, Fig, Feta, and 169

radishes
- Seasonal Herb Salad 278
- Whole Napa Cabbage Kimchi 58–59

Ranch Dip, Herby Buttermilk 116

Raspberry Sauce 366

Ravigote, Guanciale, Porcini with 200–201

Red-Eye Gravy 203

Restaurant Eve 20, 234

Reuben, Smoked Tongue 94–95

rhubarb
- Rhubarb Brownies 105
- Rhubarb Jam 105

Ribs, Korean BBQ Pear Butter 304

rice. *See also* **Shio Koji; wild rice**
- California Kimbap 122–24
- Dungeness Crab Rice 218–21
- Fish Stick Hand Roll Bar 358–60
- Horchata Paletas 311

rockfish
- Kimchioppino 337–39
- Rockfish Curry 328

Roe, Cured Salmon with Crème Fraîche and . 267

Ruddell's Smokehouse 133

Rules of the Road 27–29

Russian Dressing 95

rye berries
- Asparagus Grain Bowl Benedict 146–47
- Rye Berry Salad 146

rye whiskey
- Smoked Huckleberry Old Fashioned 190

Sage-Grilled Yardbird with
Miso-Maple Grits 243–44
Saison . . . 20–21, 28, 35, 54, 62, 97, 119, 191, 202, 295
sake
    Cured Salmon with Roe and Crème Fraîche . . 267
    Wakame-Infused Sake 191
salad dressings. *See also* vinaigrettes
    Russian Dressing 95
    Yakult-Style Dressing 291
    Yogurt Dressing 181
salads
    Barley and Wine Grape Salad 281
    Carrot Salad 181
    Confit Tuna Salad with Sea Salt Lavash . . . 126–27
    Fig, Feta, and Radicchio Hand Salad 169
    Jimmy Nardello Panzanella 168
    Kumquat and Kale 229–30
    Roasted Corn and Smoked Blue Cheese Salad . 170
    Roasted Snap Pea Salad with
    Yakult-Style Dressing 291
    Rye Berry Salad, 146
    Salt-Roasted Purple Potato Salad 238–39
    Seasonal Herb Salad 278
    Shredded Potato Salad 118–19
    Summer Squash and Plum Salad 167
salmon
    Cured Salmon with Roe and Crème Fraîche . . 267
    Lox 'n' Tacs 148–50
sandwiches
    California PBLT 183–85
    Hen of the Woods or Hamburger Sandwich . 91–93
    Oyster Po'boys with Smoked Padrón Mayo . 216–17
    Peppery Sausage Bánh Mì 245–46
    Smoked Tongue Reuben 94–95
Santa Cruz Community Farmers' Market . . . 350, 355
Santa Maria Rib Eye and Mustard Greens . . . 307–8
sardines
    Homemade "Tinned" Fish 321
    satsumas
    Goji and Hemp Overnight Oats 137–38
sauces
    Béarnaise 147
    Blueberry Sauce 283
    Coastal Cocktail Sauce 295
    Dad Sauce 91
    Fermented Hot Sauce 62
    Pizza Sauce 363
    Raspberry Sauce 366
    Smoked Chimichurri 88
sauerkraut
    Coastal Kraut 56–57
    Rye Berry Salad 146
    Smoked Tongue Reuben 94–95
sausage
    Date, Sopressata, Arugula, and
    Smoked Gouda Pizza 361–63
    Peppery Sausage Bánh Mì 245–46
    Taquito Party 364–65

Scallops, Raw, with Citronette **318**
seasonings
    Everything Seasoning 71
    Furikake 70
    Tajín-Style Spice 68
sea urchin
    Sea Urchin Butter 325
    Sea Urchin Cacio e Pepe 325
seaweed. *See also* nori
    about 195
    kombu 34–35
    Seaweed-Shiitake Miso Soup 191
    Wakame-Infused Sake 191
sesame seeds
    about 35
    Everything Seasoning 71
    Falafel Party 181–82
    Furikake 70
shallots
    about 35
    Blooming Shallots with Wasabi Dip 228
sherry
    Chamomile–Pink Peppercorn Spritz 261
    Chamomile Sherry 261
Shio Koji, 54
    Shio Koji–Cured Jerky 115
    Shio Koji–Roasted Goat Leg 282
shrimp
    Grilled Spot Prawn Cocktail 295
    Kimchi Mary 316–17
    Kimchioppino 337–39
    Shrimp and Chicken Liver Grits 84–85
    Whole Napa Cabbage Kimchi 58–59
Skenes, Josh **21**
smelts
    about 213
    Fries with Eyes 213–15
soups
    Curried Carrot Soup 80
    Seaweed-Shiitake Miso Soup 191
soy sauce, white **37**
spices, whole **37**
spinach
    Duck Egg Brie Bake 154
    Miso-Braised Gigante Beans 179–80
Spot Prawn Cocktail, Grilled **295**
squash
    Seared and Sauced Kuri Squash 241–42
    Summer Squash and Plum Salad 167
Stock, The Best Chicken **63–64**
Sundae, After-Surf **157–59**
Sweet Potatoes, Ember-Roasted **292–94**
syrups
    Pink Peppercorn Syrup 261
    Smoked Berry Syrup 190
    Tamarind Syrup 288

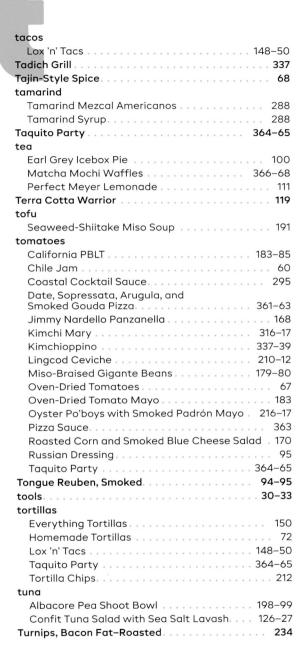

t

tacos
    Lox 'n' Tacs 148–50
Tadich Grill **337**
Tajín-Style Spice **68**
tamarind
    Tamarind Mezcal Americanos 288
    Tamarind Syrup 288
Taquito Party **364–65**
tea
    Earl Grey Icebox Pie 100
    Matcha Mochi Waffles 366–68
    Perfect Meyer Lemonade 111
Terra Cotta Warrior **119**
tofu
    Seaweed-Shiitake Miso Soup 191
tomatoes
    California PBLT 183–85
    Chile Jam 60
    Coastal Cocktail Sauce 295
    Date, Sopressata, Arugula, and
    Smoked Gouda Pizza 361–63
    Jimmy Nardello Panzanella 168
    Kimchi Mary 316–17
    Kimchioppino 337–39
    Lingcod Ceviche 210–12
    Miso-Braised Gigante Beans 179–80
    Oven-Dried Tomatoes 67
    Oven-Dried Tomato Mayo 183
    Oyster Po'boys with Smoked Padrón Mayo . 216–17
    Pizza Sauce 363
    Roasted Corn and Smoked Blue Cheese Salad . 170
    Russian Dressing 95
    Taquito Party 364–65
Tongue Reuben, Smoked **94–95**
tools **30–33**
tortillas
    Everything Tortillas 150
    Homemade Tortillas 72
    Lox 'n' Tacs 148–50
    Taquito Party 364–65
    Tortilla Chips 212
tuna
    Albacore Pea Shoot Bowl 198–99
    Confit Tuna Salad with Sea Salt Lavash . . . 126–27
Turnips, Bacon Fat–Roasted **234**

u

Umami Oil, 46

v

Vanilla Ice Cream, 157
Vasquez Farm, 355
Vidalia **18, 20**
vinaigrettes
    Cherry Blossom Vinaigrette 167
    Hippie Vinaigrette 53
vinegar. *See also* **vinaigrettes**
    about 35, 37
    Pre-Surf Fire Cider 136
    Seasoned Vinegar 52

w

Waffles, Matcha Mochi **366–68**
walnuts
    Miso, Walnut, and Chocolate Chip Cookies . . . 369
Wasabi Dip **228**
watercress
    Asparagus Grain Bowl Benedict 146–47
    California Kimbap 122–24
Watermelon Agua Fresca **349**
white chocolate
    about 37
    CA Muddy Buddies 131
    Earl Grey Icebox Pie 100
    White Chocolate, Pistachio, and
    Rose Cookies 128–29
wild rice
    Albacore Pea Shoot Bowl 198–99
    Mac 'n' Cheese with Puffed Rice Topping . 82–83
winemakers, 257, 276

y

Yakult-Style Dressing, 291
yogurt
    Homemade Yogurt 43
    Yakult-Style Dressing 291
    Yogurt Dressing 181

z

zucchini
    Summer Squash and Plum Salad 167

scott clark started his culinary career with a backpack full of his mother's borrowed knives, big dreams, and a hunger for the craft of cooking. He cooked at Vidalia in Washington, DC, and at Restaurant Eve in Alexandria, Virginia, where the kitchen showcased the Chesapeake region's ninety-seven bounties. In San Francisco's Michelin-starred kitchens Benu and Saison, he came to know and deeply appreciate the harvest of Central California and, specifically, of Half Moon Bay. Clark is now the owner and operator of Dad's Luncheonette, and he lives in Half Moon Bay with his daughter.

betsy andrews is a James Beard, International Association of Culinary Professionals, and Society of American Travel Writers award-winning journalist. She lives in Brooklyn, but she's been traveling the Central California coast and staying with family there since her childhood. She is a contributing editor at *Food & Wine*, *SevenFifty Daily*, and *Imbibe*, and she writes for many other publications. She is also a prizewinning poet; her books are *New Jersey*, *The Bottom*, and *Crowded*.

cheyenne ellis is fourth-generation Californian and the daughter of a photographer and a stuntman turned film director. She works from a home base in Bonny Doon on the Central California Coast, and splits her time between Los Angeles and San Francisco and travels the world for projects. She is most at home in nature, and her images are very much about having a good time. In Ellis's book, everyone deserves an all-access pass to happiness.

Chronicle Books publishes distinctive books and gifts. From award-winning children's titles, bestselling cookbooks, and eclectic pop culture to acclaimed works of art and design, stationery, and journals, we craft publishing that's instantly recognizable for its spirit and creativity. Enjoy our publishing and become part of our community at www.chroniclebooks.com.